CYCLING
THE GREAT DIVIDE

CYCLING
THE GREAT DIVIDE

From Canada to Mexico on North America's
Premier Long-Distance Mountain Bike Route

2ND EDITION

**MICHAEL MCCOY
AND THE ADVENTURE
CYCLING ASSOCIATION**

MOUNTAINEERS
BOOKS

This book is dedicated to the memory of Mike and Dan Moe of Laramie, Wyoming, who lived and died for adventure. They were the true trailblazers of mountain biking the Continental Divide.

Mountaineers Books is the publishing division of The Mountaineers, an organization founded in 1906 and dedicated to the exploration, preservation, and enjoyment of outdoor and wilderness areas.

MOUNTAINEERS BOOKS

1001 SW Klickitat Way, Suite 201 • Seattle, WA 98134
800.553.4453 • www.mountaineersbooks.org

Printed in the United States of America
First edition, 2000. Second edition: first printing 2013, fourth printing 2021

Copy Editor: Colin Chisholm
Design and Layout: Jennifer Shontz, www.redshoedesign.com
Maps by Adventure Cycling Association
All photographs by the author unless otherwise noted
Cover photograph: *Michael McCoy cycling the Great Divide route in southern Montana* © Chuck Haney Photography, www.chuckhaney.com
Frontispiece: *The primitive road leading to Cabin Pass, which separates the Flathead and Wigwam river watersheds of southern British Columbia* © Teddy Kisch

Library of Congress Cataloging-in-Publication Data
McCoy, Michael, 1951–
    Cycling the Great Divide: from Canada to Mexico on North America's premier long-distance mountain bike route/Michael McCoy and the Adventure Cycling Association.—Second edition.
        pages   cm
    Includes index.
    ISBN 978-1-59485-819-2 (pbk)—ISBN 978-1-59485-820-8 (ebook) 1. Mountain biking—Continental Divide National Scenic Trail—Guidebooks. 2. Continental Divide National Scenic Trail—Guidebooks. I. Title.
    GV1045.5.C69M33 2013
    917.804—dc23   2013008637

ISBN (paperback): 978-1-59485-819-2
ISBN (ebook): 978-1-59485-820-8

CONTENTS

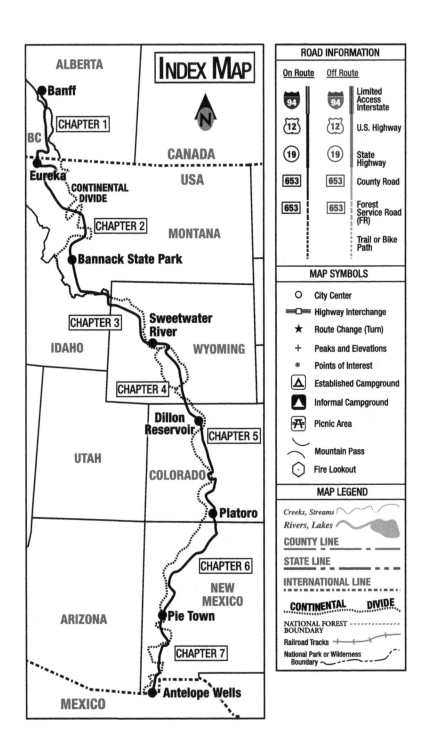

ACKNOWLEDGMENTS

Researching and mapping the Great Divide Mountain Bike Route from 1995 through 1997 was a team effort. The coach of the team was Adventure Cycling Association's then executive director Gary MacFadden. Gary, who helped dream up the vision of this route in the first place, gave me, the team captain, an astounding degree of support and flexibility regarding my timing, scheduling, and choice of where to call home. For that, he has my gratitude and respect.

But before Gary could give me the go-ahead, he was compelled to convince his own bosses—the Adventure Cycling board of directors—that this route was worth funding. Consider these words from longtime board member Matthew Cohn of Helena, Montana, written to me in June 2010: "Mac, the board of directors at the time went out on the limb to approve the use of Adventure Cycling's meager resources to develop this trail. It took two or three meetings to get everyone on board and take the leap of faith in you, Gary, and the staff. To focus our efforts on a nonroad trail 'back in the day' was taking quite a chance." Obviously, huge thanks are due to those good people on the board.

And without "Trailblazers," Adventure Cycling members and non-members who contributed by sponsoring favorite segments of the route at the rate of $100 per mile, the Great Divide route would not have become reality. The list of Trailblazers is unfortunately—make that *fortunately*—too long to list here. Moreover, the list is ever growing, as new Trailblazers come on board to support Adventure Cycling's ongoing work on the Great Divide route.

Recreational Equipment, Inc. (REI), of Seattle, was the largest single sponsor of the Great Divide route. Through their Great Outdoors Grants program, REI contributed an impressive $40,000.

Getting—and expecting—little more than a thank-you for their generosity, Flanagan Motors of Missoula, Montana, donated the use of a new Jeep Cherokee for three years. Without this gesture the costs to research the route would have been much higher.

The U.S. Forest Service (USFS) and Bureau of Land Management (BLM) were extremely supportive of our efforts. Particularly helpful were personnel at USFS Region 1 headquarters in Missoula; Ray Hanson of the BLM in western Wyoming; and Forest Service district rangers along the route in Idaho, Colorado, and New Mexico. Others offering assistance included the staff at Travel Montana; Steven Elkinton, Long Distance Trails Manager at the National Park Service in Washington, D.C.; Bob Lillie, USFS, Durango, Colorado; and Gary Nichols of the Park County (Colorado) Tourism Department.

Nonagency individuals and groups providing advice and/or assistance included the Girl Scouts of Troop 817, Whitehall, Montana, under the leadership of Judy Strom; John Gatchell of the Montana Wilderness Association; Bill Harris of the Colorado Plateau Mountain-Bike Trail Association; Michael Hutton of Timberline Bicycle Tours; Andrew Miller of the Fraser Valley (Colorado) Partnership for Trails; Philip Novotny of B.O.B. Trailers; Martha Roskowski of Salida, Colorado; and Ted Stedman of Denver. (Some of these individuals are no longer in these positions and/or reside in these places.)

Adventure Cycling staff member Julie Huck and former staffer Suzanne Hanlon led the first group tour to take place along any part of the Great Divide route, in 1996. They brought back to the office—much to my joy— some of the first verification that, yes, cyclists are going to have a lot of fun on this route. Daniel "Damby" D'Ambrosio, then editor of *Adventure Cyclist* magazine, did a terrific job of keeping the Adventure Cycling membership apprised of the Great Divide route's progress, while not enough can be said for the efforts of routes and mapping director Carla Majernik, cartographer Jennifer Milyko, and the rest of the routes and mapping staff, who prepared the Adventure Cycling maps and the maps contained in this book—both the originals and the Canada maps new to this edition.

Travel Montana, the state's tourism-promotion arm, funded a press trip in October 1994, with writers and photographers from publications including *Outside*, *Men's Journal*, *Bicycling*, and *Sports Illustrated* riding proposed sections of the Great Divide route in Montana. The resultant slew of articles helped a great deal in creating public awareness of the project.

Adventure Cycling life member Dr. Al Farrell and Steve Ready, then organizer of the annual Interbike trade show, gave assistance, monetary and otherwise, by providing Adventure Cycling a venue at which to announce the dream of the Great Divide route to the cycling world at Interbike in September 1994. Tim Blumenthal, then executive director of the International Mountain Bicycling Association (IMBA), included Gary and me among the approximately 100 individuals invited to participate in IMBA's National Mountain Bike Advocacy Summit at Biosphere II, Arizona, in January 1996. Here again we had tremendous opportunities to spread the word of the Great Divide Mountain Bike Route.

Invaluable help with field research—not to mention companionship—came from my wife, Nancy McCullough-McCoy; Ramsey Bentley, of Laramie, Wyoming (my former University of Wyoming roommate); H. Rob Holden of Missoula; Robin Hamilton of Missoula; Ray Hanson of Fort Collins, Colorado; and Joe Lehm of Madrid, New Mexico.

Much new and corrected information has come in over the years from Adventure Cycling group leaders, group members, and independent Great Divide route riders; a collective *muchas gracias* to those people. Regarding the Canada section newly added to this edition, thanks to Matthew Lee, organizer of the annual Tour Divide race that takes place on the Great Divide route. Matthew pioneered and provided information on what is now the (approximately) southern half of the Canada Section, from Sparwood, British Columbia, through the spectacular upper Flathead River watershed, to the international border at Port of Roosville.

Nearly twenty years have passed since the inception of the Great Divide route, and only a handful of employees that worked at Adventure Cycling then are still there today (you know who you are, Greg, Carla, Teri, Mike, Jenn, and Julie!). But the current staff of more than thirty possesses a collective enthusiasm for the world's longest mapped mountain-bike route that helps keep these wheels rolling. Special appreciation goes to executive director Jim Sayer and media director Winona Bateman for the support they've provided, in particular for approving the organizational resources it took to research and write this new edition of *Cycling the Great Divide*. Thanks as well to Adventure Cycling sales specialist Patrick Finley for reviewing the manuscript in advance of our submitting it to Mountaineers Books.

If there is anyone I've forgotten, my apologies . . . and heartfelt thanks!

A NOTE ABOUT SAFETY

Safety is an important concern in all outdoor activities. No guidebook can alert you to every hazard or anticipate the limitations of every reader. Therefore, the descriptions of roads, trails, routes, and natural features in this book are not representations that a particular place or excursion will be safe for your party. When you follow any of the routes described in this book, you assume responsibility for your own safety. Under normal conditions, such excursions require the usual attention to traffic, road and trail conditions, weather, terrain, the capabilities of your party, and other factors. Keeping informed on current conditions and exercising common sense are the keys to a safe, enjoyable outing.

— *Mountaineers Books*

This cyclist demonstrates the correct way to get around a muddy section for the well-being of both the trail and his bike's drivetrain. (Kathy Kessler-York)

INTRODUCTION

The Great Divide Mountain Bike Route is the world's longest mapped, off-pavement cycling route. It extends for 2,774 miles, from Banff, Alberta, to Antelope Wells, New Mexico, at the doorstep of old Mexico. From its northern terminus, the route trends upward, until reaching the crescendo of the Rocky Mountains in southern Colorado (with plenty of ups and downs in between). From there, the Rockies and the Great Divide route assume generally lower elevations as they continue south into New Mexico.

We had a primary goal of staying within 50 miles of the Continental Divide—known in Canada, aptly, as the Great Divide—whenever possible, and we were largely successful. However, the countryside surrounding that major watershed divide varies dramatically, from the forests of British Columbia and Montana, to the rocky crags and intermountain basins of Wyoming and Colorado, to the cactus-filled deserts of southern New Mexico.

A BRIEF HISTORY: BIKECENTENNIAL, BACKPACKING, AND THE GREAT DIVIDE ROUTE

The Great Divide Mountain Bike Route is a project of the Missoula, Montana–based Adventure Cycling Association. Adventure Cycling began life in 1974 as Bikecentennial, forming when a group of visionary young bicycle tourists came together with a grand plan: Let's throw a two-wheeled, 200th-birthday bash for the American Bicentennial, and invite the world to bicycle across the United States!

The event was resoundingly successful. During the summer of 1976, approximately 4,000 individuals from throughout the United States and beyond pedaled all or part of the TransAmerica Bicycle Trail. The 4,200-mile cross-country route, with beginning and ending points at Astoria, Oregon, and Yorktown, Virginia, had been mapped in a flurry of field research by Bikecentennial staffers and volunteers during 1974 and 1975.

Little did the founders realize that after the Big Summer was over, the organization would carry on, for they had envisioned the Bikecentennial as a huge, one-time event. However, America's growing legion of bicycle enthusiasts wouldn't let the idea die. Hundreds more, inspired by articles in the press and tales brought home by those who rode in 1976, wanted their own shot at pedaling across America.

Now, more than thirty-five years have passed, and Bikecentennial—
renamed Adventure Cycling Association in 1993—is stronger than ever.
Today the association claims more than 45,000 members, making it the
largest membership-based cycling nonprofit organization in North America.
Adventure Cycling has progressively researched new long-distance routes (as
well as regularly revising existing routes), to the point where the Adventure
Cycling Route Network comprises more than 41,000 miles of predominantly
rural roads ideally suited for bicycle travel. The maps created by Adventure
Cycling's cartographers are second to none.

Nor could the original planners have foreseen that one day Adventure
Cycling would plot a 2,774-mile off-pavement route for cyclists riding
mountain bikes. After all, the modern mountain bike had yet to be invented
when Bikecentennial was born. Still, the founders would probably recognize a degree of serendipity in this turn of events, because Bikecentennial's
inaugural group tour followed dirt and gravel roads much like those of the
Great Divide route.

The 1975 Lolo Ruff Stuff Ramble was Bikecentennial's initial trial for
group tours to be operated the following summer. The tour was suggested
by the late Sam Braxton, a bicycle builder in Missoula. Sam had taken to
building "rough-stuff" touring bikes using 26-inch rims (the standard touring
bikes of the early 1970s were equipped with 27-inch wheels). He outfitted
the wheels with fatter-than-standard, 1⅜-inch tires. He also modified the
gearing to suit the rigors of hauling heavy loads up steep pitches and over
rough terrain. Braxton, who passed away in 1989, is rarely, if ever, mentioned
among the inventors of the mountain bike. But his name should be up there
with the likes of Gary Fisher and Joe Breeze, for Braxton's hybrid bikes were
years ahead of their time.

The route chosen for the Lolo Ruff Stuff Ramble was based on a trip
Braxton and his wife Shirl had undertaken on their own beefed-up bicycles
in the summer of 1974. Always on the lookout for uncommon adventure—the
couple had met while on a Mountaineers outing in Washington State—the
Braxtons learned about the historic route, bicycled it, and then raved about
it to Bikecentennial staff members. It sounded like an ideal candidate for
Bikecentennial's kick-off tour.

The main attraction of the Lolo Ruff Stuff Ramble was the rugged Lolo
Motorway, a narrow dirt road running the high ridges above the Lochsa River,
just across the Montana state line in Idaho. Hacked from the wilderness in the
1930s by Civilian Conservation Corps crews, the motorway approximates the
route used in the eighteenth century by west-slope Indians on their buffalo-
hunting forays to the prairies east of the Bitterroot Mountains. Later, in 1805,

The miles zip by with plenty of smiles on a warm, sunny day in the Canadian Rockies. (Nicholas Jensen)

Lewis and Clark followed this route as the Corps of Discovery struggled through the game-poor, downfall-abundant Bitterroots ... and later still, in 1877, it was used by Chief Joseph and the several hundred other Nez Perce Indians who were fleeing U.S. troops commanded by General Oliver O. Howard.

Like the Lolo Ruff Stuff Ramble, the TransAmerica Bicycle Trail, as it was originally laid out, encompassed plenty of dirt and gravel stretches. Unfortunately, off-the-rack touring bicycles were not up to the rigors of off-road riding like Braxton's modified bikes were. Consequently, after receiving countless complaints from cross-country cyclists who hated the off-pavement portions of the route, Bikecentennial eventually mapped paved alternatives skirting all of the dirt and gravel sections. Today, the TransAmerica Bicycle Trail follows hard-surfaced roads exclusively.

What goes around, sometimes, truly does come around. The goal of the designers of the Great Divide Mountain Bike Route in the mid-1990s was to avoid pavement at nearly any cost. With the bombproof, lightweight mountain bikes now available—with their super-fat tires, low gearing, powerful brakes, sophisticated suspension systems, and other improvements and innovations—bikes and their riders were more than ready for the challenge of off-pavement touring ... which is why Adventure Cycling got back into the business of mapping unpaved touring routes.

Backing up a few years, in 1985 we at Bikecentennial headquarters took note of an exceptional, two-part article that ran in consecutive issues of the now-defunct magazine *Bicycle Rider.* "Last summer," stated the article's introduction, "two brothers may have changed the traditional notion of touring as a highway sport. From June 24 to August 28, 1984, Mike and Dan Moe of Laramie, Wyoming, pedaled, pushed, coasted, and carried bicycles for 2,500 miles, from Mexico to Canada, along the rugged mountain wall of the Continental Divide. Their trek exemplifies an exciting renaissance in touring, that of long-distance mountain biking."

Tragically, the ever-adventurous Moe brothers died in a 1995 mishap in the Arctic Ocean, when a bowhead whale capsized the motorboat in which they were riding. They left a legacy, however, for it is fair to say that the Moes planted the seed that grew into the Great Divide Mountain Bike Route.

Also in 1985, on July 20, a friend drove my wife, Nancy, and me to the Tri-Basin Divide in southwest Wyoming. That's the point where water flows either toward the Colorado River, the Columbia River, or the Great Basin. There we grabbed our Cannondale mountain bikes—they were the first two Cannondale fat-tire bikes sold at Sam Braxton's shop in Missoula—out of the truck and loaded them with way too much gear, all packed into (or on top of) rear-mounted panniers. Then we struck out on a five-day camping trip, riding on dirt roads and trails through the Wyoming and Salt River ranges, up the valley of the Green River, and along the Gros Ventre River from its headwaters to where it flows into the Snake River in Jackson Hole. The trip was hard, fun, and a real adventure. I knew I had found a new passion.

The crystallizing moment may have been on a day in 1990, when executive director Gary MacFadden and I sat enjoying a lunch of Mexican food at our favorite downtown Missoula restaurant. Brainstorming for new ideas, one of us said to the other something like, "Let's map a mountain-bike route along the Continental Divide from Canada to Mexico."

Now, some accounts of this magic moment have included reports that an excessive quantity of margaritas was involved. Not true! I was there, so I should know.

As intriguing as it sounded in 1990, the idea was shelved as Adventure Cycling worked on other, more pressing matters, such as purchasing and renovating a headquarters building for a growing staff. Then, early in 1994, Gary and I were having lunch again, when he asked, "Mac, do you remember that long-distance mountain-bike route we discussed a few years back?"

Yes, I surely did, and we heartily agreed that the time was right to do it. Why? For one thing, we had just finished adding a decade-long wish list of road routes to the Adventure Cycling Route Network. We were looking for that next big TransAmerica Bicycle Trail–sized project to tackle. Second, we realized that our organization could and should take the lead in helping to bridge the gap between bicycle touring and mountain biking. To this point, since the advent of mountain biking around 1980, the two had been treated largely as mutually exclusive activities by enthusiasts and the cycling press alike. Finally, the concept fit snugly with our new name, Adventure Cycling Association. What could be more adventurous than bicycling from Canada to Mexico, following little-used roads and back tracks where cyclists would encounter more deer and elk than humans?

In the July 1994 *Adventure Cyclist*—the magazine's name had been changed from *BikeReport* just weeks earlier—we ran a two-page spread, written by yours truly, under the bold headline "Ready for the Longest Mountain Bike Trail in the World?"

"Imagine mountain biking from Canada to Mexico, through some of the most stunning landscapes on earth," the piece began, "along dirt roads and two-tracks reserved for the occasional fisherman's rig, Forest Service pickup truck...and Adventure Cycling mountain biker."

In the story, I explained the origin of our dream of an off-pavement route paralleling the Continental Divide, and why we wanted to make it happen: "Historically, cycling enthusiasts have done one or the other—either loaded up with panniers and camping gear, that is, and lit out on the open road, or headed into the hills on a mountain bike for a day's ride on dirt. Very few have toured off-pavement carrying a full complement of gear. We want to change that."

The Adventure Cycling staff quickly became enthusiastic about the possibilities offered by this cycling route paralleling the Continental Divide. It could, we predicted, become to off-road bicyclists what the Appalachian Trail is to hikers. We pictured riding the route as a blend of bicycle touring, mountain biking, and backpacking. We called it "bikepacking." (Since then, the term has evolved, and today "bikepacker" is typically applied to mountain bikers who go super-light, foregoing heavily loaded panniers or trailers—and the comforts they hold—by employing a system of innovative rackless packs.)

We chose to name the project the Great Divide Mountain Bike Route, in part to distinguish it from the Continental Divide National Scenic Trail, a hiking route primarily composed of rugged single-track trails. We agreed that we would try to avoid tough single-tracks such as these, knowing that riding most mountain trails while carrying or pulling a heavy load is prohibitively difficult. Moreover, we wanted to help alleviate, rather than contribute to, the conflicts that were erupting in many areas because of growing numbers of hikers and mountain bikers using the same trails.

Rather than following trails, then, we would link together the sorts of existing low-use roads woven throughout USFS and BLM lands in Montana and elsewhere in the Rockies. Wherever the yet-to-be-identified route encountered private lands, we believed, it would still be possible to follow public right-of-way roads, thereby entirely avoiding the challenges of building new trails and/or trying to obtain new rights-of-way across private lands.

The task of researching the Great Divide route fell on me in 1994. "It's a tough duty, but somebody's gotta do it," became my mantra for the next four years. Still, it was anything but a one-man show. The project quickly captured the imagination of hundreds; consequently, things jelled and got done amazingly fast. For instance, dozens of agency personnel and local cycling enthusiasts jumped in to help plot the route in advance and help with field reconnaissance.

Keeping the home fires burning and funding wheels turning were Gary, routes and mapping director Carla Majernik, Adventure Cyclist editor Dan D'Ambrosio, and all the other Adventure Cycling staff members. These folks helped spread the word about the project, began drafting route maps, and instituted creative, highly successful programs aimed at raising funds to pay for route research and map development.

As it turns out, the Great Divide Mountain Bike Route comprises roughly 86 percent dirt and gravel roads, 12 percent paved roads, and 2 percent single-track trails. Now that it's been around for nearly two decades, we realize that rather than tackling the whole thing in a summer many cyclists launch series of shorter, three- and four-week outings on the route. This is often the case with other long-distance trails like the TransAmerica Bicycle Trail and the Appalachian Trail (AT). Those who hike the entire AT, whether in pieces or on one long outing, are referred to as "thru-hikers." Borrowing from the heritage of that legendary and historic American footpath, we call those who pedal the entire Great Divide route "thru-bikers."

Then there is the other extreme: through-bikers who cover the Great Divide route as fast as possible. The Tour Divide race mentioned in the acknowledgments has grown to become something of a cult classic among endurance mountain bike racers, and the 2012 version attracted an international field of more than a hundred riders. Currently, the men's record is 15 days, 16 hours, and 4 minutes, pedaled by Jay Petervary in 2012. (Round-the-world record holder Mike Hall covered the distance more than a day faster in 2013, but wildfire detours in New Mexico voided his mark.) No less impressive is the women's record of 19 days, 3 hours, and 35 minutes, attained by Eszter Horanyi of Crested Butte, Colorado, also in 2012.

The number of through-bikers, both fast and slow, is long and growing. Consider one of the slower ones, Rich O'Brien, a retired schoolteacher from Mankato, Minnesota, who linked together two summers of riding in 1997 and 1998 to bag the route. The intrepid O'Brien wrote this to us shortly after completing his adventure:

The author (left) with Jay Petervary, who established a new record in 2012 by riding the Great Divide route in 15 days, 16 hours, and 4 minutes (Nancy McCoy)

"I have walked the Appalachian Trail, I have biked solo across the U.S., I have paddled most of the Mississippi River. The Great Divide ranks right up there with these other adventures. Overcrowding on the AT is making it less and less an experience of wilderness. Thus comes the Great Divide bike trail to the rescue. The differences between the hiking and the biking make the Great Divide unique enough so as to light fires in the imaginations of those who hear about what it all has to offer. . . . In time the Divide biker will experience what the AT hiker calls 'trail magic,' a sort of nebulous definition of the serendipitous good things that happen along the way."

And then there's Matthew Cohn, mentioned above in the acknowledgments as one of the Adventure Cycling board members who had to be persuaded the idea of the Great Divide route was more than half-baked. On June 4, 2010, he wrote these words to me: "This year we will finish the last segment of the ride (Pie Town to Antelope Wells). I think our group is setting a new record for the longest time to complete the trail . . . twelve years to be exact. The route has been amazing and the riding is unforgettable. Frankly, it has ruined me for road touring."

Fast or slow, there's plenty of trail magic to be found. Here's hoping the spell will be cast over you soon, on your own Great Divide route adventure.

IS THE GREAT DIVIDE ROUTE FOR YOU?

Obviously, an expedition on the Great Divide Mountain Bike Route is not for everyone. Nor is it for all bicyclists; it's not even for every cyclist harboring a dream of a months-long adventure.

Some serious trail-loving mountain bikers, on learning that the Great Divide route is composed primarily of dirt and gravel roads, have asked,

"What's the adventure in riding where you can drive?" To them we say, "Just try it." Many of the roads followed are so remote, so lacking in traffic, that it's hard to imagine why they were built in the first place. But there they are, and we've taken advantage of them. (We like to believe they were built for mountain biking, even though the engineers and road crews didn't realize it at the time.)

Granted, for those interested only in the thrill of single-track (which, if you read the mountain-bike magazines, you might think is the only kind of mountain biking there is), or, conversely, only in the mile-gobbling speed attained by cycling on paved roads, the Great Divide route may hold little interest. But if you have—or can get into—the right frame of mind, the route offers a wonderful blend that is rather like a hybrid of road riding and mountain biking. You can simply *cruise* on a lot of these old roads, and rarely worry about traffic. It's a liberating style of bicycling that truly must be experienced to be understood. (Regarding the dearth of single-track, consider these words from mountain-bike endurance rider John Stamstad, the first to speed-ride the route in 1999: "Anyone who complains that there is not enough single-track doesn't know what it feels like to ride a fully loaded bike eight to fifteen hours a day.")

Moreover, although the majority of the Great Divide route does follow a road of some sort, including low-traffic frontage roads paralleling major highways, these roads pass scores of trailheads leading to hundreds of the best single-track trails in the Rocky Mountain West. If you think of primary, paved roads as arteries crisscrossing the countryside, then the back roads of the Great Divide route are like veins along the spine of the Rockies. These veins provide ready access to an endless network of capillaries, which are the single-track trails and two-track roads webbing the backcountry. Some of the capillaries are, of course, off-limits to bicycles because they run through wilderness areas. Many others, however, are perfectly legal for bicycling.

You shouldn't consider setting out on a Great Divide Mountain Bike Route expedition without prior long-distance cycle-touring and/or back-packing experience. Riders need to have the utmost confidence in both their equipment and their self-reliant backcountry travel skills. Compared to road touring, the primary difference on the Great Divide route—besides that of riding dirt versus paved surfaces—is that you will encounter far fewer people and towns. A road tour, such as a crossing of the United States on the Trans-America Bicycle Trail, is largely about discovering the charm of small-town America. A trip along the Great Divide route, in contrast, is a journey into the rough-hewn world of nature. The biggest thing the two have in common is the countless hours you will spend in the saddle to reach your destination.

Beyond that, though, those who have ridden the TransAmerica Bicycle Trail tend to remember things like soda fountains, picturesque town squares, the scent of fresh-cut hay wafting on the breeze, and friendly locals. These things are less common on the Great Divide route (though the smaller number of locals encountered *are* generally friendly!). You'll be more apt to recall the vision of a grizzly bear tearing through a high avalanche clearing on the prowl for huckleberries; running out of water and finding some just when it is getting too close to too late; herds of pronghorn antelope and wild horses kicking up dust in the wide-open spaces of Wyoming's Great Divide Basin; and the absolute *have-I-landed-on-Mars?* solitude of New Mexico's fantastically eroded Chaco Mesa country.

If these things are for you—and you can live without ice cream for days on end—then by all means, have at it!

GETTING READY AND GEARING UP

An expedition on the Great Divide Mountain Bike Route is no mean feat, either to plan or to execute. The 2,774-mile route encompasses vast expanses of exceedingly remote and often thirsty country, requiring the bikepacker to think and act more like a backpacker than a bicycle tourist.

Breakdowns of the mileage (with fractions rounded off) look like this: Canada holds 257 miles of the Great Divide route, 65 of them in Alberta and 192 in British Columbia. Montana contains 710 miles of the route; Idaho, 72 miles; Wyoming, 489 miles; Colorado, 545 miles; and New Mexico, 701 miles. Along the length of the Great Divide route you will cross from one side of the Continental Divide to the other at least thirty-two times. The lowest elevation attained is 2,577 feet above sea level, near the Canadian border. The highest, a lofty 11,910 feet above sea level, is reached at Indiana Pass, a few miles south of and nearly a mile above the town of Del Norte, Colorado.

This book breaks the Great Divide route into seventy suggested riding days; eight days for Banff, Alberta, to Eureka, Montana, and sixty-two days for the rest of the U.S. portion. The schedule outlined herein is by no means the only way one can divide up the mileage, but it is one way that should work well. The route and riding days are divided into seven chapters; each corresponds to one of the seven map sections available through Adventure Cycling. You will, however, note that the chapters don't always begin or end precisely where the corresponding maps do. This is because we've attempted to end each of the seventy days either at a good campsite or in a town with camping and/or motels available, and not all of the beginning/ending points of the seven map sections fall in such places.

Adventure Cycling's full-color, waterproof, folding maps feature

Spanning the Rockies from Canada to Mexico, the Great Divide route takes on some of the wildest non-wilderness country in North America. (Ben Yandeau)

navigational, services, historic, and general information for the route. It is imperative that you obtain and pack along these maps, because they show the route and the services along it in considerably greater detail than do the maps in this guidebook. (This is, incidentally, in line with the caveat Mountaineers Books makes with all of their guidebooks: That is, users should carry supplemental maps and not rely solely on the diagrammatic renderings in their books.) The Great Divide Mountain Bike Route maps are available through Adventure Cycling Sales (800-721-8719 or www.adventurecycling .org/store). Other maps useful for planning purposes include the USFS and BLM maps listed on the Adventure Cycling maps, as well as the DeLorme atlases for Montana, Idaho, Wyoming, Colorado, and New Mexico (207-846-7000 or delorme.com). Similarly, for the Canada section good planning resources are the "Kootenay Rockies" and "Canadian Rockies" volumes of the *Backroad Mapbooks*, available at www.backroadsbooks.com.

Out of respect for the remote nature of the country traversed by the Great Divide route, we advise against traveling the route solo. Unlike the touring bicyclist who sticks to paved roads, on most of the route you won't have convenient access to services or to motorists who in a pinch can provide assistance. The injury or mechanical breakdown that is little more than an inconvenience when on the road can readily become an emergency situation in the backcountry, for the unprepared or unaccompanied.

You will be faced with several stretches of two to four days in duration that offer no food stores or other services. These are well flagged and described in the text; however, be sure always to read ahead a few days so that one of these segments doesn't catch you off guard. (In fact, it is a good idea to read this entire book before setting out.) It will be of little use to learn that no groceries are available for 100 miles if you are already 40 miles into that century-long stretch.

Essential Items

When preparing for any length of outing on the Great Divide route, from day ride to through-ride, think like a backpacker: Plan ahead, and consider where you might run into problems. Knowing where the potential for trouble lies will help keep you out of it. To begin, always pack along the mountain biker's Ten Essentials:

1. Water—more than you think you'll need
2. Food—more than you think you'll need
3. Loud plastic whistle
4. Space blanket for body-heat retention
5. Helmet and leather gloves
6. Map and compass and/or GPS receiver
7. Waterproof matches or butane lighter
8. Headlamp
9. Foul-weather gear
10. Sharp Swiss Army–type pocketknife

Other indispensables include high-quality sunglasses and sturdy cycling shoes. Many but not all riders prefer clipless pedals and shoes with recessed cleats over old-fashioned toe clips. Whichever you choose, be sure your shoes are comfortable for walking as well as riding.

Regarding bicycle tools, cyclists vary greatly in what they like to carry, and it's usually in direct correlation to their adeptness (or ineptness) at bicycle mechanics. You could try to carry one of every bicycle tool made, but most would be nothing but excess weight if you're not trained in using them.

At a minimum, carry:
- Allen keys to fit all of your bike's Allen bolts
- Six-inch locking pliers
- Two spare tubes (even if you use tubeless tires)
- Spare foldable tire
- Three tire irons
- Tire pump to fit your valve-stem type
- Patch kit
- Chain-rivet remover
- Spoke wrench
- Spare spokes
- Spare Allen bolts
- Chain lubricant and rag

▶ Roll of black electrical tape. (Question: What's one thing you'll never hear an experienced bicycle traveler say? Answer: It can't be fixed with electrical tape.)
▶ Bike owner's manual, or smart phone application, with troubleshooting information and diagrams

Anyone, even those with very little background in bicycle mechanics, can practice preventive maintenance. By regularly doing so you can greatly reduce the chances that serious repair will be needed at some later date. Of foremost importance on the Great Divide route are (1) keeping your bicycle relatively clean and free of mud clots and (2) checking your bike each morning before heading out to ensure that everything that is supposed to be tight is tight. Allen bolts—whether they're securing water-bottle cages, holding together chain rings, or keeping your saddle in place—have a way of shaking loose on bumpy riding surfaces. A shot of Loctite thread-locking compound on the bolts can go a long way toward preventing things from vibrating loose. If you're running tubeless tires, be sure to use an internal tire sealant like Stan's No-Tubes to reduce the chance/severity of flats.

Like tools, first-aid supplies are of little use if you don't know what they're for. Prior to your expedition, get some training in first aid by signing up for a course through your local Red Cross chapter and/or by reading a book on backcountry medicine, such as *Wilderness & Travel Medicine: A Comprehensive Guide,* by Eric Weiss, MD (Mountaineers Books, 2011). Pack the book along with your first-aid kit.

First-aid supplies should include:
▶ Large triangular bandage
▶ A 3-inch elastic bandage
▶ Assortment of gauze patches and adhesive strips (including butterfly bandages, effective as temporary closures)
▶ Moleskin for blisters
▶ Collapsible mini-scissors
▶ Spenco 2nd Skin for burns, blisters, road rash
▶ Adhesive tape
▶ Sunscreen (at least 30 SPF)
▶ Aspirin or other pain reliever
▶ Lip balm with sunscreen
▶ Tweezers
▶ Baking soda for insect bites
▶ Insect repellent

- Antihistamine (such as Benadryl) for allergic reactions
- Roll of 2-inch gauze
- Antiseptic soap
- Antibacterial ointment
- Hydrogen peroxide or rubbing alcohol
- Compact splint
- Instant cold pack for sprains, strains, and broken bones
- Energy bars for emergency food

Choosing Your Ride

If rumble strips, those annoying shoulder bumps designed to bring drowsy motorists back to their senses, are the bane of the road cyclist, then washboard surfaces are the nemesis of those tackling the Great Divide route. One rider told me that midway on his adventure he had to lay over in Breckenridge, Colorado, to have his fillings replaced.

It is never that bad; still, especially later in the summer when some gravel roads have gone ungraded after enduring substantial quantities of traffic, washboard can become a real pain in the neck ... and in other places, too. History tells us—coming from cyclists who have reported back to us after riding the route—that the best defense is a bike equipped with both front and rear suspension systems. (Know, however, that full-suspension bikes

A good-looking group ready and raring to leave the pavement behind and hit pay dirt (Nancy McCoy)

weigh more and have extra parts that can break. They also require the use of a trailer or specialized racks for panniers.) However, in recent years we've seen the introduction of 29-inch-wheeled bicycles specifically designed for Great Divide route–type riding that come stock with no shocks at all. One of these bikes, the Co-Motion Divide, is even named after this route! The best advice is this: Ask around, at bike shops and online forums, and test ride a few different bikes. Or, if you already own a sturdy mountain bike, know that it will probably work just fine.

Some riders prefer pulling trailers, such as the B.O.B. (Beast of Burden), while others don't. A trailer does have several advantages over panniers, including that it is easily detached and it distributes a substantial amount of the load over its own wheel, thereby reducing stress on your bicycle's frame and wheels. Again, ask around and test out the various options.

Your bike should be equipped with knobby tires, handlebar bar-end extensions to provide a variety of hand positions, an accurately calibrated cyclometer, and a low gear of at least 23 inches. If you use a rack-and-pannier system rather than a trailer, avoid "low-rider" front racks, which provide inadequate ground clearance for off-road touring. Panniers should be constructed of durable, heavyweight, water-resistant Cordura. A solid mounting system is mandatory to prevent panniers from bouncing around and shaking loose. There is a whole new generation of handlebar- and frame-mounted packs available today, both a spinoff and enabler of the ultralight bikepacking movement (check out the Cyclosource online at www.adventurecycling.org /store). Last but not least, remember to bring your helmet.

Bikepacking Gear

The Great Divide route is one of the most challenging bicycle adventures you can undertake. Services are few and far between, so you will be largely dependent on what you bring with you, and what you bring will be subjected to extreme wear and tear. Spend a few dollars extra to get the most durable gear you can find. Careful selection and pretesting of equipment will pay huge dividends over the long ride.

Other than your bike and mode of carrying gear (i.e., panniers versus trailer versus frame packs), prepping for a ride on the Great Divide route can be likened to preparing for a cross between a backpacking and bicycle-touring trip. Here is an equipment list for starters; you'll want to add to and subtract from it based on your own experience and preferences.

- ▶ Two pairs of padded riding shorts
- ▶ Two short-sleeved shirts of polypropylene or other wicking fabric

- One long-sleeved shirt of wicking fabric
- Waterproof, breathable rainsuit/windsuit (jacket with hood and pants)
- Polyester-fleece jacket
- Wool or polyester-fleece pants
- Polypropylene/Lycra-blend tights
- Long johns, stocking cap, cycling socks, and gloves or mittens of wicking fabric
- Cotton T-shirts, underwear, and socks for camp wear
- Two bandannas
- Waterproof shoe covers
- Athletic shoes for camp wear and stream crossings
- Bathing suit, towel
- Four water bottles and/or large back-mount hydration bladder
- High-quality water filter
- Down- or synthetic-filled sleeping bag, rated to at least 20 degrees Fahrenheit
- Inflatable sleeping pad
- Lightweight tent
- Waterproof ground cloth
- Backpacking stove and fuel bottles, cook set, eating utensils
- Various-sized waterproof stuff sacks
- Toiletries
- Other things you might not think of that will come in handy: extra bungee cords, insect repellent, baby wipes (great for personal hygiene during extended showerless periods), camera, binoculars, extra Ziploc-style plastic bags, chamois cream or Bag Balm (to prevent chafing), toilet paper, pencil and journal, camp chair (there are nifty models that convert your sleeping pad into a back support), and a good read for those rainy, tent-bound days. A lot of folks these days pack along their reading materials on their tablet or smart phone. Speaking of....

To Cell or Not to Cell

Though it's certainly less true than it was a decade ago, some outdoor enthusiasts still feel that carrying a cell phone into the backcountry is akin to wearing a raincoat in the shower—that is, it defeats the purpose of what you're doing and why you're there. However, lives have been saved because expedition members were carrying cell phones. Choose for yourself; just remember, one way or the other you must take responsibility for your own well-being. And remember also that in many of the remote places the Great Divide route visits, there is no cell reception.

HEADING OUT

Locator-directional signs will often be found at important intersections. However, bear in mind that simply because a road is given a number on the map doesn't mean you'll find a corresponding sign on the ground—often they've been stolen or vandalized, or they may have never existed.

To mark the miles, rig your bike with a high-quality cyclometer, widely available at bike shops. Compared to cycling on the pavement, it is much more difficult to estimate distance traveled when riding on rough dirt and gravel surfaces. Moreover, in the woods and barren wilds of the Continental Divide country there typically are not a lot of signs or landmarks to help orient you. This is why the route descriptions throughout this book are keyed to odometer (mileage) readings. As previously mentioned, in addition to this guidebook you should carry the Adventure Cycling maps of the Great Divide route. (Consider going one step further and also pack along the USFS/BLM maps listed on the Adventure Cycling maps.) Regularly check your odometer reading against the route descriptions, and you'll keep well apprised of your whereabouts. It is also possible to download the GPS files for the Great Divide route at the Adventure Cycling website (www.adventurecycling.org). The waypoint files are keyed to the maps of the route; there is a waypoint for each turn in the narratives and each facility listed in the maps' service directories.

Educate yourself about no-trace travel and camping practices. Haul out all of your trash (or use the trash cans available at some campgrounds). Carry a camp stove for cooking. If you must build a campfire, use an existing fire ring rather than creating a new one. Be sure your fire is completely snuffed out before leaving it, and avoid building fires altogether when conditions are particularly hot, dry, and/or windy. Especially when camping at a "dispersed site"—the term used by land managers to distinguish nondesignated (but legal) campsites from established campgrounds—look for bare earth or a sandy spot to pitch your tent rather than crushing delicate vegetation.

Ruts caused by tires cutting into the tread surface can become pathways for water, helping to create or intensify erosion problems. Stay on the designated route and off the surrounding countryside—even off side trails and roads when conditions are wet and muddy.

The vast majority of the Great Divide route follows dirt and gravel roads open to motorized travel—not that you'll see many vehicles on the rugged old logging and mining roads that characterize much of the route. It is also possible that you will occasionally encounter hikers or equestrians. Treat either with the respect you would wish for if you were in their shoes or saddle. When meeting saddle or pack animals, dismount from your bicycle and stand to the lower side of the trail. Talk to the riders as they pass, and don't make any sudden noise or movement that may cause a horse to spook. When approaching equestrians from behind, call out a greeting and ask the riders how best to proceed around them.

In the mountains and high deserts spreading away from the Continental Divide, rapid changes in weather are the norm. Be prepared for and expect just about anything, from searing heat to high winds to wet snow.

Hypothermia, a lowering of the body's core temperature, is the number-one killer of outdoor recreationists. To avoid hypothermia, dress—and undress—in layers, trying to maintain a point of equilibrium where you're neither cold nor sweating heavily (which will dampen your clothes and cause dehydration, both of which can compound the problem). Wear a light wicking layer such as polypropylene directly against your skin, and drink water often. Most cases of hypothermia occur between 30 and 50 degrees Fahrenheit, so it's a very real threat when mountain biking in the high country, especially with the wind-chill effect of riding downhill at higher speeds (no doubt after working up a sweat gaining the other side of that mountain pass).

Sunburn, heat exhaustion, and heat stroke are concerns during the hot days of summer. Cover up with lightweight clothing, and on anything left bare apply a high-SPF sunscreen. Drink lots of water (between one and two gallons per day, depending on the temperature and length of the ride), and take frequent rest breaks in the shade to lower your body temperature.

Altitude sickness is a possible concern at the high elevations of Colorado and northern New Mexico, although through-bikers will become gradually acclimated as they ride south. Take care to stay well hydrated and to consume nutritious foods, concentrating on a diet high in complex carbohydrates.

Lightning storms can be killers, so don't be caught riding on an exposed ridge on a summer afternoon if thunderheads are possible. If you do get caught in a lightning storm, avoid lone trees, open areas, and the bases or edges of cliffs. Safer locations include heavily timbered areas, and beneath or between big rocks in boulder fields.

Giardia lamblia, a one-celled animal that thrives in cold water and causes the severe intestinal illness giardiasis, is a potential inhabitant of all surface waters on the Great Divide route. The water-borne cysts are deposited in or near streams via animal droppings and human waste. Always pack along more water than you think you need for the day's ride, and carry a high-quality portable water filter. Use it any time you're forced to drink stream or other surface water. The filters are widely available at outdoor-equipment stores.

As in other activities requiring good balance and quick motor skills, mountain-biking accidents occur more often when the rider is worn out. To

A wolf track in the mud. Canis lupis, *or signs of them, may be encountered along the route anywhere from Canada to northwest Wyoming. (Julie Huck)*

minimize fatigue, consume plenty of food and water throughout the day, and take frequent rest breaks. Don't go at it too hard or too long, especially if it is early in the journey and you're unaccustomed to the high elevations of the Rocky Mountains.

From early spring until midsummer, wood ticks are common in the brush of forested areas and in the sagebrush deserts. While ordinarily just a nuisance, they can carry potentially serious diseases, including Rocky Mountain spotted fever and Lyme disease. Perform a thorough self-inspection if you've been beating the brush, in order to locate any creepy-crawlies before they dig in. (Most books on wilderness medicine discuss tick removal.)

Potentially dangerous black bears are found in every state traversed by the route, and the more aggressive grizzly bear is a resident of the northern Rockies, from Canada roughly to the vicinity of Pinedale, Wyoming. Great Divide route riders often report encountering bears, including grizzlies. The USFS recommends these practices for cycling and camping in bear country:

▶ There is safety in numbers, so don't bike alone.
▶ Learn to recognize the signs of grizzly bear activity, such as tracks, scat, and partially eaten or buried animal carcasses lying along the trail. If you see these signs, don't linger.
▶ Make more noise than usual, and consider attaching a bell to your bicycle.
▶ Never approach a bear to take a photo or for any other reason.
▶ Keep a clean camp. All food, drinks, garbage, and scented toiletries should be stored in a bear-resistant container or vehicle, or hung at least 10 feet off the ground and 4 feet from any vertical support.

It is common practice among outdoor enthusiasts to carry canisters of bear spray for personal protection. The repellent, actually a highly concentrated and pressurized pepper-based product, can be purchased at sporting-goods stores in the northern Rockies, including Canada. Be sure also to obtain a lesson in using the spray from a salesperson, because the highly toxic repellent is hazardous. (The repellent is to be used only during a probable bear attack—you don't want to spray it around camp, or it can become a bear attractant.)

During autumn, big-game hunters use a lot of the territory covered by the Great Divide route. In fact, in much of the Continental Divide country you will encounter more people during hunting season than at any other time of year. If you intend to ride during big-game season, dress in bright colors and make more noise than usual. Hunting seasons vary from state to state and province to province, so check with the appropriate land-management agency regarding specific dates.

As previously mentioned, we do not recommend solo travel on the Great Divide route. But if you must go it alone, bear in mind that you need to be doubly prepared for any emergency situation. Always leave a detailed itinerary with a friend, and regularly check in with that person. If a search party must be dispatched, the chances of finding you will be greatly enhanced if they know where you were scheduled to be and when. Turning once again to the world of technology, another option is to carry a device such as the SPOT Personal Tracker. This GPS messenger utilizes satellite technology to pinpoint your location, and works even where cell phones do not.

Which Direction to Travel and When to Set Out

Through-biking north to south. It is no coincidence that both this book and the Adventure Cycling maps lead the rider in a north-to-south direction of travel. Adventure Cycling concluded during the route-planning phase that it would be preferable to begin in the north, primarily because it would offer a more favorable weather window for those riding the entire route in a summer. For instance, one can begin riding at Banff in mid-July, soon after the snows at the higher elevations of Canada and northwest Montana have melted; arrive in the high country of Colorado in August; and finish up in the Chihuahuan Desert of New Mexico in late September or early October, after things have cooled down a bit. Another advantage of riding north to south is that it permits you to acclimate more gradually to the exceptionally high altitudes of Colorado.

A potential downside of this strategy is that monsoonal rains are common in New Mexico in late summer, with July and August typically the wettest months. These can make some portions of the route impassable, necessitating travel on paved alternatives. However, to do it the other way—ride the route from south to north, that is—and to take advantage of cooler spring weather in New Mexico, you would need to leave by May. This means that you would arrive at the high-elevation reaches of northern New Mexico and southern Colorado when, in many years, snowdrifts still clog much of the route.

These things said, quite a few cyclists have successfully ridden the route south to north. In fact, Great Divide route veteran Mathieu van Rijswick of the Netherlands has researched the climatological data and makes a convincing argument that the route can be ridden south to north from late May through early August. You can find his research at www.crazyguyonabike.com.

Still, the majority will start at the top and ride to the bottom. If you have the luxury of riding the route whenever you want, setting out from Banff in mid-August could present the best overall conditions. (No guarantees: This is Mother Nature after all!) By the time you get to the high country of Colorado it will be early autumn, when the days typically are warm and the nights cool, and the quaking aspens are wearing their brilliant fall foliage. When you reach New Mexico in early October, chances are the weather there will have dried out and cooled off.

Doing it in pieces. Not everyone can take two months or more out of their lives to ride the Great Divide route. That is why many cyclists break the route into sections and complete it over the course of two, three, even four summers. Detailed below is a good way to divide the route into four segments, with a nod toward convenience of access to and from the break points. Also included are mileages and the best time of year to ride each section:

Segment 1—Banff, Alberta, to Butte, Montana. 708 miles. July through September.
Segment 2—Butte to Rawlins, Wyoming. 747 miles. July through September.
Segment 3—Rawlins to Abiquiu, New Mexico (good access to Santa Fe/Albuquerque). 725 miles. July through September (October for northern New Mexico).
Segment 4—Abiquiu to Antelope Wells, New Mexico. 594 miles. May through June, and October.

Getting to and from the trailheads. The idea of easy access to remote areas could be termed a "geographical oxymoron." Accordingly, the convenience of getting to and from the route never was a factor in determining the path followed by the Great Divide route.

The descent from Flathead Pass in southern British Columbia. Certain sections of the downhill are far rougher than this. (Teddy Kisch)

To reach the northern end of the route you'll most likely want to fly to Calgary International Airport, then arrange for a shuttle to the route's beginning point in Banff.

Getting home from the other end is a bit more challenging, yet there are options. Adventure Cycling maintains a list of shuttle services all along the route, which you can access at www.adventurecycling.org/gd-shuttle. If you are unable to track down a shuttle operator even after checking out the current list, the best option will be to backtrack the 46 miles from Antelope Wells to Hachita, then ride east on State Highway 9 to El Paso, Texas (100-plus miles from Hachita). Columbus, New Mexico, located roughly halfway between Hachita and El Paso, offers camping at Pancho Villa State Park.

A Final Note

If there is one thing Adventure Cycling has learned since mapping the Great Divide route, it is that things can change quickly out there in the wilds. New signs are added, while others disappear; grocery stores open and close; forest roads are paved, while hard-surfaced roads deteriorate to gravel. Other roads are realigned, gated shut, or eradicated to allow nature to reclaim them.

The number of things that have changed from the time the route was researched in 1995 through 1997, to the autumn of 2012 when this edition was researched, was quite an eye-opener for me. And they'll no doubt continue to change. While we were preparing this manuscript, a pair of proposed projects came to our attention that could have profound effects on sections of the route: One, a gold-mining operation near Butte, Montana, that would have large trucks hauling ore on Highland Road (Day 22); and two, the approval by Secretary of the Interior Ken Salazar of potentially the largest wind farm in the world, on BLM lands south of Rawlins, Wyoming (Day 39). In addition, as this book went to press, we received reports that portions of the Canada route between Banff and the Flathead Valley suffered damage from severe flooding. This is a good reminder to always check for the latest updates on the Great Divide route map addenda section of Adventure Cycling's website.

Please keep this in mind at all times. Consider this guide as the state of the route when the book went to print, and expect the unexpected.

RULES OF THE TRAIL

Always keep IMBA's* Rules of the Trail foremost in mind, whether you're riding on the Great Divide route or elsewhere:
1. Ride on open trails only.
2. Leave no trace.
3. Control your bicycle.
4. Yield trail appropriately.
5. Never scare animals.
6. Plan ahead.
*IMBA = International Mountain Bicycling Association, 303-545-9011; www.imba.com.

The Canada section, added to the route in 2004, is characterized by cold streams, deep forests, and stark mountain crags. (Ben Yandeau)

CHAPTER 1

BANFF, ALBERTA, TO EUREKA, MONTANA

267.5 MILES
Days 1 through 8 (eight days)
One Continental Divide crossing

Beginning in the busy but beautiful town of Banff, Alberta, the Canada Section of the Great Divide Mountain Bike Route takes you through some of the most spectacular terrain on Earth. Somehow, when traversing the Canadian Rockies, you truly feel like you are *in* the mountains and not just looking at them. This is true along other portions of the route to the south as well, but it seems doubly true here in the route's far northern reaches.

Considering the bustling, cosmopolitan ambiance that surrounds you in Banff, you may be shocked by how quickly you leave the city behind when you begin riding. Almost instantly, one trades ducking cars and busses for thinking more about cougars and bears. It's as though you've entered the forest primeval, a heavily wooded setting that can feel like rain forest—especially if it's raining.

The first 70 miles or so of the Canada Section is like a string of pearls. The roads and trails are the string, and the dazzling mountain parks are the pearls: Banff National Park, Spray Valley Provincial Park, and Peter Lougheed Provincial Park in Alberta; and, across the Great Divide in British Columbia, Elk Lakes Provincial Park. The Alberta portion also constitutes the northwestern part of an immense, multi-use recreation region known as Kananaskis Country, or "K-Country" in the local parlance.

Elk Lakes Provincial Park's glaciers and namesake lakes form the headwaters of the Elk River, whose valley the route follows for the next 40 miles, to the town of Elkford. From there you head east to wrap around the far side of Fording Mountain and down the Fording River valley, regaining the Elk Valley where the Fording empties into the Elk River north of Sparwood.

South of Sparwood, the route follows mapping that was newly researched and added in 2010. It includes about 100 miles of wild-country riding through British Columbia's Flathead and Wigwam river valleys—and includes a series of dirt and gravel roads composing what is sometimes referred to as the "Grizzly Bear Highway." The moniker is no fluke; the Flathead Valley in British Columbia is home to the largest population of inland grizzlies on the North American continent.

If you prefer something a little *less* wild, the original route from Sparwood to the international border, now known as the "Fernie Alternate," is depicted on Adventure Cycling's map of the Canada Section. It passes through more towns and settled areas, and also includes a greater quantity of paved roads. Another option, if you want to ride the main route but not sleep in a tent, would be to do two very long days from Sparwood to Eureka, of 54 miles and 70 miles, and stay indoors at the Butts Patrol Cabin. (Even then be prepared to camp, because the cabin is available on a first-come, first-served basis.) It's also possible to sag this trip with a truck and even a trailer—the route itself is not passable, but there are two-wheel-drive roads heading out from the Fernie area that access the Lower Harvey Creek and Ram-Wigwam Recreation Sites.

When announcing this major route change in British Columbia, Adventure Cycling's routes and mapping director, Carla Majernik, had this to say: "The Flathead is the last major valley in southern Canada to be completely uninhabited. The new routing fits perfectly with the spirit of the rest of the Great Divide route—challenging and remote."

Tour Divide race organizer and repeat winner Matthew Lee originally proposed and researched the route change, piecing together jeep roads and game trails to bring the Canadian leg of the race through the Flathead basin. "Tour Divide racers are truly champions for the Great Divide route and for bicycle travel," Lee said. "They may run the route at breakneck speed, but their hope is to inspire others to ride part, or all of it, at their own pace and experience the jaw-dropping natural beauty this route has to offer."

Jaw-dropping beauty, indeed. In fact, you may find that your mouth is rarely closed—and the same can be said for your camera's shutter—the entire way from Banff to Eureka.

A map note: Unlike in the United States, where the watershed divide is called "Continental Divide," on the Canada maps it's labeled "Great Divide," because that's what they call it in the great white north. So don't get confused with the black-and-white maps in this book, thinking the line delineating the Great Divide is the route. Also, we have divided the route from Banff to Eureka into eight riding days. This is relatively conservative, and the days might prove too short for strong riders. (Loaded riders have done it in six days or even fewer.) However, since a lot of people will be starting their grand Great Divide route through-biking adventures here, we thought it better to err on the side of too easy—permitting riders to ease into the saddle—rather than too hard.

Finally, if you plan to cross the U.S.–Canada border, whether heading south or north, be sure each member of your party has a valid passport.

Day 1

BANFF TO SPRAY LAKES WEST CAMPGROUND

20.4 miles

It's ironic, perhaps, that the world's longest mapped mountain bike route, which strings together some of continent's wildest country, begins virtually in the morning shadow of one of the most breathtaking man-made structures

The Fairmont Banff Springs Hotel, visible from the route's northern terminus, is quite unlike anything else you will encounter over the next 2,774 miles. (Julie Huck)

in North America: the Fairmont Banff Springs Hotel. (Warning: Don't expect to find anything like this at the other end of the route!)

Rising above its timbered surroundings like a colossal dream castle, the Banff Springs Hotel opened on June 1, 1888, as one in a series of the Canadian Pacific Railway's grand railroad hotels. The original structure, built near the convergence of the Bow and Spray Rivers, appeared quite different than today's version; in fact, the original wooden hotel burned down in 1926, after which the hotel was rebuilt larger and more like its current appearance. It had its ups and downs in the ensuing years, even closing its doors for a three-year period during World War II. The 245-room Manor Wing was added in the

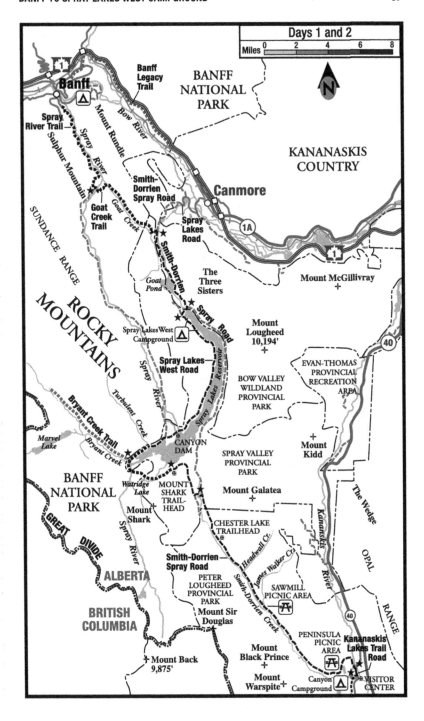

mid-1980s, in preparation for the expected overflow of tourists arriving for the 1988 Winter Olympics in Calgary and nearby Canmore.

Consider stocking up on a few days' worth of food before departing Banff, for the only place to shop between there and Elkford—110 miles and four days away, if you follow the plan set forth here—is the small Boulton Creek Trading Post, located 60 miles from Banff (there are also showers available at the nearby Boulton Creek Campground).

Today's ride is short because no one ever (well, almost never) gets going as soon as they think they will on the first day of an adventure like this. The Spray River Trail, actually a decommissioned roadbed, takes you out of town and into the wilderness. It's lovely and easy riding, but after about 6 miles you'll turn onto the Goat Creek Trail, which is a bit more challenging surface-wise and a lot hillier. There will likely be some hills that necessitate walking if you're pulling a B.O.B. or otherwise hauling a heavy load. After 6 miles on that trail you'll turn south onto the Smith-Dorrien Spray Road, a wide gravel byway that often carries a fair quantity of tourist traffic (and can therefore be quite dusty).

After leaving the Smith-Dorrien Spray Road, you'll cross a dam and enter the Spray Lakes West Campground. The camping begins at about 18 miles, but a string of campsites continues along the reservoir for a good 2 miles, so you might want to resist grabbing the first available site, as there may be a better choice just up the road.

DAY 1 ROUTE

0.0 In the parking lot behind the Fairmont Banff Springs Hotel, begin riding south on the Spray River Trail.

3.6 Notice bridge to the left crossing the Spray River (do not go that way).

6.2 Bear left onto the Goat Creek Trail. A couple of tenths of a mile later, cross the Spray River bridge and begin climbing.

6.8 Top of climb on ridge between Spray River and Goat Creek. The track becomes narrower.

7.5 Cross Goat Creek bridge. Waterfall to right.

8.5 Cross second in a series of three small bridges.

9.5 Cross bridge number three.

11.5 Goat Creek Trail kiosk.

12.0 Turn right onto Smith-Dorrien Spray Road.

15.0 Curve left to cross outlet and stay on main road.

17.1 Spray Lake Ranger Station on right.

17.2 Turn right toward Spray Lakes West Road and ride across dam.

17.5 Curve left, passing campground host's site.

17.9 Spray Lakes West Campground along left side of road.

20.4 Gate. The road is barricaded shut to motor traffic beyond this point. In addition to the sites in the Spray Lakes West Campground, informal camping opportunities can be found between here and Canyon Dam, 7 miles south on the route.

Day 2
SPRAY LAKES WEST CAMPGROUND TO CANYON CAMPGROUND
36.3 miles

Expect some narrow and exposed sections of old roadbed early today as you ride beside Spray Lakes Reservoir, with occasional stretches of talus that has sloughed off the slopes above. After that comes some tricky routefinding as you make your way around the south end of the lake before accessing the Mount Shark trailhead on snow-free (you hope!) cross-country ski trails.

Yesterday, today, and tomorrow you traverse some of the most magnificent scenery in the entire chain of Rocky Mountains. Yet some of it feels more civilized, more settled, than the route in Canada south of Sparwood, as well as along many sections of the U.S. route. One reason for this is quite obvious: Great Divide Canada links together a string of national and provincial parks, which attract a lot of visitors and offer visitor services.

At about mile 19 today you'll enter Peter Lougheed Provincial Park and remain in its borders until crossing the Great Divide at Elk Pass on Day 3. The park is a recreational paradise, with camping, climbing, fishing, hiking, cycling, and other activities in the summer, and a great selection of Nordic ski trails in the winter.

Originally known as Kananaskis Provincial Park, it was renamed in honor of the man who served as the premier of Alberta from 1971 to 1985. Born in Calgary in 1928, Peter Lougheed played football for the University of Alberta and then, in the early 1950s, for the Edmonton Eskimos of the Canadian Football League. After marrying, he earned an MBA at Harvard, working in construction and law before turning his attention to Canadian politics in the early 1960s. As a Progressive Conservative, he was elected first to the legislature and then as premier. Lougheed's tenure was marked by a "provinces' rights" battle against the federal government, largely over the control of Alberta's natural resources. He helped establish the Alberta Heritage Savings Trust Fund, investing oil revenues in health care and other long-term projects. Lougheed died of natural causes in September 2012, in the Calgary hospital named after him.

"Rarely does the passing of a Canadian provincial premier spawn a nationwide outpouring of admiration and affection," read his obituary in the *Economist*. "But Peter Lougheed, a former premier of the western province of Alberta who died on September 13th at the age of 84, was a rarity. During his 14 years in office...Canadians came to know this rather slight man (he was only five-foot-six) as one who played a big role in their country's politics. Rarer still, Mr. Lougheed managed to succeed without making enemies; tributes from across the political spectrum over the past week refer to his integrity and civility. Stephen Harper, the prime minister, described him as 'quite simply one of the most remarkable Canadians of his generation.' "

A man worthy, no doubt, of having his name grace a park so spectacular and well-loved by Canadians.

DAY 2 ROUTE

0.0 Continue along Spray Lakes West Road, from the point where it's barricaded shut to motor traffic.

6.9 Pass through a gate and ride across Canyon Dam. The Spray River Canyon is to your right.

7.1 Do not go right; instead, walk down a steep, short hill, push or ride across the flats, and then push up another short hill. Continue into the woods on an old dirt fire road.

7.9 Go left after climb.

8.1 Go left, then ride downhill.

9.0 Thirty-yard stretch of rocky road.

9.6 Ride across Turbulent Creek bridge. Note waterfall up slot canyon to the right. Trail turns narrower, although it's still along an old roadbed.

10.8 Round bend to view massive Mount Shark.

11.2 Turn right at T-intersection, then note Bryant Creek Trail sign.

11.6 Bear left toward Palliser Trail onto rougher track after cresting small hill. Do not go onto better trail heading uphill to the right.

11.7 After steep little hill, turn left at junction onto better trail. Cross Bryant Creek bridge.

12.2 Bear left and cross bridge over Spray River. Start steep, 0.75-mile uphill, a pusher for many riders.

13.0 Leave Banff National Park. Begin roller-coaster section through timber.

13.6 Continue straight where steep trail drops right toward Watridge Lake.

14.0 Cross footbridge over unsigned creek and continue on main trail, amid a network of Nordic ski trails.

15.8 Veer right to avoid gate and enter the Mount Shark trailhead parking area. Turn left to climb along wide gravel road.

A rider walks his bike over rugged terrain in the vicinity of the Canyon Dam, which holds back the Spray River and creates Spray Lakes Reservoir. (Kathy Kessler-York)

17.1 Mount Shark helipad to right.

18.0 Start down.

19.0 Cross Smuts Creek. Mount Engadine Lodge is off route 0.25 mile to the right.

19.1 Turn right, returning to the wide gravel Smith-Dorrien Spray Road. Enter Peter Lougheed Provincial Park about 0.25 mile later.

23.0 Chester Lake trailhead.

26.7 Sawmill Picnic Area.

35.3 Turn right onto paved Kananaskis Lakes Trail Road toward Boulton Creek Trading Post.

36.0 Peter Lougheed Provincial Park Visitor Centre on left. Turn right onto paved bike path paralleling road.

36.3 Canyon Campground.

Day 3

CANYON CAMPGROUND
TO WEARY CREEK RECREATION SITE

24.9 miles

Today's ride takes you up and over Elk Pass, the one and only crossing of the Continental Divide (a.k.a. Great Divide) on the Canada Section. In the past, residents of Elkford and the surrounding area have stumped for continuing British Columbia Highway 43 up the Elk River and over Elk Pass, thereby creating a shorter all-weather route to Calgary. We're told—and are happy to report—that it's not likely to happen. (However, the author was informed by a campground host in Peter Lougheed Provincial Park that the primitive road over Elk Pass is the official four-wheel-drive escape route for those living in upper K-Country, in the case of wildfire or other natural disaster.)

And so it remains that to drive from where you begin today's 24.9-mile ride to where you end it, you would have to travel approximately 200 miles— something you'll want to keep in mind and plan ahead for if you have a sag wagon accompanying you on your adventure.

At mile 10.9, if you turn right off the route, in about 0.25 mile you'll come to a trailhead that is the major staging area for the Elk Lakes Provincial Park. It's an alpine and subalpine scene so stunning that it seems like it should be a *national* park. In fact, the landscape has been likened to that of the Lake O'Hara area in Yoho National Park, located northwest of here in British Columbia. There's beautiful camping along the shores of Lower Elk Lake, a little less than a mile west of the trailhead. (Bicycling is not permitted on the trail leading to the lake, so you'll need to walk your steed.) There's also a cabin located just north of the trailhead area maintained by the Alpine Club of Canada (visit www.alpineclubofcanada.ca).

Surrounding the Upper and Lower Elk Lakes are lofty Mount Aosta to the south and Mount Fox to the north; and, to the west, the massive Petain, Castelnau, and Elk glaciers. Many of the names worn by the peaks and glaciers here celebrate the French leaders of World War I: Foch, Petain, Joffre, and others. Much of the park is above treeline, though at the lower elevations you'll see stands of lodgepole pine, alpine fir, and Engelmann spruce. Shrubs common to the lower lands include buffalo berry, white rhododendron, and juniper, while fertile wet meadows support gooseberry, Saskatoon berry, and wildflowers like Indian paintbrush, elephant's head, and blue violet. The lakes are embraced by mature old-growth forest, providing habitat for cavity-dwelling birds and small mammals. Large mammals to watch for include those that you would expect to see in a wild northern

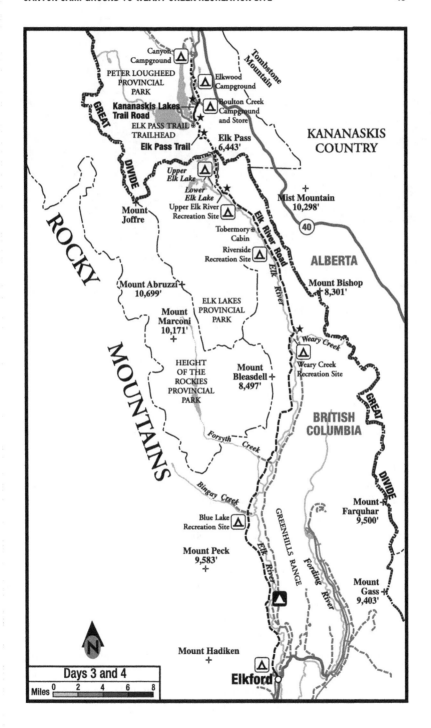

Little-traveled gravel byways like this one are a joy to bicycle, with bears and cougars bigger concerns than busses and cars. (Julie Huck)

wilderness such as this: elk, deer, moose, mountain goats, bighorn sheep, and both black and grizzly bears.

The park is contiguous with Height of the Rockies Provincial Park to the west and northwest; and, of course, with Peter Lougheed Provincial Park to the north. Both Height of the Rockies and Peter Lougheed border Banff National Park to the north. This is a very large continuum of high-mountain wild country.

Once you head south on the Elk River Road at 10.9 miles, you'll find the riding to be a fun, roller-coaster affair. It sometimes looks like you're approaching an uphill, but it all just seems to flow in a general downslope manner. At 13.9 miles you'll pass the Tobermory Cabin, another option for an indoor overnight.

If you notice signs that read "RAPP" and wonder what it stands for, here it is: Report All Poachers and Polluters. Good advice.

DAY 3 ROUTE

0.0   Leave Canyon Campground on the bike path, heading south.

1.2   William Watson Lodge on right.

3.5   Boulton Creek Trading Post. Bike path ends; turn right and then left onto Kananaskis Lakes Trail Road. If you're short on supplies, stock up here on two days' worth of food and water (unless you're counting on filtering surface water, of which there's plenty).

4.7 Turn left into Elk Pass Trail parking area. Access the trail immediately to the right of the restrooms. Go around gate; trail starts out as a good gravel road.

5.2 Uphill grade turns significantly steeper.

5.4 Go under powerline and curve left. You'll more or less follow the powerline all the way to the Elk Lakes Provincial Park trailhead.

6.0 Cross bridge over unnamed creek. At three-way junction, bear left up steep hill nearly 0.4 mile in length.

6.3 Go under powerline, curving right.

8.2 Elk Pass, elevation 6,443 feet; Continental Divide. (First crossing of the divide on the Great Divide Mountain Bike Route.) Leave Alberta and Peter Lougheed Provincial Park; enter British Columbia.

10.9 Walk around gate and turn left onto Elk River Road. Elk Lakes Provincial Park trailhead 0.25 mile to right.

13.7 Upper Elk River BC Forest Service Recreation Site is off route 0.25 mile to the right. Primitive camping.

13.9 Tobermory Cabin, BC Forest Service. Includes cots and woodstove; available on a first-come, first-served basis.

18.0 Riverside BC Forest Service Recreation Site. Primitive camping.

24.2 At Y-intersection, bear right onto unsigned gravel Elk River Road (left is the Kananaskis Powerline Road).

24.9 Weary Creek BC Forest Service Recreation Site. Primitive camping.

Day 4

WEARY CREEK RECREATION SITE TO ELKFORD

28.0 miles

Today's entire ride is through the Elk Valley, with heavily timbered mountains reaching high into the sky on both sides of the road. The Elk is a 140-mile-long river that flows into the Kootenai River (*KOO-te-nai*) at Lake Koocanusa about 10 miles north of the international boundary. Its tributary streams include the Fording River, encountered on Day 5, and the Wigwam River, with which you'll become intimate on Day 8. The Elk River is considered one of the best fly-fishing streams in western Canada.

Considering the pristine mountain country you've been pedaling through since leaving Banff, the vision of the Fording River open-pit coal-mining operations of Teck, Canada's largest diversified mining company, will come as quite a shock. It's the largest resource-extraction activity you'll encounter on the entire Great Divide Mountain Bike Route, and you can't miss it: You'll see it high on the mountainside to your left as you reach the approximate halfway point between last night's campground and Elkford. If you happen to camp at the dispersed sites mentioned at mile 21.8 today, you'll see that it's even more impressive at night, with giant trucks crawling over the mountain and illuminating what otherwise would be dark skies.

Marking its fortieth anniversary on March 15, 2012—the first Vancouver-bound railcar loaded with coal departed Fording River on that date in 1972—the mining operation today employs more than 1,200 workers, making it a major contributor to the region's economy. It's the largest of Teck's five Elk Valley coal mines. And by "large" we mean *huge*: The Fording River operations encompass some 50,000 acres of coal lands, with more than 10,000 acres having been mined, currently being mined, or scheduled for future mining.

Coal resources in the Elk River region are found in Jurassic-period rocks of the Kootenay Formation. Mining of the valley dates back to around 1885, when the railroad tracks arrived. Now with a means to move the coal,

Lunchtime on the trail: A time to relax, refuel, and reflect on the stunning surroundings (Michael Whitfield)

numerous small underground operations have fired up, giving rise to communities like Fernie, Michel, and Corbin (an isolated outpost you'll pass through on Day 6). The underground mines eventually yielded to open-pit operations like those seen today.

The Fording River's reserves of coal, used mainly to produce coke for the global steelmaking industry (a relatively small amount also goes to thermal uses), are projected to last another seventy-five years at the current rate of removal. Both dragline and shovel-and-truck methods are utilized to remove overburden and expose the numerous coal seams, which range in thickness from about three to fifty feet. After loading and hauling away overburden in monster trucks, dozers are used to clean the surface of the coal seam and then push the coal down to a flat-bench loading area. There it's loaded into trucks to be hauled to the crusher. According to Teck, the company's detailed mining plan is complemented by a long-term reclamation program for Eagle Mountain, where the lion's share of the mining is centered.

Elkford is a newish town, incorporated in 1971, that grew up as a result of the coal industry. Even so, it has already dealt with its share of boom times and busts, also direct results of what's happening in the world of coal. Because of the week-on/week-off schedule followed by a lot of the coal-industry workers, many of them, especially single people, commute in from other towns. Consequently, a lot of the wages earned locally are spent elsewhere. Offsetting this to some extent is the fact that Elkford's other natural resources—wilderness and outdoor recreation—are being discovered by a growing number of Canadians, some of whom purchase houses here as retirement homes or vacation getaways.

As far as overnight options go, Elkford has a couple of motels and the Lions Municipal Campground, which boasts more than six dozen "wilderness" sites, hot showers, and complimentary firewood for registered campers.

DAY 4 ROUTE

0.0 Leave Weary Creek Recreation Site, heading south.

12.1 Cross Forsyth Creek.

15.4 Blue Lake BC Forest Service Recreation Site is on right (beautiful primitive camping).

21.8 Dispersed camping spots (with outhouse) in nice meadow along river to the left. (Traffic between here and Elkford can be a little greater than on points north along Elk River Road.)

24.6 Continue straight as road widens.

26.1 Cross cattle guard and enter rural outskirts of Elkford.

27.4 Ride onto pavement.

28.0 Elkford; junction with Fording River Road.

Day 5

ELKFORD TO SPARWOOD

31.1 miles

Today's ride takes you up the big hill out of Elkford on pavement and onto the enjoyable Fording River Road. From then on, elevation gained, it's largely a cruiser. You'll ride along downward-trending roads the rest of the way to Sparwood, as you follow first the Fording River and then the Elk River. The paved, low-traffic Lower Elk Valley Road, accessed at 20.6 miles, is simply a joy to zip along for 8 miles—but don't get too complacent, as there can be the occasional vehicle coming from either direction. Here's a potential side trip you may want to consider: As you climb out of Elkford on Fording River Road, after about 3 miles you'll see the trailhead for Josephine Falls on the right. This popular hike heads to an overlook where the Fording River cascades more than 80 feet down a steep canyon. It's a hike or ride of only about 1.5 miles, largely through a logged-out area (there are woods where you can stash your bike if you choose to hoof it). The story goes that the waterfall was "discovered" by a Professor Osborne—although we suspect aboriginal people saw it before him!—who named it for his teenage daughter after she hooked a large trout at the base of the falls. From the waterfall, further hiking options lead to Lost and Lily lakes. Note: In June 2013, a key section of the Fording River Mining Road washed out. Use Provincial Highway 43 to Sparwood; it offers a decent shoulder and decreases the mileage by 8.6 miles.

After pedaling onto the gravel Fording Road, you'll pass around the back (east) side of Fording Mountain, following the Fording River for much of the way. These are private timber lands, so you may encounter logging operations along the way. The road is generally high grade, although in places it sometimes sustains long-lasting damage from landslides and other causes.

Sparwood, the easternmost town in British Columbia, has at least one motel, a B&B, and the Mountain Shadows Campground. The latter is located on the east side of Provincial Highway 3, about a mile south of "downtown" (you'll understand the quotation marks after seeing it for yourself). If you have a good map, or ask a local for directions, it's possible to reach the campground by way of quiet residential streets west of the highway. If you do stay at Mountain Shadows, try for a site away from the highway, which can be busy all night. The commercial campground's wonderful hot showers make the road noise worth enduring.

Highly recommended before you ride to camp: a root beer float and onion rings at the Sparwood A&W. True, you may have been out in the wilds for less than a week, but you'll fondly recall this little taste of civilization for

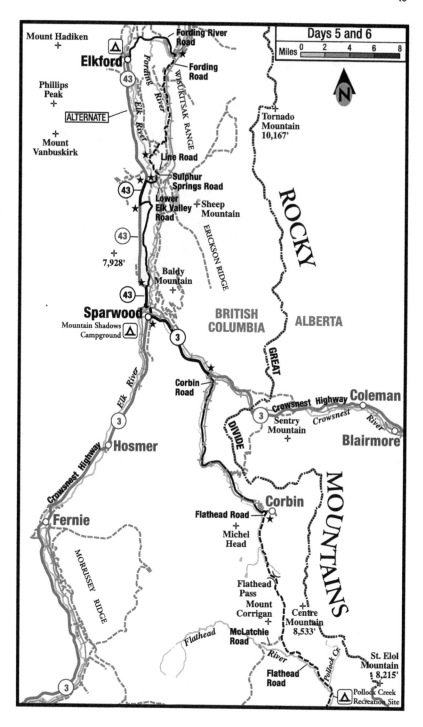

Riders and their bikes are dwarfed by the massive tires of the Terex 33-19 Titan, once the world's largest tandem-axle dump truck. (Doug Werme)

the next several days. On display outside the restaurant is an old continuous miner, a bizarre-looking piece of heavy machinery outfitted with a large rotating steel drum with tungsten-carbide teeth that scrape coal from a seam.

Indeed, Sparwood is in the heart of coal country. In July and August you can even arrange to board a bus at the town visitor center to take a tour of the Elkview Mine, one of Canada's largest open-pit operations. And, speaking of superlatives, you can't miss spotting the immense Terex 33-19 Titan on display in the center of town. Built in 1973 at the General Motors diesel division in London, Ontario, for twenty-five years it was the largest and highest-capacity tandem-axle dump truck in the world (it was supplanted by the somewhat larger Caterpillar 797 in 1998). The Titan has a payload capacity of 350 tons and weighs more than half a million pounds empty. This model is said to be the only 33-19 ever built. On retirement it was restored and placed on static display here in Sparwood.

DAY 5 ROUTE

0.0 Back at the junction in Elkford, turn east to begin climbing on the paved Fording River Road.

2.3 The gradient diminishes.

4.5 Pass through congested area of mining activity (it's the access area for Teck's Fording River operations, described in yesterday's narrative).

6.0   Immediately after crossing bridge, turn right onto unsigned Fording Road. Go straight, crossing the railroad tracks. Route turns into high-grade gravel road paralleling powerlines and railroad tracks to the left.

9.9   Curve left on the main road where another road of nearly equal quality drops to the right.

11.4 Come in just above water on a cliffside bench.

12.5 Cross bridge spanning Fording River as you continue losing elevation.

15.7 Curve left onto wider and potentially dustier road. (This road also goes right, but that would require a right-hand turn of more than 90 degrees.)

16.9 Continue straight as Line Road goes left.

17.1 Cross Fording River, then turn right onto gravel Sulphur Springs Road.

17.8 Turn right onto paved Line Creek Mine access road. Cross Elk River.

18.6 Turn left onto Provincial Highway 43, a primary highway that you'll follow for 2 miles. (A new wide shoulder was under construction in summer 2012.)

20.6 Turn left toward "Airport 5 Km." onto Lower Elk Valley Road.

28.7 Turn left, returning to Provincial Highway 43.

30.1 Pass high over the Elk River and railroad tracks, entering Sparwood. Be sure to use the bike/pedestrian lane, which is isolated from the busy highway by concrete barriers.

30.7 Ride high over Michel Creek and then another set of railroad tracks.

31.0 Continue straight at the stoplight (or turn right into Sparwood to access the residential streets leading to Mountain Shadows Campground, as described in the narrative above).

31.1 Junction, Provincial Highway 3/Crowsnest Highway.

Day 6

SPARWOOD TO POLLOCK CREEK RECREATION SITE

39.5 miles

In Sparwood you're faced with a decision: You can follow the main route through the upper Flathead and Wigwam river valleys, or you can take the Fernie Alternate. The alternate, which was the original and one-and-only route until 2010, is about 40 miles shorter than the new main route and much tamer. Riding the alternate is more like bicycle touring, while tackling the main route is akin to real mountain biking. The alternate first requires riding approximately 16 miles along the busy Provincial Highway 3, which leads from Sparwood to the lively resort town of Fernie. From there, it's predominantly backcountry road riding—on both pavement and gravel—to the international border. (Note: Riding the Fernie Alternate requires that you obtain Adventure Cycling's Canada Section map, as the alternate is not detailed here.)

If you plan to follow the main Flathead-Wigwam route, keep in mind that you won't have another opportunity to purchase supplies until Eureka, Montana, located 125 rugged miles from Sparwood. And be sure to review the "bear aware" tips found on page 28—as mentioned in the introduction to this chapter, the "Grizzly Bear Highway" region holds the largest population of inland grizzlies on the North American continent. Keep your eye out for fresh bear signs—and if you spot some, make even more noise than usual.

The region traversed on the Flathead-Wigwam route is not only remote and spectacular but ecologically unique and significant, to the degree that it spawned the formation of a conservation campaign called "Flathead Wild." This is a coalition of environmental groups in southeast British Columbia and northwest Montana led by Wildsight, a group that works to maintain

The southbound descent of Flathead Pass dishes up some interesting conditions where the road and streambed have become one. (Nicholas Jensen)

biodiversity and healthy human communities in Canada's Columbia and Rocky Mountains ecoregion. The Wildsight website (www.wildsight.ca) states that the Flathead Valley "is one of the most biologically important places on Earth. The valley is home to a free-flowing river with exceptional water quality and is unmatched in North America for the variety, completeness, and density of carnivore species like grizzly bears that live and breed there.... Despite its relatively untouched state and the mining and oil and gas development ban announced by the B.C. government, this area—and the species found here—are still urgently in need of permanent protection."

Toward that end, Flathead Wild is pursuing a vision to create (1) a new National Park Reserve Area in the southeastern third of British Columbia's Flathead River Valley, and (2) a new Southern Rockies Wildlife Management Area connecting habitat through the Flathead, Wigwam, Elk, and Bull river valleys.

"We are excited about the reroute of the Great Divide," Casey Brennan, Southern Rockies program manager for Wildsight, told Adventure Cycling in 2011. "These are important and spectacular trans-boundary watersheds that will provide travelers with an unparalleled wilderness experience." He emphasized that the route, and the riders it attracts, is a great example of sustainable tourism and a perfect activity for the rugged B.C. Flathead River Valley. You can learn more about this important conservation initiative in the Day 7 narrative.

Though you will enter the wild country described above before the day is over, the riding starts out with 7 miles along the busy Crowsnest Highway, which offers a good shoulder. After that there's another 14 miles of pavement on the Corbin Road. It has only a small shoulder but generally carries little traffic (you may need to pull off the road now and then to let a coal truck pass). From Corbin it's a climb of about 6 miles to gain Flathead Pass over a narrow gravel road, much of it quite closed-in with thick willows. Be sure to make lots of noise in these areas to notify bears of your presence. On the other side of the pass you'll encounter some "interesting" riding conditions: very rocky, with areas of severe erosion where the road and the streambed have become one. Expect to dismount now and then, and to get your feet wet.

If you have trouble at Pollock Creek Recreation Site finding a suitable branch to hang your food bag from—a primary "bear aware" tactic—an enterprising solo cyclist from Holland told us that he managed to store his bag at the nearby Flathead River bridge, on a metal structure designed to protect the bridge's wooden pillars from logs floating downstream.

Or, if you'd like to push on, Lower Harvey Creek Recreation Site, just over 5 miles farther, has some beautiful streamside sites in an open meadow.

From there, Butts Patrol Cabin, a possible indoor option (remember, it's first come, first served), is another 10 miles down the road.

DAY 6 ROUTE

0.0 From Sparwood, ride east on Provincial Highway 3/Crowsnest Highway.

7.0 Turn right onto paved Corbin Road at "Teck Mining Coal Mtn." sign.

14.1 Cross bridge.

18.5 Cross bridge.

21.8 Corbin. At gated mine entrance, turn right onto the narrow, gravel Flathead Road and begin climbing.

24.6 Note road going left; stay on main road.

27.5 Flathead Pass, elevation 5,895 feet.

29.0 Cross small bridge.

30.0 Cross another small bridge.

33.1 Pass McLatchie Road coming in on the right.

39.4 Cross Flathead River on major bridge.

39.5 Pollock Creek Recreation Site. Primitive camping.

Day 7

POLLOCK CREEK RECREATION SITE TO RAM-WIGWAM RECREATION SITE

44.1 miles

Today's ride takes you up and over Cabin Pass, a climb of approximately 12 miles that is steep in places. The payoff for all the effort is that your surroundings become ever more spectacular the higher you go.

About a mile after turning onto Cabin Road you will cross Howell Creek. It was in the vicinity of the confluence of Cabin and Howell creeks that a large coal-mining operation was proposed nearly four decades ago. You have many years of hard work by a host of conservation groups to thank for the pristine nature the area retains today.

As mentioned in yesterday's narrative, a coalition of groups from both sides of the border has proposed creating the Flathead National Park Reserve, adding about a third of the Canadian Flathead's acreage to the complex of national parks made up by Glacier National Park in the United States and Waterton Lakes National Park in Canada. "In addition," it's stated on the website of the Crown of the Continent Geotourism Council, "the coalition seeks to establish a Wildlife Management Area that would allow traditional uses outside the national park while establishing fish and wildlife conservation

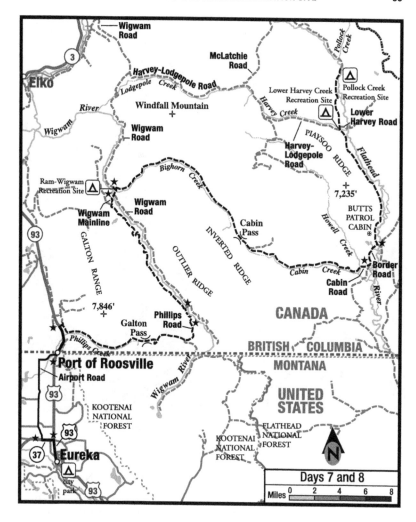

as the highest priority. This proposed WMA would include much of the Flathead, Wigwam, and Elk valleys in British Columbia."

The Crown of the Continent Geotourism Council is a self-described network "working together in the region that includes and surrounds Waterton–Glacier International Peace Park in southwestern Alberta, southeastern British Columbia, and northwestern Montana. Established in 2007, the partnership's focus to date has been collaboration with National Geographic Society on the Crown of the Continent MapGuide and the development of its website."

According to that website (www.crownofthecontinent.net) the Flathead River in British Columbia and Montana (where it's known as the North Fork

Sarah Raz and Josh Tack, shown here on the Great Divide route south of Banff, left their positions at Adventure Cycling in 2012 to bicycle from Alaska to Mexico. (Julie Huck)

of the Flathead and creates the western border of Glacier National Park) has been called "the grizzliest place in the interior of North America." The website says, "In addition to dense populations of grizzly bears and cougars, this is the first place in the western United States that wolves naturally migrated south from Canada after nearly 50 years of absence. As you might expect, all those carnivores are fueled by healthy populations of whitetail and mule deer, as well as elk and moose, and these in turn thrive on a broad diversity of plant communities across this wide-bottomed, low elevation valley."

Dr. John Weaver of the Wildlife Conservation Society has written, "A unique community of carnivore species resides in the transboundary Flathead region that appears unmatched in North America for its variety, completeness, use of valley bottomlands, and density of species that are rare elsewhere."

The website goes on to explain that in February 2010 a historic Memorandum of Understanding (MOU) signed by Montana Governor Brian Schweitzer and British Columbia Premier Gordon Campbell represented a giant step in keeping the Flathead wild in perpetuity. The agreement, signed just before the 2010 Winter Olympics in Vancouver got underway, bans oil and gas drilling and mining in the transboundary watershed.

More than a year later, in November 2011, the province of British Columbia passed a law complementing the 2010 MOU, banning oil drilling, natural gas extraction, and mining from the Flathead basin. Cash was part of the deal: The Nature Conservancy (U.S.) and Nature Conservancy Canada (they're different groups with similar names) agreed to join forces to raise nearly $10 million to pay British Columbia for the costs of mineral exploration already completed. Among the threats over the years: Cline Mining Company's plans to develop an open-pit mine in the headwaters of the Flathead; a 2007 announcement by British Petroleum Canada to develop a 50,000-acre coal-bed methane project in the Elk and Flathead valleys; and a 1974 plan announced by Sage Creek Mining Ltd. for a large coal-mining operation on Cabin and Howell creeks.

In September 2012 the conservancies announced that they had successfully raised the $10 million through private donors. John Lounds, CEO of Nature Conservancy Canada, said the money will be paid to the British Columbia government to help put in place environmental protections, and that some will go to resource companies impacted by the deal. It's unusual, he added, for a nonprofit to pay money to a government, but that in this case it makes sense because it allows for full implementation of the 2010 MOU.

"Nature does not recognize international borders," Lounds said on announcing the success of the fundraising effort. "We are extremely proud to be able to achieve globally significant conservation in partnership with governments, conservation groups, and businesses on both sides of the border."

DAY 7 ROUTE

0.0   From Pollock Creek Recreation Site, continue riding south.

1.5   Pass Packhorse Creek Outfitters on left.

2.6   Cross small bridge.

5.2   Pass Lower Harvey Road on left; then, on right, Lower Harvey Creek Recreation Site and Harvey-Lodgepole Road.

7.3   Cross small bridge.

13.5   Small cabin on right.

15.2   Turn right on Border Road.

15.6   Pass Butts Patrol Cabin on right (optional indoor overnight; first come, first served).

17.1   After the 77 kilometer marker, turn right uphill onto unsigned, lower-quality Cabin Road. After the turn, immediately see an 88-kilometer marker. The next 12 miles are uphill, steep at first and then stairstepping as you get closer to Cabin Pass. (Two miles up the road you just turned off is Howell Creek Campground.)

18.3   Cross Howell Creek

23.2   Cross creek on large bridge.

29.2   Cabin Pass. Use care descending; road is bumpy and scree-covered in places.

32.0   Cross bridge spanning Bighorn Creek.

44.0   Turn sharp left onto Wigwam Road.

44.1   Ram-Wigwam Recreation Site. Primitive camping.

Day 8

RAM-WIGWAM RECREATION SITE TO EUREKA

43.2 miles

For the first 12 miles of today's ride you'll be on a closed road traversing the bench on the west side of the Wigwam River. It's rolling terrain, with a few steep hills thrown in, through forested areas and occasional clear-cuts. Following that you'll come to a stretch of trail that is fast becoming infamously legendary among Great Divide route riders: The roughly 0.5-mile single-track/bushwhack linking the Wigwam Mainline and the high end of Phillips Road.

After traversing some wetlands (watch for blazes on the trees marking the trail), and no doubt getting your feet wet and legs muddy, you'll climb radically up a trail for about 0.25 mile. You will want to carry your trailer or panniers up on one trip, then return to the bottom and haul your bike up. You will also encounter some precarious spots where you do *not* want to fall. Once you get to the top of the steep climb, it's still a ways through the woods to arrive in the clear-cut where you'll find a landing that is the end of the Phillips Road.

After passing through a gate at 16.5 miles you'll begin the tough 5-mile climb to Galton Pass. The ensuing descent to the valley some 3,500 vertical feet below is steep, rocky, rutted, and littered with scree. There's also the chance of encountering cattle, as well as uphill truck or motorcycle traffic. In other words, use extreme caution.

On meeting Provincial Highway 93, you'll ride south 2.4 miles to the international border. (Still have that passport? You'd better.) After entering

Traversing an area of wetlands that leads to the precipitous trail climbing out of the Wigwam River drainage to Phillips Road (Julie Huck)

the United States, you'll enjoy 11 flat miles of farm road and highway, then... Eureka, at last!

Before reaching Eureka you'll pass the Nature Conservancy's Dancing Prairie Preserve, which protects an island of remnant prairie. Characterized by kettle-and-moraine topography, the preserve holds a mosaic of native grasses and wildflowers that thrive in the gravelly soils left behind by receding glaciers. Among other plants, it is home to approximately 90 percent of the world's rare Spalding's catchfly (the Palouse prairie of Washington, Oregon, and Idaho holds the remainder). You can recognize the foot-tall perennial in July and August by its white flower and lime-green foliage that feels sticky to the touch.

DAY 8 ROUTE

0.0 From Ram-Wigwam Recreation Site, ride south.

0.4 At fork, bear right at "Wigwam Mainline" sign. Go around closed gate; cross Wigwam River on a bridge.

6.8 Cross a bridge.

9.0 Cross another bridge.

12.2 Begin descending.

12.8 Watch for rock cairn on right not long after passing a 65-kilometer marker. Turn right onto single-track trail heading into woods (if you come to the river, you've gone too far).

13.4 Climb the steep hill described above, then find your way through the woods on trail.

13.9 Emerge into a clearing, the upper end of Phillips Road. Continue on road.

16.5 Go around gate; continue straight onto the better-surfaced road (road going left is of lower quality). Climb toward Galton Pass.

19.9 Switchback right.

21.5 Galton Pass, 6,319 feet. Use extreme caution on 3,500-foot descent.

26.4 At fork, bear left continuing downhill.

29.6 Switchback left.

29.9 Turn left onto Provincial Highway 93.

32.3 Port of Roosville, U.S.–Canada border. Continue south on U.S. Highway 93.

32.6 Turn right off highway onto Airport Road (paved).

40.3 Turn left onto State Highway 37.

41.3 Turn right onto U.S. Highway 93.

42.5 Enter Eureka.

43.2 South end of downtown; Tobacco Valley Historical Village (this is where you'll leave town). Camping and water pumps available at city park. Eureka has all services.

The northeast flank of Richmond Peak (Day 15) rightly has a bit of a reputation. (Tony Neaves)

CHAPTER 2

EUREKA TO BANNACK STATE PARK, MONTANA

548.4 MILES
Days 9 through 24 (sixteen days)
Five Continental Divide crossings

This section of the Great Divide Mountain Bike Route passes through five national forests: Kootenai, Flathead, Lolo, Helena, and Beaverhead-Deerlodge. The northern half is characterized by steep mountains and seemingly endless stands of western larch, Douglas fir, lodgepole pine, and other coniferous species. Wherever big timber thrives you'll often find logging trucks, as well, so in these forested reaches of the north, remain vigilant for the possibility of monster rigs sharing the route. The southern half of the section, while still offering plenty of timbered areas, is more memorable for its wealth of mining remains and broad valleys teeming with Hereford cattle and variously sized and shaped haystacks. Vistas from high places up north in the Whitefish Range and along Richmond Peak near Seeley Lake may lead you to believe you've been magically whisked away to Alaska; the big spreads and ghost towns of the south are the embodiment of Big Sky Country, evoking the Old West.

The riding begins modestly enough amid the quiet pastoral farm country of the Tobacco Valley, located south of the international border at Port of Roosville. But on leaving the low country surrounding Eureka and entering the Kootenai National Forest, things quickly turn wilder. You'll climb past clear-cuts and through stands of old-growth timber, a setting that in many ways feels more Pacific Northwestern than Rocky Mountain in character. Watch for critters like bears, moose, gray wolves, bald eagles, and pileated woodpeckers.

From the Whitefish Divide the route drops steeply down the valleys of Yakinikak and Trail creeks, places so wild that grizzly bears too unruly to live elsewhere are occasionally relocated here by wildlife officials. You'll then ride for several miles through the valley of the Flathead River's North Fork, which serves as the western boundary of Glacier National Park. After recrossing the Whitefish Divide at Red Meadow Pass, you'll follow dirt roads through state-forest lands to the year-round playground of Whitefish, home to the Whitefish Mountain Resort, one of Montana's top destination ski areas.

From Whitefish the Great Divide route follows a series of paved and gravel roads through the agrarian, mountain-ringed upper Flathead Valley. A rather complex network of old logging roads subsequently takes you through or above the Seeley-Swan Valley to Seeley Lake. The next town visited is Lincoln, south of which you'll begin seeing signs that the resource-extraction industry of choice—for a long time that of removing timber from the mountain slopes—is switching to that of removing minerals from within them. Helena, Montana's capital, is one mining town that made it big, having avoided the ghost-town fate met by so many other old camps now littering the surrounding hills. From Helena it is on to the unique city of Butte, by way of Basin, north of which defunct mines with names like Hattie Ferguson and Morning Glory line the way. Helena and Butte are the two largest cities visited on the entire Great Divide route.

From Butte you'll head to the fly-fishing outpost of Wise River, then ride the paved Pioneer Mountains National Scenic Byway as it wends between the east and west units of the sublime Pioneer Mountains. Finally, a descent past Elkhorn Hot Springs spits you out into the irrigated green valley of Grasshopper Creek, which you follow to the ghost town of Bannack.

Day 9
EUREKA TO TUCHUCK CAMPGROUND
30.7 miles

In Eureka you'll want to stock up on groceries for at least two days, as you won't see another grocery store on the route until the end of Day 11 in Whitefish. (There is the option on Day 10 of detouring into Polebridge, which has a minimally stocked store.) From Eureka, 10 miles of mellow riding on paved roads take you through a landscape alternating between bucolic, open farmland, and dense forests, the latter only hinting at the wild country soon to come. Finally, at 22 miles you'll hit pay dirt, ascending the moderately graded FR 114 for 6 miles to the Whitefish Divide, then coasting down that road for another 5.6 miles to the Tuchuck Campground, a Kootenai National Forest site nestled along Yakinikak Creek in a marvelously wild setting. Once again, this area is home to both black and grizzly bears. Because much of today's ride is on pavement and the distance is moderate, it's relatively easy. Stream water is plentiful, but—as always—be sure to filter it before drinking.

The glacially formed Tobacco Valley, in which Eureka resides, earned its name either from the indigenous Kootenai Indians, who ostensibly grew tobacco in the area, or from failed attempts by area missionaries to raise the same crop. While the climate may not be ideal for growing tobacco, Eureka, at an elevation of just 2,577 feet above sea level, is mild by Montana standards. Eureka claims the distinction of being both the lowest (altitude-wise) and highest (regarding its position at the top of the map) town on the U.S. portion of the Great Divide route.

Forestry and farming come together in the Tobacco Valley, where a primary crop is Christmas trees. In fact, Eureka calls itself "Christmas Tree Capital of the World" (hard to dispute, although other towns in the United States and beyond call themselves that too). Don't miss visiting the sprawling Tobacco Valley Historical Village, situated at the southwest end of downtown.

They're in two different countries, but southern British Columbia and northwestern Montana are often indistinguishable. (Kathy Kessler-York)

On site are the Peltier log home (Eureka's first residence), the old Rexford train depot, and several other buildings, including a hand-hewn log ranger station and the old Fewkes Store, all of them linked by a stout boardwalk. In addition to highlighting the logging legacy of the region, displays and artifacts interpret the history and prehistory of the area's Kootenai Indians.

The Kootenai regarded themselves as one people, but they were actually divided by the Kootenai River into two tribes, the Upper and Lower Kootenai. The two subgroups resided in different parts of the region, where each developed a distinct language and its own traditions. Before acquiring horses in the mid-1700s, which radically changed their lifestyle, both the Lower and Upper Kootenai fished the Kootenai River, utilizing traps and individual fishing tools. They also gathered plants such as bitterroot and camas root, and hunted for big-game species, including deer, bighorn sheep, elk, bear, and mountain goats. The Kootenai altered the native landscape by burning underbrush every year to open up the forests and make hunting easier.

DAY 9 ROUTE

0.0 From the Tobacco Valley Historical Village, ride southwest to cross railroad tracks and river in about 0.25 mile. Continue uphill on unsigned Old Highway/Tobacco Road.

0.6 Follow road signed "Old Highway."

7.3 At T-intersection turn left onto Barnaby Lake Road.

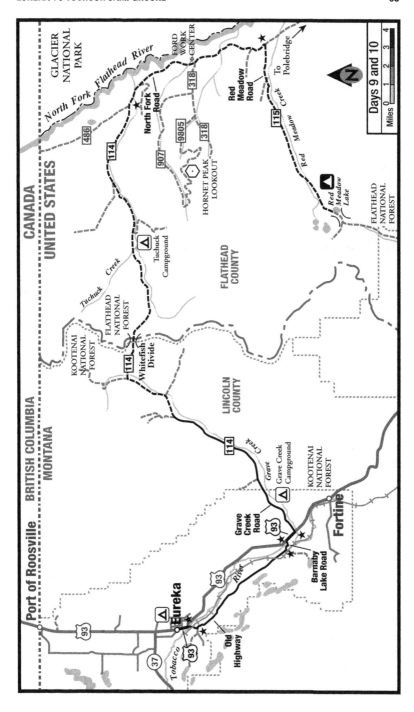

8.0   Turn right onto U.S. Highway 93.

8.9   Turn left onto Grave Creek Road.

11.9 Grave Creek Campground.

13.1 Continue straight on FR 114/Grave Creek Road.

19.1 Curve right; pavement ends.

23.0 Turn right off main road, following sign reading "N. Fk. Flathead 17 miles/Forest Road 114." Uphill grade steepens.

25.1 Crest Whitefish Divide and begin descending through a wild valley.

30.7 Tuchuck Campground.

Day 10

TUCHUCK CAMPGROUND TO RED MEADOW LAKE

30.1 miles

Today's ride is relatively easy, both in terms of terrain and mileage. From Tuchuck Campground you'll ride along Trail Creek down gravel-surfaced FR 114 to its junction with FR 486, also known as the North Fork Road. For nearly 10 miles you'll follow this relatively major gravel road along the North Fork of the Flathead River, which forms the western boundary of Glacier National Park—and is the same river you encountered on Day 6 in British Columbia, where it's known simply as the Flathead River. At 18.4 miles you'll make the westerly turn up FR 115 and begin climbing on gravel beside Red Meadow Creek to the night's destination of Red Meadow Lake. Alternatively, at 18.4 miles you could opt to leave the route and ride into Polebridge, located 5.5 miles from this point. Funky, fun, and home to the unique North Fork Hostel, Polebridge serves as the western side door into Glacier National Park. Potential off-route rides from this outpost lead to destinations in the park that include spectacular Kintla and Bowman lakes, and Lake McDonald and Going-to-the-Sun Road via the Inside North Fork Road. Polebridge boasts a minimally stocked grocery store and a café; if you opt to bypass the settlement, you will find no services on today's ride. Stream water is abundant.

As you pedal through the primeval forests that embrace today's route, keep an eye out for wildlife such as bear, moose, elk, and cougar. There are also two other animals you conceivably could glimpse in the Kootenai National Forest, but only if you're lucky enough to win the lottery: the rare Canadian lynx and the woodland caribou. Signs found by biologists have led to speculation that the latter occasionally slip across the Canadian border into these far-northern, forested reaches of the United States.

At mile 13.5, near the Ford Work Center, you'll see FR 318 going west. If by chance you're feeling particularly energetic—or if you plan to shorten the day's mileage by overnighting in Polebridge—consider taking a side trip 8.5 miles up FR 318 and FR 9805 to the trailhead for Hornet Peak Lookout. From here it's an uphill hike of a mile-plus to the top of 6,744-foot Hornet Peak. Gracing the peak is a 1922 D-1 standard fire lookout, said to be the last of its kind standing. Rather than sitting atop a high tower, as many later-built lookouts do, Hornet is simply a log cabin with a shingled, aerie-like cupola perched on top. Early Forest Service workers constructed the lookout using on-site timber, which they felled with crosscut saws and then squared and notched with broadaxes.

Wild huckleberries, one of nature's tastiest treats, grow abundantly in the forests of northwest Montana, generally ripening in early August. (Kyle Karlson)

More recently, through a partnership involving the Flathead National Forest and the nonprofit North Fork Preservation Association, volunteers performed renovation work on the lookout, injecting new life into the old beauty. (The lookout can be reserved for rustic overnight accommodations by calling the Hungry Horse Ranger District at 406-387-3800.)

An equally rewarding benefit of expending the energy to gain Hornet Peak is the incomparable view it affords of the western reaches of Glacier National Park. Long, narrow glacial lakes glisten between fingers of heavily forested ridges, the lakes' upper, eastern ends reaching to meet ice- and snow-clad mountains. To complete a loop rather than backtracking, you can enjoy the incredible downhill cruise to FR 907, which parallels Tepee Creek back to FR 318, meeting it at a point 2 miles west of the Ford Work Center.

As you head west up Red Meadow Road toward the day's destination, you'll pass through remains of the 1988 Red Bench Fire, which blew up during the same dry summer as the big Yellowstone fires. Nearly 40,000 acres of lodgepole pine, most of it dead or dying due to mountain pine beetle infestation, burned as firefighters worked tirelessly to suppress the conflagration. The fire burned so hot that it even killed a large number of ancient ponderosa pine and western larch trees that had survived numerous other fires during the previous 350 years. Blackened, skeletal trees reach for the sky, while on the ground below sprout fireweed and a new generation of conifers. Additional fires have burned in the general vicinity since 1988.

DAY 10 ROUTE

0.0 From Tuchuck Campground, continue east on FR 114.

9.1 Turn right onto North Fork Road/FR 486.

13.5 Ford Work Center.

18.4 Turn right onto FR 115/Red Meadow Road.

30.1 Red Meadow Lake. Primitive camping.

Day 11

RED MEADOW LAKE TO WHITEFISH

29.7 miles

Today's 30-mile ride begins in virtual wilderness and ends in bustling Whitefish, a place that's about as civilized as things get in Montana. Although the surrounding terrain is exceedingly steep, the roads followed are quite moderate in grade and mostly downhill to boot: After the short, easy climb from Red Meadow Lake to the Whitefish Divide, you'll lose a half-mile of elevation en route to Whitefish. Don't worry about whizzing past services before you notice them, because none are found until you get to Whitefish. The first 22 miles of the ride are along dirt and gravel roads of the Flathead National Forest and the Stillwater State Forest, and the final 8 miles follow pavement.

The steep slopes hanging high above the earlier portions of the ride are commonly striped and fanned with avalanche chutes. Interestingly, it's usually not the force of an avalanche's cascading snow that breaks and uproots trees; rather, it is the powerful winds—estimated to approach 130 miles per hour, moving in advance of the tons of sliding snow—that smash through the forests. Brimming in summer with herbs, shrubs, and berries, these natural forest clearings provide a buffet of dining opportunities for grizzly bears. The bears favor juicy, young plants, which are more nutritious than older plants, so their tendency is to move upslope as summer progresses and the snowline recedes, thereby taking advantage of plants that sprout as soon as the snow disappears. Grizzlies also use the avalanche openings as travel corridors and for bedding down.

A couple of miles after departing Red Meadow Lake you'll leave the Flathead National Forest and enter the Stillwater State Forest, created in the late 1910s by terms of a land swap between the federal government and

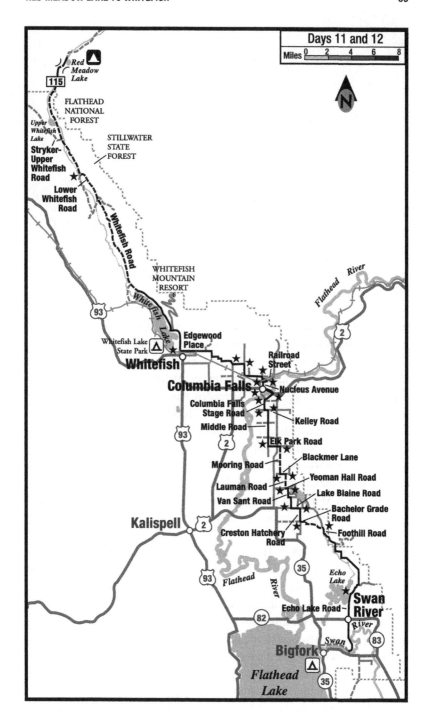

Some cyclists pack their gear in panniers, some in frame-mounted packs, and others—like this rider—in trailers such as the B.O.B. (Julie Huck)

the State of Montana. Some 40,000 acres of timber in the forest burned in a 1926 fire, precipitating construction of a full-time ranger station and equipment warehouse. This ushered in a new era of forest management in Montana. Recent critics have decried that the Stillwater State Forest has been overmanaged—overlogged and overroaded, that is—and underprotected. See if you notice any striking differences in the character of the forests after leaving the Flathead National Forest for the Stillwater.

If Steamboat Springs, Colorado, which you'll visit later in your adventure, is where cowboying meets schussing (as all the ski magazines seem eager to point out), then Whitefish is where logging and skiing join forces. The Whitefish Mountain Resort, one of Montana's three major destination ski resorts, provides an imposing backdrop for old "Stumptown," as frontier Whitefish was called.

Known until 2008 as The Big Mountain, the resort has operated commercially for more than sixty years. Like many ski areas, it began as the haunt of local ski pioneers. In the 1930s woolen-clad members of the loosely knit Hell-Roaring Ski Club, named for a creek drainage on the mountain, began shuffling into the hills above Whitefish on primitive skis with traction-providing ropes attached to the bottoms. At some point the skiers would remove the ropes, point their solid-wood skis downhill, and let 'em run. Falling, controlled and otherwise, was their main means of stopping and changing directions. Eventually, club members built a pair of warming/overnighting huts and persuaded the Forest Service to extend an access road that already went partway up the mountain. A lot of Whitefish folk got hooked on skiing in this manner, and the sport was poised to become business. On March 31, 1947, several investors formed Winter Sports, Inc.—they had turned down the proposed name of Hell-Roaring Ski Corporation, believing it would scare away potential visitors—and on December 14 of that year The Big Mountain opened for business, charging two dollars per rope-tow ticket.

DAY 11 ROUTE

0.0 Continue riding west on FR 115 from Red Meadow Lake.

2.1 Leave the Flathead National Forest and enter the Stillwater State Forest.

5.6 Upper Whitefish Lake.

6.0 Continue straight; Stryker Road goes right.

10.4 Turn left toward Lower Whitefish Road.

12.6 Continue straight.

21.6 Continue straight.

22.1 Ride straight onto pavement, looking down on Whitefish Lake.

29.7 Pass road on left signed "Edgewood Place"; leave route and ride over railroad bridge into downtown Whitefish. All services. Camping is available at commercial campgrounds and at Whitefish Lake State Park, located about a mile west of town.

Day 12
WHITEFISH TO SWAN RIVER CROSSING
40.4 miles

Today's ride provides a break from the wild, densely forested—and unforgivingly hilly—mountains of northwest Montana. From Whitefish to Bigfork you will ride mostly on a maze of beeline roads traversing the flats between the Swan Mountains and the Flathead River. They are the sort of "right-angle" roads, laid out on east–west and north–south axes, which typify farm country. Although Bigfork, the suggested overnight destination, is located 2 miles off the route, it's highly recommended that you go there. It's a gorgeous little town, brimming with boutiques and cafés; moreover, Bigfork sits at the mouth of the Swan River on the northwest shore of immense Flathead Lake. It would be a shame to be this close to the largest freshwater lake west of the Mississippi and not even lay eyes on it.

Long one of the most popular businesses in Bigfork, among visitors and locals alike, is Eva Gates Homemade Preserves (www.evagates.com), established in 1949. The place is best known and loved for its delicious preserves made from the huckleberries that grow wild on the mountain slopes above town and elsewhere in northwest Montana. If it happens to be late July or early August when you are riding through, you can probably find your own bounty of the berries. On returning to the mountains tomorrow, check the forest floors and brushy openings adjacent to the road for the ripening fruits. Depending on the weather of the previous few months, you may find a few small "hucks" here and there on the bushes, or they might be ponderously awaiting the picking, dangling by the hundreds from their greenery like shiny purple marbles. (Another factor affecting huckleberry production is forest fire, or lack of it: In order to remain fertile, huckleberry bushes appear to need to burn at least every few decades.)

Huckleberries are the favorite late-summer/early fall food of black bears and grizzly bears. Sample a few and you'll agree that bears have excellent taste! And make plenty of noise just in case you're intruding on a bruin in his personal patch. Bears rely heavily on hucks to provide the carbohydrates needed to fatten up before going into hibernation, so a low-yield year is bad news for bears, indeed. Following a huckleberry-poor autumn, old or otherwise infirm bears have a slimmer chance of living through the winter, and pregnant females can give birth to fewer cubs. It's also more common during poor-crop autumns for bears to go scratching for food in other, more hazardous places, such as the apple trees in their human neighbors' backyards.

DAY 12 ROUTE

0.0   Return to north side of railroad bridge and ride east onto Edgewood Place.

2.7   Road curves right.

5.5   Just beyond a right-hand curve, turn left onto paved Tamarack Lane.

6.5   Turn right at T-intersection, following Tamarack Lane.

9.0   Turn right at 4-way junction onto 4th Avenue NW.

9.8   Cross five sets of railroad tracks, then turn right onto Railroad Street.

10.1   Turn left onto unsigned Nucleus Avenue and pass through downtown Columbia Falls. The town has all services.

10.7   Turn left at stoplight onto U.S. Highway 2.

11.4   Cross the Flathead River and turn right at end of bridge onto paved River Road.

12.2   Turn left onto Columbia Falls Stage Road (paved).

13.1   Turn left onto Kelley Road (paved).

13.3   Turn right onto Middle Road (paved).

16.3   Turn left onto Elk Park Road (paved).

17.3   Ride across a main road, and 0.25 mile later turn right onto Mooring Road (gravel).

19.6 Turn left onto Blackmer Lane (paved).

20.1 Turn right onto Lauman Road (gravel).

21.4 Turn left at T-intersection onto Yeoman Hall Road (paved).

21.6 Turn right onto Van Sant Road (gravel), which curves left, then right.

23.4 Turn left onto Lake Blaine Road (paved).

24.2 Turn right onto Creston Hatchery Road (paved).

25.2 Turn left onto Bachelor Grade Road (gravel).

27.5 Turn right at T-intersection onto unsigned Foothill Road (paved). Ride with extra caution over next few miles, as the road is winding and sometimes busy with traffic.

35.1 Turn left at T-intersection onto paved Echo Lake Road.

37.3 Swan River. Café, art gallery, mini-mart, service station. Cross State Highway 83.

40.4 Just before crossing the Swan River on bridge, leave the route by riding west onto the old road that leads 2 miles to Bigfork. All services, including camping, and a wealth of shopping and dining opportunities.

The sock says it all: "Montana Dirt Girls." Here a trio of MDGs break for lunch on the trail in the Treasure State. (Julie Huck)

PEOPLE YOU'LL MEET: RON AND JAN BRUNK

In 1980 Ron and Jan Brunk bicycled into Whitefish in search of a new home. "In about two days," recalls Jan, "we decided this was the place we were meant to be." The town's economy was depressed at the time, so the couple got work where they could find it. Ron began repairing bikes part-time in the back of the Glacier Mountaineering outdoor store. "I soon started getting so busy," he says, "that we either had to go full-time with the bike business or back away from it completely." Choosing the former option, in 1982 the Brunks purchased a small building in downtown Whitefish and opened the doors of Glacier Cyclery.

Seventeen years after discovering Whitefish, in celebration of their seventeenth anniversary the Brunks pedaled out of town—this time on vacation, and on the Great Divide Mountain Bike Route. Impressed by what they saw, they soon "purchased" several miles under Adventure Cycling's Trailblazer program. "Our favorite," Ron says, "is the mile straddling the Whitefish Divide, up near Red Meadow Lake."

Recently, the Brunks added "Nordic" to the shop's name, and Glacier Cyclery & Nordic now provides Whitefish-area residents and visitors the proper tools to enjoy the outdoors year-round.

Day 13

SWAN RIVER CROSSING TO CEDAR CREEK CAMPGROUND

33.0 miles plus 2 miles returning to route from Bigfork and 1 mile off route to Cedar Creek Campground at day's end

Before leaving Bigfork you'll want to buy groceries for one or two days, depending on whether or not you plan to have dinner at Holland Lake Lodge on Day 14. Stock up on water, too, for much of the day will be spent high on ridges where surface water is rare. Back into the mountains, you'll ride on roads that are winding and everchanging in direction, the antithesis of the Flathead Valley roads you followed yesterday. After leaving the pavement and entering the Flathead National Forest, you'll be compelled to tackle a long, sometimes steep climb of approximately 6 miles, on a hard-packed gravel road that ascends the ridge separating Flathead and Swan lakes. After topping out you'll freefall for several miles on similarly surfaced

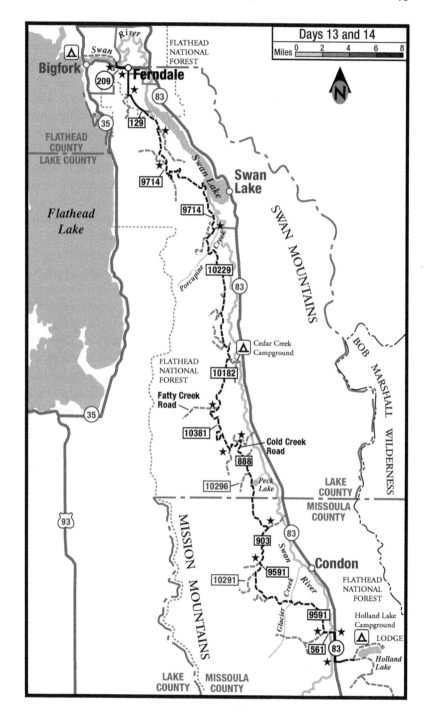

roads before beginning along a series of rolling, primitive dirt roads tucked between the foot of the Mission Mountains and State Highway 83. Surface water is abundant on the final third of today's ride; services are nonexistent throughout the day.

Today, and tomorrow too, you'll see lots of forest and plenty of clear-cuts. Some older clear-cuts have assumed the character of natural openings, and you may actually be grateful for these, as they permit across-the-valley views of the majestic Swan Mountains that otherwise would be obscured by trees. One species you can't help noticing here and elsewhere in northwest Montana is the beautiful western larch. The tree has a rich reddish-brown trunk that grows tall and impossibly straight. David Thompson, who came early into these parts as a fur trader for the North West Company, wrote about one immense western larch he ran across in the Kootenai River country in 1808, with a "thirteen feet girth and one hundred and fifty feet clean growth" ("clean growth" meaning the trunk below where branches begin appearing).

The largest of several Pacific Northwest tamarack species, the western larch is one of a rare breed of deciduous conifers; that is, it sheds its needles each autumn. After turning golden, the needles drift to earth, glimmering in the sun like fairy dust and carpeting the forest floor with color. The trees appear dead and somber in winter, but come spring fresh larch needle growth provides the otherwise dark-green forest with wonderfully bright splashes of spring green. Mature western larch are particularly impressive: Fully two-thirds of their height can consist of clear, straight trunk, before limbs start branching out on the upper third. Individual trees can grow as tall as 200 feet, although 150 feet is more common.

The straight grain and relatively dense wood of the western larch makes it the favorite of savvy firewood cutters in these parts. Its strong, decay-resistant qualities also make the tree ideal for use in items such as telephone poles and mine timbers. Prehistoric Indians brewed a tea from its bark (purportedly as a treatment for tuberculosis, coughs, and colds), chewed its solidified pitch like gum, took advantage of its solid wood for fashioning bowls, and used the tree's rotted wood for smoking buckskin. It's also said that the Kootenai Indians preferred the larch for the center pole in performing sundance ceremonies. Tribes east of the Rockies typically employed cottonwoods for the purpose.

DAY 13 ROUTE

0.0 From where you left the route, cross the Swan River on a bridge, then turn left onto State Highway 209.

1.2 Ferndale. At St. Patrick's Episcopal Church, turn right onto unsigned Crane Mountain Road toward Swan River.

Vince and Angie Vincent of Utah covered the northern half of the route in 2011 and the southern half in 2012. They did not carry their bikes the entire way. (Don Vincent)

3.2 Turn left at the Y onto FR 129 toward Bug Creek.

4.8 Pavement ends.

5.6 Bear right uphill away from "Dead End" sign and begin extended climb.

11.4 Turn left downhill onto FR 9714 toward Yellow Creek.

12.6 Switchback left.

21.0 Turn right at T-intersection onto FR 10229 toward Porcupine Creek.

22.1 Drop left onto more primitive road toward "Fatty Creek Road—12 miles." The ensuing stretch passes through some impressive stands of old-growth western larch, Douglas fir, and white pine.

29.1 Continue straight, following Fatty Creek Road sign.

33.0 Leave route and ride 1 mile east to Cedar Creek Campground, small and pleasant but potentially mosquito-abundant. (Previous Great Divide route riders have reported that the best campsite is on the second road, closest to Swan River.)

Day 14

CEDAR CREEK CAMPGROUND TO HOLLAND LAKE

37.9 miles plus 1 mile returning to route from Cedar Creek Campground and 1 mile plus off route to Holland Lake at day's end

Today you'll continue winding south-southeastward through the Swan Valley, cutting across several drainages that crease the east slope of the Mission Mountains. The uphills and downhills are many but moderate along this maze of old dirt- and gravel-surfaced logging roads. After about 34 miles you'll turn onto State Highway 83, the Swan Highway, and spin along it for 1.6 miles before making the turn toward Holland Lake Lodge. In another 2.6 miles you'll come to the turn-off to the resort, near which there's also a pleasant Forest Service campground. The picturesque lodge is perched above the shore of shimmering Holland Lake, with a big, green lawn reaching between lodge and lake. Beyond loom the glorious mountains of the Swan Front. Holland Lake Lodge is a semi-dude ranch, but in addition to hauling pilgrims into the mountains on horseback they can accommodate drop-ins for meals and for rooms and cabins, space permitting. You might want to plan on having both supper and breakfast at the lodge's restaurant. You can also buy a shower or a sauna soak here, and the resort rents canoes for paddling on placid Holland Lake.

If you can swing it, consider taking a hike while in the area, for you're in the middle of one of the biggest concentrations of wilderness in the contiguous United States. Look at a map of the area to see that to the west lies the USFS-administered Mission Mountains Wilderness and the adjacent Mission Mountains Tribal Wilderness, which lies within the Flathead Indian Reservation. The Missions offer a woolly Alaska-type wilderness experience, with bushwhacking required to get to many of its more remote areas ... and plenty of grizzly bears.

On the other side of the valley, to the east, is the Bob Marshall Wilderness. Adjoining "the Bob" on the southeast is the Scapegoat Wilderness, and to the north the Great Bear Wilderness. Combined, the triad of wilderness areas encompasses some 1.5 million acres. Add to that the nearly 1 million wilderness acres of Glacier National Park, separated from the Great Bear only by a road corridor, and you have a wilderness complex of 2.5 million acres. That's larger than Yellowstone National Park.

The Bob, crown jewel of Montana's wilderness areas, was named after Bob Marshall, a forester and pioneer leader of the American wilderness preservation movement. Marshall hoofed hundreds of miles through the wild country surrounding the South Fork of the Flathead River, gathering

Occasional dismounting and pushing are not only acceptable, they are sometimes required if you want to get from Point A to Point B. (Julie Huck)

information that he would turn into a recommended plan for saving much of the area from development. In 1940, shortly after Marshall's untimely death, the federal government set aside for protection nearly a million acres surrounding the South Fork. After Congress passed the Wilderness Act in 1964, the Bob received additional protection as a component of the National Wilderness Preservation System.

The well-maintained trail between Holland Lake and Gordon Pass is a popular west-slope route into the Bob, used by both backpackers and horse-packers. One destination, rising some 25 miles northeast of Holland Lake as the raven flies, is the Chinese Wall, a 1,000-foot-high escarpment along which the Continental Divide runs for miles. Forming part of the boundary between the Bob and the Sun River Game Preserve, the Chinese Wall is home to bighorn sheep, shaggy-white mountain goats, and golden eagles, which nest along its lofty cliffs.

DAY 14 ROUTE

0.0 From where you left the route, ride west on dirt road.

4.4 Turn left onto FR 10381 (road may be gated).

9.5 Turn left toward "Swan Highway."

11.2 Turn right onto Cold Creek Road/FR 888.

14.0 Continue straight where FR 10296 goes right.

15.0 Peck Lake on left. Big clear-cuts over next couple of miles provide open views of the Swan Mountains and Mission Mountains.

19.2 Turn right onto FR 903.

22.6 Drop left onto FR 9591. This road is closed and blocked; cross creek and go around boulders.

23.2 Turn left to continue on unsigned FR 9591; FR 10291 goes straight. The single-track stretch has been gated and is filling in with grass.

26.1 Pass through gate and continue straight.

28.4 Ride straight through clearing; you'll see an 11-mile marker where roads go left and right. Cross Glacier Creek.

32.6 Turn left at T-intersection onto FR 561.

33.7 Turn right onto State Highway 83.

35.3 Turn left onto paved road leading east toward Holland Lake Lodge.

37.9 Leave route, continuing around north side of Holland Lake to the Forest Service campground or to Holland Lake Lodge.

Day 15

HOLLAND LAKE TO SEELEY LAKE

32.0 miles plus 1 mile plus returning to route from Holland Lake Lodge and 2 miles off route to Seeley Lake at day's end

After leaving Holland Lake this morning there are no services until the end of the day, off route a couple of miles, in the town of Seeley Lake. Confronting you immediately after setting out is a substantial climb, followed by a wonderful 2.5-mile stretch of gated, grassed-over road . . . followed by another, even tougher, climb of 5.5 miles. By the time you reach the top of that hill, at 16.9 miles, your legs will definitely be awake. (Note: At 9.3 miles into the day's ride, seriously consider making the 0.5-mile side trip to Clearwater Lake, a hidden gem perfect for a picnic or a swim.) But the best and most challenging part of the day is yet to come: After going around a gate at

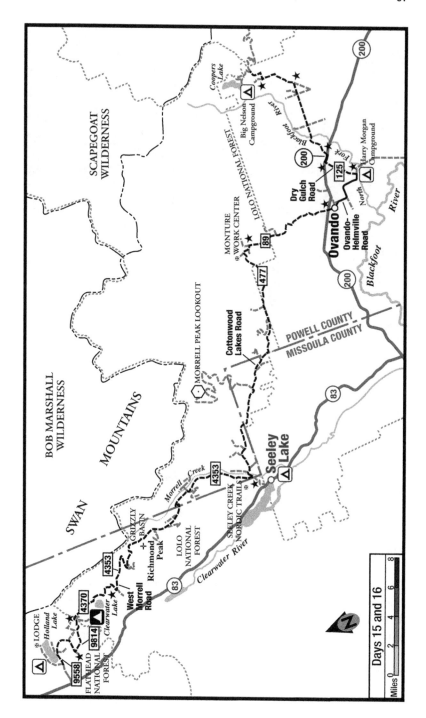

Mountain-bike handlebars, beargrass, and a single-track trail traversing a timbered hillside: A Montana mountain still life (Julie Huck)

18 miles you'll begin a 4-mile segment of old road bed, exceedingly rough and eroded in places, that winds around the northeast flank of Richmond Peak into a marvelous alpine basin. The stretch has become famous... or infamous, perhaps, since Great Divide route riders seem either to love it or hate it. It definitely requires patience to negotiate, as downfall, overgrowth, rocks, and washouts all team up to hinder progress. Even those who complain about the conditions, though, rave about the scenery: It looks like a piece of Glacier National Park that was picked up and moved 60 miles south. Keep

your eyes peeled for bears on the move through the avalanche chutes striping the slopes across the way in aptly named Grizzly Basin. Once you cross a second gate at 21.8 miles, you'll follow hard-surfaced gravel roads downhill along Morrell Creek for the next 10 miles.

At 32 miles you'll make a turn off route to head for Seeley Lake, the name of both a big lake and the lively little resort town on its banks. At the junction where you turn you'll notice the trailhead for the Seeley Creek Nordic Trails. Although laid out primarily for cross-country skiing—some of the best Nordic skiing in Montana is found here—the Seeley Creek Nordic Trails were simultaneously planned with the mountain bicyclist in mind, and Adventure Cycling personnel were consulted to help with trail planning. The system offers some terrific single-track and two-track riding, in case you're not too worn out to give it a try.

Another, decidedly different sort of trail experience you can enjoy in the Seeley Lake area is a float down the mellow Clearwater Canoe Trail. Beginning 5 miles north of town, the "trail" was designated and christened by the Lolo National Forest administration, which wanted to locate and promote a quiet stretch of river that any canoeist, even a neophyte, could safely handle. This 4-mile stretch of the Clearwater proved perfect, with its deep channel and lack of logjams, the bane of canoeists on many similar-sized streams of the region. Along the willow-embraced water trail, which encompasses a marsh-type environment that's common to the lake states but rare in the Rockies, you can see and hear an unusually large number of songbird species in spring. Other possible wildlife sightings include common loons, moose, beaver, painted turtles, bald eagles, and ospreys. Canoe rentals and shuttles to and from the trailhead can be arranged in Seeley Lake. You'll also want to buy groceries for the next two days.

DAY 15 ROUTE

0.0   From where you left the route, ride uphill onto FR 9558 toward "Owl Packer Camp."

0.5   Take middle option toward Owl Creek, continuing uphill.

3.9   Turn left onto FR 9814; "Snowmobile Trail #15" is marked with an orange diamond.

4.1   Continue straight onto lesser-traveled dirt trail.

4.3   Cross gate onto overgrown road.

5.8   Stay low/straight as another road heads uphill to the right.

6.9   After cresting steep hill, cross over gate and turn left onto gravel FR 4370.

9.3   Note trail on right; it leads 0.5 mile to Clearwater Lake, which has primitive camping.

12.5 Turn left at T-intersection onto West Morrell Road/FR 4353. Begin steep 5.5-mile climb.

16.9 At four-way junction, turn sharp left. FR 4353 becomes a trail; ride around boulders to access it.

18.0 Cross gate; road becomes exceedingly rough in places as it winds around the northeast flank of Richmond Peak into a spectacular alpine basin. Rocks and downed trees over the next 3.8 miles make travel arduous.

21.8 Cross gate and proceed onto high-grade gravel road.

22.5 Continue straight downhill.

26.3 Continue straight on FR 4353.

32.0 Trailhead, Seeley Creek Nordic Trails. Leave route and ride 2 miles west into Seeley Lake. All services, including Forest Service campgrounds.

Day 16

SEELEY LAKE TO BIG NELSON CAMPGROUND

42.7 miles plus 2 miles returning to route from Seeley Lake and 2 miles off route to Big Nelson at day's end

Buy groceries for a couple of days before leaving Seeley Lake, for the next reasonably stocked store is in Lincoln, at the end of Day 17. Today you'll begin skirting the southern end of the Bob Marshall and Scapegoat Wilderness Areas for several miles on good gravel roads; then, after a paved interlude of nearly 4 miles along State Highway 200, it's back onto gravel. You'll ride across the North Fork of the Blackfoot River's flat floodplain, which is occupied by numerous cattle ranches, then begin climbing back toward forested slopes. Leaving the route at 42.7 miles, you'll continue for 2 miles to the night's destination of Coopers Lake and the Lolo National Forest's Big Nelson Campground. Generally, the riding is not difficult, yet the distance and gravel roads combine to make for what can be a long day in the saddle. Plenty of surface water can be found throughout the ride.

As you tackle the first several miles, look high into the hills to the north and try to spot the Morrell Peak Lookout. You could ride to it, but it requires a climb of more than 3,000 vertical feet. The road you're riding on has been used over the years for a pair of Montana's most popular wintertime sporting events: the OSCR cross-country ski race, which in its early days ran from near Ovando to Seeley Lake (today the course sticks to the Seeley Creek Nordic Trails and surrounding forest roads), and the 350-mile Race

Ovando, a small community with a big heart, loves its bicycling visitors. Rustic camping is available at two locations in town. (Doug Werme)

to the Sky. The latter, Montana's preeminent sled dog race, draws mushers and mutts from near and far.

Chances are that by this time on your trip you've spotted at least one bald eagle, a once-endangered bird whose numbers have increased substantially in recent years. The bald eagle is a member of the family Accipitridae, which also includes hawks, vultures, falcons, and ospreys. Raptors, as family members are also known, have big hooked beaks, vise-grip talons, and outstanding vision. Adult bald eagles weigh between nine and twelve pounds, with the female substantially outsizing the male, and their wingspan can surpass 6 feet. In captivity the birds have lived as long as forty years; in the wild, fifteen to twenty years is more common. Like their golden eagle cousins, bald eagles mate for life, and together the male and female build their nesting site, or aerie. Constructed of grasses and medium- and small-sized sticks, the nest is continually repaired and added to over the years, so it can grow as large as 4 feet in diameter and every bit as deep.

Whereas golden eagles prefer nesting on cliffsides in mountainous and prairie country, bald eagles nest in trees and close to water, since fish are their primary food source. The female typically lays two eggs (although one or three is possible) in March, then incubates them for about a month and a half while the male brings home the bacon. On hatching, eaglets are helpless little things, weighing approximately three-and-a-half ounces. In the eagle family, sibling rivalry is carried to an extreme: The first-born, with its head-start spurt in growth, often ends up killing his or her younger, smaller competitor. At ten or eleven weeks the bird's weight will have increased an amazing fortyfold, with the larger females weighing in at around nine pounds. About this time they make their first clumsy attempts at flying, which often consist of a sort of hopping and flopping to and from nearby branches.

DAY 16 ROUTE

0.0   From where you left the route, continue straight/east toward Cottonwood Lakes.

18.5   Curve right (Monture Work Center is to the left).

19.0   FR 477 becomes FR 89.

20.9   Leave Lolo National Forest.

26.0   Cross State Highway 200 onto paved Ovando-Helmville Road.

26.4   Ovando (limited services). Continue right toward Helmville Road.

26.7   Turn right, following Ovando-Helmville Road.

29.9   Harry Morgan Campground. Turn left onto unsigned, narrow Dry Gulch Road/CR 125.

32.6   Turn right onto State Highway 200.

33.0   Immediately after guardrail, turn left onto unsigned gravel road; shortly, you'll see a sign pointing you toward Big Nelson Campground.

35.8   Continue straight at crossroads.

37.8   Continue straight toward Big Nelson Campground.

38.7   Turn left toward Coopers Lake and Big Nelson Campground.

41.2   Go right toward Big Nelson Campground.

42.7   Leave route and ride 2 miles northwest to Big Nelson Campground (free camping on Coopers Lake).

Day 17

BIG NELSON CAMPGROUND TO LINCOLN

22.1 miles plus 2 miles returning to route from Big Nelson

Feel free to dawdle along the shores of Coopers Lake this morning, for today's ride is short and easy—after the first uphill stretch anyway. After regaining the route you'll climb through the Helena National Forest, tackling a testy "little" hill of 6.4 miles before summiting and enjoying a mostly downhill ride the rest of the way to the full-service town of Lincoln. At 10.9 miles you'll pass Reservoir Lake, a popular trailhead—particularly for equestrians—for excursions into the Scapegoat Wilderness. Some decent campsites can be found in this area. From there, good, all-weather gravel roads, along with a mile-plus of paved State Highway 200, deliver you to Lincoln.

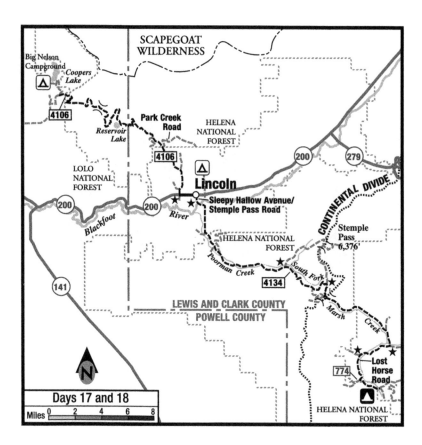

Once you see the timbered crannies and hidden hollows surrounding this woodsy burg, you may understand why "Unabomber" Ted Kaczynski chose the area as his hideout of twenty-five years. Kaczynski was generally considered a harmless recluse by Lincoln-area residents who knew him, but that apparently wasn't the case, even if you disregard his "work" outside the area: A book by Kaczynski's former neighbor and friend Chris Waits ties acts of violence to the man, including vandalism and the killing of locals' pets.

The original version of Lincoln was situated about 5 miles northwest of the present town. An early placer mining camp, the town took its name from its location in Abe Lincoln Gulch. The first mine in the gulch, which was established during Civil War times, was named Springfield, after the popular president's home in Illinois. Now settled along the upper Blackfoot River, Lincoln is still a center of mining and logging, as well as a supply point for hunters, horseback riders, and hikers heading into the Scapegoat Wilderness. Come winter, snowmobiling and cross-country skiing are popular pursuits

Riders from Winthrop, Washington—Ina Clark, Wiley Seckinger, and Rob Seckinger—take a breather on the trail outside Lincoln, Montana. (Andrew Sufficool)

in the snow-smothered surroundings. Not to mention dog-sledding: Lincoln is home to four-time Iditarod champion Doug Swingley.

DAY 17 ROUTE

0.0 From where you left the route, head east onto FR 4106 toward Dry Creek. Begin long climb.

6.4 Crest summit; proceed downhill toward State Highway 200.

10.9 Reservoir Lake.

16.4 Continue straight (Park Creek Road goes left).

19.0 Continue straight.

20.7 Turn left onto State Highway 200, which has a good shoulder.

22.1 Lincoln. All services.

Day 18

LINCOLN TO HELENA NATIONAL FOREST CAMPSITE

29.2 miles

There are no services between Lincoln and Helena, so be sure to procure groceries for two days before setting out. As you pedal from the west to the east slope of the Rockies today, you'll make the second (first in the United

States) of the Great Divide Mountain Bike Route's more than two-dozen Continental Divide crossings. In this area, though, you'll be confronted with the fact that "Continental Divide country" does not necessarily equate with "pristine," as a lot of this high country outside Helena has been overlogged, overmined, and overroaded. The first 7 miles of the ride are along a wide, potentially dusty gravel road. At 11.3 miles you'll turn off the main road to start up a primitive dirt track following the South Fork of Poorman Creek, a 4.4-mile stretch entailing steep uphills and several stream crossings. (For an easier but longer route continue on the main road over Stemple Pass, rejoining the narrative at mile 15.7. This route entails some tricky routefinding because of the abundance of unsigned side roads, so be sure to carry a good forest map.) After crossing the Continental Divide at 16.4 miles you'll descend on a good gravel road through the canyon of Marsh Creek, where the desert-like slopes are evidence that you're finally on the eastern, more arid side of the Rockies. Just beyond 16.6 miles—where the route description directs you to "veer left where FR 485-D1 drops right along the Continental Divide"—watch for a spring off to the left side of road; it's a good water source. After 29.2 miles of riding you'll reenter and cross a corner of the Helena National Forest, after several miles of riding on private lands where it is illegal to camp without permission.

Occasionally during the next couple of days, and then in several other locations south of here in Montana and other states, you'll notice wooden signposts emblazoned with the letters "CD." These mark the route of the Continental Divide National Scenic Trail, a hiking trail that runs intermittently along the spine of the Rockies. Although the CDNST was added to the National Trails System back in 1978, much of it still exists only as a concept or as a general corridor. The few individuals who have hiked the Continental Divide from Canada to Mexico have picked their own way in many areas, linking existing trails and even hiking some trail-less, cross-country segments. Only the trail sections in Montana and Idaho are entirely identified, while a great deal remains open to question in Wyoming, Colorado, and New Mexico. When completely mapped, the CDNST will extend along the Continental Divide for approximately 3,100 miles, from Antelope Wells, New Mexico (also the southern terminus of the Great Divide route), to the Canadian border at the top of Glacier National Park.

DAY 18 ROUTE

0.0 In Lincoln turn south at the blinking traffic light onto Sleepy Hallow Avenue/Stemple Pass Road.

11.3 Turn right onto FR 4134 up the South Fork of Poorman Creek.

15.7 Turn right onto main road.

16.4 Veer left, following the higher road over the Continental Divide (second crossing of the divide on the Great Divide Mountain Bike Route).

16.6 Veer left where FR 485-D1 drops right along the Continental Divide. (Just beyond this mileage, watch for spring off to left side of road; good water source.)

21.2 Continue downhill along Marsh Creek.

23.0 Ride straight downhill, passing log home.

24.1 Turn right at T-intersection toward Prickly Pear Creek.

26.7 Cross cattle guard, then turn left onto Lost Horse Road.

28.2 Pass Willow Lodge and curve left.

29.2 Camp somewhere in this vicinity after reentering public lands of the Helena National Forest.

Katie Monaco of Missoula, Montana, whips up a trailside feast. (Julie Huck)

Day 19

HELENA NATIONAL FOREST CAMPSITE TO HELENA

33.4 miles

On today's ride you'll cross the Continental Divide two times, at miles 6.1 and 18.2, before commencing the rapid descent into Helena. The first crossing entails a respectable climb of about 3.5 miles; the approach to the second crossing at Priest Pass is less noteworthy. However, from that pass prepare for a major descent, as you will lose nearly 2,000 feet of elevation over the ensuing 15 miles into Helena. The roads followed during the first 10 miles of the day's ride are variable; some of them are of dirt and can get mucky when wet. The next 15 miles follow good gravel roads, and the final 9 miles into Helena are along paved U.S. Highway 12.

The area of the Continental Divide you'll ride through today is webbed with roads, littered with the remains of defunct mines... and filled with compelling history. As you're riding in and above the Dog Creek valley and approaching Mullan Pass—which you don't go over but do go very near—at some point you'll cross the ghost of the tracks of the 25th Infantry Bicycle Corps. On June 16, 1897, the soldiers of the 25th Infantry pedaled through this area before cresting Mullan Pass and dropping to their night's destination of Fort William Henry Harrison, located at the northwest edge of Helena.

The 25th Infantry was one of four black Indian-fighting regiments organized by the U.S. Army in the wake of the Civil War. The blacks became known as "Buffalo Soldiers" to the Indians they were sent west to quell. In 1897, by which time the Indian wars had quieted, the 25th was stationed at Fort Missoula. Among the regiment's white officers at the time was an early-day cycling enthusiast, Lieutenant James A. Moss, who firmly believed the two-wheeled contraption could, in certain conditions, prove effective as a mode of troop transport. "The bicycle," he wrote, "has a number of advantages over the horse—it does not require much care, it needs no forage... it is noiseless and raises little dust, and it is impossible to tell direction from its track."

Yearning to demonstrate the validity of his theory, Moss requested from General Nelson Miles permission to mount a 1,900-mile bicycle expedition, from Fort Missoula to St. Louis. Permission granted, Moss picked twenty black soldiers to ride with him on one-speed Spalding safety bicycles, outfitted with balloon tires and handlebar-mounted gear packs. They departed Fort Missoula on June 14. On the third day, outside Elliston, the troops pedaled up the Mullan Road, a wagon track built in the late 1850s and early 1860s to connect the Missouri River port of Fort Benton with Fort Walla Walla,

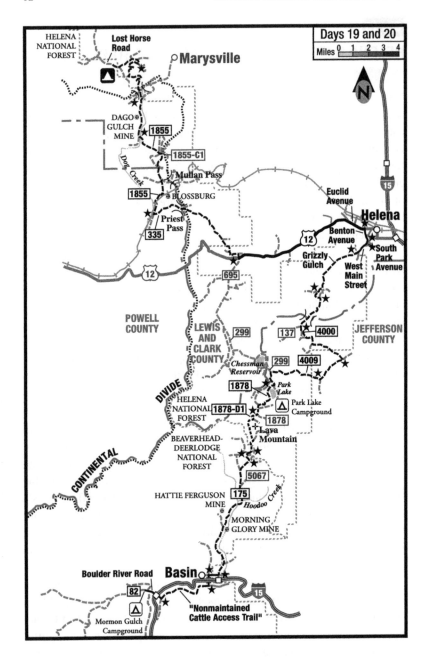

Washington. It was a wet, muddy climb to the Continental Divide. By the time they got there, two inches of new snow covered the ground, so the trip down was nearly as arduous as the ride up had been.

The Great Divide route occasionally follows a rail-trail where trains once ran; it also intersects with still-active rail lines. (Ben Yandeau)

Beyond Helena and Fort Harrison, the 25th Infantry was dealt plenty of hardships, including mosquito infestations, wheel-sucking soils, thunderstorms, oppressive heat, and sickening alkaline waters. Amazingly, they arrived in generally good condition in St. Louis on July 24, forty-one days after leaving Fort Missoula. Moss regarded the trip as a success, but his dream of seeing hundreds of bicycle-mounted troops never materialized, as vehicles powered by internal-combustion engines soon revved up on the roads.

DAY 19 ROUTE

0.0 Continue riding southeast on Lost Horse Road.

1.1 Continue straight up toward Empire Creek.

2.7 Pass large mining remains on left, then turn right toward Ophir Creek and Marysville. Commence steep climb.

6.1 Come out of the woods into a treeless area crossed by three roads that form a triangle. This is an unsigned crossing of the Continental Divide (C.D. crossing #3). Continue straight to the next corner, where two roads exit—take the left-hand road, which is unsigned FR 1855. (Do not go toward Ophir Creek or Lost Horse Creek.)

6.6 Continue straight.

9.4 Turn left to cross Dog Creek, following FR 1855 toward Blossburg.

11.2 Crest watershed divide; curve right to avoid riding onto FR 1855-C1.

13.3 Continue straight on FR 1855 toward Blossburg.

15.8 Turn left onto FR 335 toward Priest Pass.

18.2 Cross Priest Pass and the Continental Divide (C.D. crossing #4).

23.9 Turn right at highway department gravel-storage area.

24.1   Turn left onto US Highway 12.

31.0   Enter outskirts of Helena. Route becomes Euclid Avenue.

33.4   Turn right toward downtown Helena on Benton Avenue. (Several motels are located straight ahead, off route.)

Day 20

HELENA TO MORMON GULCH CAMPGROUND

44.7 miles

Before striking out today, stock up on two days' worth of food, as you won't find another full-blown grocery store until Butte at the end of Day 21. After departing Helena through its most historic corner, you'll reenter the Helena National Forest by way of Grizzly Gulch, climbing—gradually for the most part—to a low divide at 8 miles. You'll then continue along good gravel roads to about 20 miles, where you'll begin a stretch of about 7 miles that follows a potentially confusing series of old two-tracks and newly cut trail skirting the west flank of Lava Mountain. Pay close attention to the route description through this area, or there's a good chance you'll become temporarily lost. After finding your way from the Helena National Forest into the Beaverhead-Deerlodge National Forest, things become somewhat more straightforward. Once you come in alongside Cataract Creek, you simply follow it downstream through its sometimes-narrow canyon to the frontage road paralleling Interstate 15. After passing through the outskirts of Basin (minimal services are available just off route here), you'll ride onto a curiously signed "Nonmaintained Cattle Access Trail," which you'll follow for a ways before passing under I-15 and riding onto Boulder River Road.

Before that, however, don't be surprised if you end up staying in Helena for a day, after you begin uncovering the bounty of history and color the town has to offer. Prospectors poured into the valley of Prickly Pear Creek after hearing of a July 14, 1864, gold strike in Last Chance Gulch, made by a group known as "the Four Georgians." (A large share of those early gold miners were Southerners, or at least Confederate sympathizers.) Helena, like Virginia City, Bannack, and dozens of other southwest Montana mining camps, grew first as an unplanned and unattractive collection of tents, wickiups, and other sorts of temporary shelters. Piles of dirt and gravel were scattered about everywhere, and the streets of powder instantly turned to muddy quagmires after rain or snow. It wasn't long, though, before a few hand-hewn log cabins started popping up. Still, paint was a rarity, so the buildings appeared old before they were completed.

The runoff from an exceedingly deep snowpack in the winter of 2010–11 caused rivers in southwest Montana to flow out of their banks.

By 1866 the gold boom in Montana was over; many former boomtowns dried up, while a few hung on. Helena was one of the latter: Here placer mining, a low-tech method of mining carried out by lone individuals or unorganized groups of miners, gave way to the mining of hard-rock quartz lodes. Capital, cooperation, and long-range vision were required of this more equipment- and labor-intensive mode of mining. Roads were built for transporting equipment, corporations were organized, and banks were born. Suddenly, Helena residents realized that their young town had blossomed into a center of enterprise, and by 1867 several solidly built stone buildings lined the city streets. Eventually, Helena stole the distinction of territorial capital from Virginia City (which earlier had robbed Bannack of the title). Helena became the state capital after Montana gained statehood in 1889. The wealth, meantime, continued to grow: It was reported that by the time Montana became the forty-first state, Helena claimed more millionaires per capita than any community in the country.

Topping your list of places to visit in Helena should be the Museum of the Montana Historical Society, located at 225 North Roberts Street, just across from the state capitol. Highlights include a wing focused on the work of F. Jay Haynes, who at the turn of the century was the official photographer of both Yellowstone National Park and the Northern Pacific Railroad; and the Mackay Gallery of Charles M. Russell Art. The latter holds some sixty oils, watercolors, sculptures, and pen-and-inks by Charlie Russell. Nicknamed "America's Cowboy Artist," Russell was arguably the most famous Montana resident ever. If you're an insatiable fan of his evocative Western works, also mosey over to the floor of the House of Representatives in the capitol, where you'll find hanging the huge painting with the long name of *Lewis and Clark Meeting the Flathead Indians in Ross' Hole*. You can also hop aboard the Last Chance Tour Train outside the museum for an hour-long trip taking in several other historic Helena sites.

Granville Stuart, a man whose name seems to pop up all over early Montana history, was among the first to placer mine for gold along aptly named Cataract Creek, a tributary of the Boulder River. In the creek's tight canyon you'll pass some impressive old mine remains, including those of the Morning Glory, which was active well into the twentieth century. The town of Basin was founded in 1880 by a pair of miners at the site of an earlier settlement named Cataract, which appeared following an 1862 gold strike. Basin grew up primarily as a supply center for area miners. In the late 1880s the Montana Central Railroad was constructed through the area, giving the town a boost in the form of rail links to the outside world. In the small downtown you'll note buildings typical of Western mining towns of the late nineteenth century, with their characteristic second-story false fronts. (A few buildings in Basin are in fact from the nineteenth century, but the majority were built after a 1903 fire took out most of the town.)

One of the more interesting attractions in the Basin area is a defunct mine that has been transformed into an enterprise known as the Merry Widow Health Mine (www.merrywidowmine.com). It's one of a handful of old uranium mines in the Boulder-Basin area where folks come to bask in an atmosphere of radon gas. The low-level radioactive gas is reputed to have therapeutic effects for a list of maladies—arthritis, migraines, asthma, diabetes, allergies, and lupus to name just a few. Believers theorize that the radon stimulates the pituitary gland to manufacture a greater quantity of health-enhancing hormones. Still, before you partake of a treatment, be sure to read the fine print—it is curious that radon is the same gas that thousands of residents of the Rocky Mountains and other parts of the country have paid good money in attempts to rid their basements of.

DAY 20 ROUTE

0.0 From where you left the route, ride south on Benton Avenue, which soon becomes Park Avenue.

0.5 Continue straight across Lawrence Avenue; Last Chance Gulch pedestrian mall is one block to the left.

0.9 Turn left onto Reeder's Alley, then right onto South Park Avenue, which becomes unsigned West Main Street. Continue straight up the canyon.

1.6 Bear right onto gravel Grizzly Gulch (the paved road going left follows Orofino Gulch).

5.8 Bear left at unsigned fork.

6.3 Turn right at T-intersection toward Park Lake and begin steeper climb.

8.0 Crest watershed divide; start down.

8.6 Continue straight toward Park Lake on FR 4000 (FR 137 goes right toward North Fork Travis Creek).

9.3 Bear left where a private road goes right.

10.3 Curve left where another private road goes right.

11.7 Continue through area of rural homes.

12.9 Turn right toward Park Lake.

14.9 Turn right onto FR 4009 toward Park Lake.

18.7 Curve left, continuing on FR 4009 toward Park Lake (FR 299 goes right to Chessman Reservoir).

19.9 Cross cattle guard and turn right onto FR 1878 toward Frohner Meadows (Park Lake Campground is 1 mile off route).

22.8 Continue left; cross cattle guard.

22.9 Turn right onto 1878-D1, a rough four-wheel-drive track, at the point where FR 1878 goes straight up North Fork Quartz Creek. Next 2 miles are steep and rough.

23.6 Follow the uphill fork to the right instead of dropping left.

23.8 Bear left on main track.

24.9 Follow sign for "Lava Mountain Trail #244."

25.1 Continue on trail.

26.1 Enter large meadow.

26.5 After steep downhill, turn right at T-intersection.

26.9 Cross cattle guard, entering Beaverhead-Deerlodge National Forest. Immediately turn right at four-way junction.

27.5 Turn left onto main road after steep downhill.

28.3 Bear left at junction.

31.0 Bear right around corner where FR 5067 goes hard left.

32.1 Cross Hoodoo Creek.

33.7 Hattie Ferguson Mine on right.

34.7 Morning Glory Mine on left.

38.9 Turn right onto paved frontage road.

39.2 Turn left and pass under Interstate 15. Downtown Basin is off the route, straight ahead at this point. Minimal services, including a restaurant and motel (and camping at the unique Merry Widow Health Mine).

39.4   Turn right onto paved frontage road.

39.8   Ride onto gravel road signed "Nonmaintained Cattle Access Trail."

43.8   Curve left onto pavement.

44.0   Turn right and pass under I-15.

44.5   Ride onto gravel following "Boulder River Rd. No. 82" sign. Wide, well-maintained gravel road.

44.7   Mormon Gulch Campground on left. Open valley with stands of aspen and dying pine trees.

Day 21

MORMON GULCH CAMPGROUND TO BUTTE

34.7 miles

Today's ride follows a route new in 2013 that bypasses a piece of I-15, which previously was the only stretch of interstate highway marring the Great Divide route's interstate-free status. The route meanders into Butte through a historic neighborhood, then enters Uptown and zips past the Mother Lode Theater and, farther along, the Berkeley Pit Observation Site.

Butte boasts one of the most colorful histories of any city in the Rocky Mountain West. The city sits on the slope of a high arc defined by the Continental Divide, atop what remains of the Richest Hill on Earth. Much of the hill, beginning in 1955, was excavated and carried away to smelter. The excavations left behind a gaping, oozing wound on the skin of the earth. Known as the Berkeley Pit, it is one of this unique city's primary tourist attractions. More than a mile wide and 1,600 feet deep, the pit has been filling with toxic water since 1982, when mining operations stopped and so did the pumping of water that seeps in through hundreds of miles of tunnels running through Butte Hill. What to do with the toxic soup that continues getting deeper is a real problem.

Other Butte-iful things you should do: Sample a scrumptious pasty (*PASS-tee*), a meat-and-potatoes pie of Cornish-miner derivation that many consider the official food of Butte. Then find your way up through the neighborhood/mini-village of Walkerville (easiest to do from the point where you turn onto Excelsior Avenue at mile 29.0, below), and to the Granite Mountain Mine Memorial. It marks the site of the 1917 Speculator Mine fire, which took the lives of 168 miners, making it the worst hard-rock mining tragedy in America's history. On the floor of the memorial you'll see plates representing the various labor unions of an earlier Butte—and there were lots of them, one for nearly any conceivable profession, it seems. Butte's nickname at the

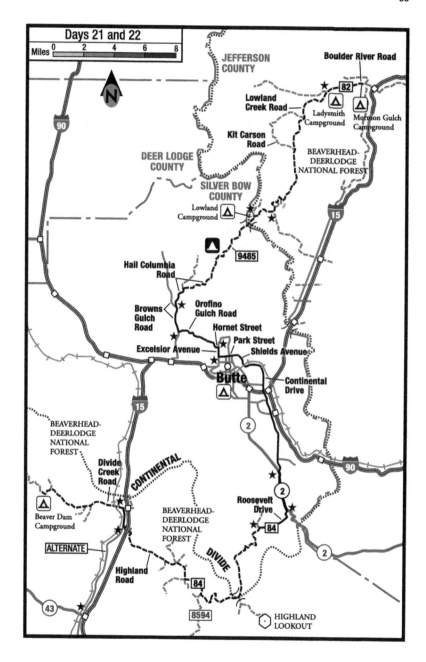

turn of the century was the "Gibraltar of Unionism," and the city sent the single largest delegation to a 1906 meeting in Chicago of the International Workers of the World.

The author setting out on a self-contained solo ride on the Great Divide route in southwest Montana, summer 2011 (Nancy McCoy)

DAY 21 ROUTE

0.0 Continue riding from Mormon Gulch Campground.

2.6 Ladysmith Campground on left. Just past here, bear left at Y onto Lowland Creek Road. (Sign says "Boulder River Rd. No. 82" pointing right.)

7.5 Kit Carson Road to the right. Begin gradual climb.

11.3 Maney Lake parking area to the left.

12.4 Sheepshead Freedom Point to the left. About a quarter mile later, turn right at "Lowland CG 2" sign.

14.2 Turn left at T-intersection onto FS 9485 following "Lowland Campground" sign. FS 509 goes right.

14.5 Lowland Campground on right.

15.1 Cross Continental Divide Trail #147 (C.D. crossing #5). Begin downhill.

17.9 Ride into narrow canyon. Road becomes rougher and steeper.

18.5 Informal, dispersed camping sites on left and right along creek for next 0.5 mile.

20.0 Cross cattle guard onto unsigned Hail Columbia Road. Begin to see occasional homes.

22.2 Ride onto pavement, then bear left at Y. FS 411 goes right.

24.1 Cross small bridge; unsigned Browns Gulch Road comes in from the left. Road becomes a wider two-lane.

25.8 Turn left onto Orofino Gulch Road.

28.8 Bear left onto Hornet Street. Enter Butte.

29.0 Turn right onto Excelsior Avenue.

29.6 Turn left at light onto Park Street.

30.3 Cross Main Street in Uptown Butte. Park Street soon becomes Shields Avenue.

31.1 Berkeley Pit Observation Site.

32.6 Road becomes Continental Drive.

34.7 Amherst Avenue on right. This leads 12 blocks west to a concentration of motels and other services in the vicinity of the Harrison Avenue I-90 interchange.

Day 22
BUTTE TO BEAVER DAM CAMPGROUND

35.4 miles

Be sure to buy groceries for at least two days before leaving Butte; stock up on water, too, for during much of today you'll be in high, streamless country near the top of the watershed. Following an initial 9 miles of pavement, you'll climb on good gravel roads through an ever-changing landscape of timbered hillsides, open aspen parks, and sage flats before beginning, at mile 24.4, the 4-mile dive to Interstate 15. The ride from Butte to Beaver Dam Campground is truly a feast of the senses; you may be surprised to find such sublime mountain terrain in close proximity to Butte, which is ... well, not necessarily the most attractive city in Montana. Be aware that at 28.6 miles into today's ride you'll need to choose whether or not to continue along the main route, which climbs, then descends Fleecer Ridge (Day 23). This will be difficult to comprehend until you confront it, but it's true: The descent from Fleecer is one of the two or three toughest hills to negotiate on the entire Great Divide route—and that includes uphills and downhills. If you'd rather bypass Fleecer Ridge (which is beautiful and unforgettable), simply follow the paved alternate, beginning at mile 28.6, detailed below the main route description. From that same juncture on the main route it's another 7 miles to Beaver Dam Campground, including 1 mile of pavement and 6 miles of gravel.

There's a lot more to do in Butte than mentioned in yesterday's narrative. You can also visit the opulent Copper King Mansion (219 West Granite) and the Arts Chateau (321 West Broadway), and sip an imported brew at the Irish Times Pub (2 East Galena) in the old Butte Daily Post building. While in Uptown you may also enjoy browsing through some of the many antique and junk stores. If possible, try to dedicate at least a half day to visiting the superlative World Museum of Mining & Hell Roarin' Gulch, situated up the big hill at the west end of Granite Street. At the Butte–Silver Bow Chamber of Commerce Visitor Center, located off Montana Street next to the KOA Kampground, you can board Old Number 1, a gas-powered trolley-car replica, for a tour taking in the mining museum and most of the other attractions mentioned here, as well as others.

Don't be surprised to find yourself pedaling into Butte and immediately disliking the city's outward looks, but then—if you follow the advice above and in the Day 21 narrative—riding out of town in love with Butte's brash brand of beauty and never-say-die spirit.

DAY 22 ROUTE

0.0   Return to Continental Drive and ride south.

0.4   Ride over Interstate 90.

1.7   Pass U.S. High Altitude Sports Center, which hosts World Cup and other speed-skating events.

6.0   Turn left onto State Highway 2.

8.3   Turn right off highway onto FR 84/Roosevelt Drive.

11.2   Bear left at unmarked intersection in area of rural homes.

12.6   Enter Butte watershed protection area; no camping for next 3.8 miles.

A makeshift campsite in southwest Montana. Generally speaking, you can camp anywhere on BLM lands unless posted to the contrary.

17.1 Crest Continental Divide at unsigned junction (C.D. crossing #6). Continue straight/right; a left leads to Highland Lookout. Enter sage/aspen park, with far-ranging views of the Pioneer Mountains.

20.0 Ride straight toward Interstate 15.

22.0 Bear right toward I-15; sign reads "Butte 15 miles."

23.3 Continue straight toward I-15.

24.4 Top a rise and begin long, steep descent to I-15.

28.1 Pass under I-15.

28.6 Turn right onto paved frontage road. (Alternate route begins here; see below.)

29.5 Cross cattle guard and turn left at T-intersection onto gravel Divide Creek Road.

30.1 Go straight to cross railroad tracks where a right leads into the Big Hole River water-treatment facility.

32.0 Continue straight toward Beaver Dam Campground.

35.4 Beaver Dam Campground.

**EASIER, PAVED ALTERNATE ROUTE TO WISE RIVER
BEGINNING AT MILE 28.6 ABOVE:**

0.0 Turn left onto frontage road.

8.5 Turn right onto State Highway 43.

18.7 Rejoin main route at mile 14.0, Day 23, where Jerry Creek Road goes right.

Day 23

BEAVER DAM CAMPGROUND TO LITTLE JOE CAMPGROUND

36.4 miles

What comes down, as you certainly did yesterday, must go up, and up it is—up, up, up for 6 miles on gravel and dirt roads surmounting Fleecer Ridge. The precipitous drop on single-track from the ridge is one of the most memorable places on the Great Divide route. "On single-track" may be an exaggeration: Many riders have commented that they've been forced to leave the trail—typically a no-no, but here a must—and walk their bike down the sage-covered slope to safely get to the bottom.) The descent delivers you to the valley of Jerry Creek, which you'll parallel on a fun gravel road to its confluence with the Big Hole River. Two subsequent miles on State Highway 43 bring you to the outpost of Wise River, where the river of the

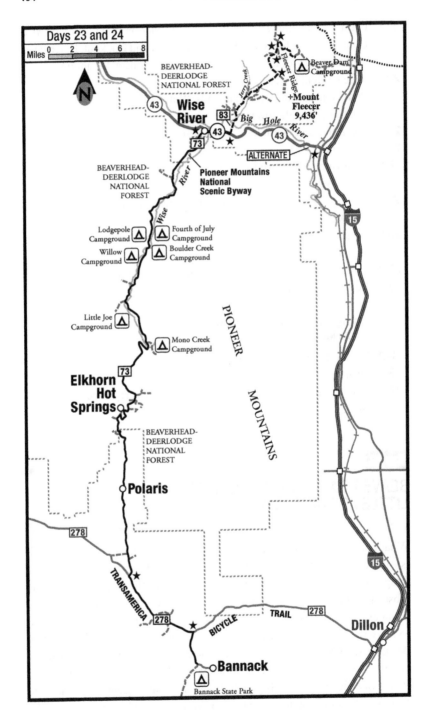

Phillip Lorenc from Waukegan, Illinois, participating in Adventure Cycling's 2009 Cycle the Divide Montana tour

same name empties into the Big Hole, a river legendary in the world of fly fishing. Depending on your itinerary and plans, in Wise River you'll want to buy groceries for two or three days. From Wise River you'll ride south onto the Pioneer Mountains National Scenic Byway, possibly the finest and most scenic road ride in all of southwest Montana. You'll be riding uphill but generally at a moderate grade. After experiencing it you will probably agree that this road is an invaluable component of the Great Divide route despite the fact that it's paved.

Anglers take note: When you arrive at the Big Hole River you are at the epicenter of the one of world's most desirable fly-fishing destinations. Lewis and Clark named the Gallatin, Madison, and Jefferson—the three rivers that come together to form the Missouri—after the U.S. secretary of the treasury, the secretary of state, and the president ("the author of our enterprise," as they called Thomas Jefferson). Less enduring were their virtuous name choices for the three forks of the Jefferson, which they declared the Wisdom, Philanthropy, and Philosophy rivers. Today those rivers are known as the Big Hole, Beaverhead, and Ruby. The Big Hole River town of Wisdom, meantime, kept the original name, while it is thought that the name Wise River came from the fact that the stream is a tributary of what formerly was called the Wisdom River.

Have you got all that? It doesn't much matter; what does matter is that you're about to enter a piece of the prettiest backcountry in all of Montana. Note that although the recommended campground is Little Joe, several additional Forest Service campgrounds line the way. A rustic indoor option, with hot spring pools and a restaurant, can be found by continuing 12.3 miles past Little Joe to Elkhorn Hot Springs.

DAY 23 ROUTE

0.0   Continue riding up-drainage from Beaver Dam Campground.

2.5   Turn left at junction toward Jerry Creek.

3.1   Bear right onto better road.

3.5   Turn left toward Fleecer Trail 94/Indian Creek Saddle. See far across valley, to the road you came down yesterday.

4.7   Cross cattle guard.

5.5   Cross cattle guard into broad meadow and begin up steep ridge coming off Mount Fleecer.

6.0   After passing a large stand of trees on your right on the first hill crest, turn right, aiming toward a row of dead pine trees.

6.1   Go around a fence (it's on the ground) and onto steep downhill track.

6.8   Extremely steep downhill section for roughly 0.5 mile.

7.2   Take hard left to pass through creek and then bend right, riding downstream along creek.

7.4   Continue straight downhill where another road goes left.

7.6   Road surface improves.

8.0   Cross Parker Creek.

8.1   Bear right/downhill on main road, after meeting it at a switchback.

9.4   Ride across creek on bridge, then bear left.

11.3 Ride straight downhill.

14.0 Turn right onto State Highway 43.

16.1 Wise River. Turn left onto FR 73/Pioneer Mountains National Scenic Byway (paved). All services in town, including well-stocked mercantile.

20.6 Road turns from chip seal to blacktop at Beaverhead-Deerlodge National Forest boundary.

36.4 Little Joe Campground.

Day 24

LITTLE JOE CAMPGROUND TO BANNACK STATE PARK

36.0 miles plus 0.5 mile off route to Bannack

After leaving camp, 8.6 additional miles on the paved Pioneer Mountains National Scenic Byway will bring you to a big rip down a hill on gravel. You'll then zip past—or maybe even zip into and get soaked at—Elkhorn Hot Springs. From there you'll continue coasting through a tight, timbered canyon before entering the wide-open floodplain of Grasshopper Creek. Just after the point where you break into the open, you'll encounter a motel on the right and a country store on the left. At 25.4 miles a left turn onto Country Road 278 leads, in 7.6 miles, to the southerly turn onto pavement taking you to Bannack State Park, reached at 36 miles.

Along Grasshopper Creek, on July 28, 1862, the White's Bar gold strike was made by a group of Colorado "Pike's Peakers." It was the first recorded claim in the Montana Territory (although this area at the time was part of

Sarah and Josh (see photo on page 56) spotted farther south on the Great Divide route as they continue their 2012 Alaska-to-Mexico adventure (Julie Huck)

the Dakota Territory, but that's another story), and it fanned the flames of Montana's first big mineral boom. The Grasshopper diggings drew prospectors from all directions, and within a year the burgeoning town of Bannack claimed some 3,000 individuals. The populace included prospectors, of course, but also entrepreneurs both above and beneath the law, drawn by the opportunity to divest successful miners of their newly found riches. Blacksmith shops, saloons, a bowling alley, a Chinese restaurant, and much more quickly appeared in town.

Bannack was named territorial capital in 1864, when the Montana Territory was split from the Idaho Territory (which it became part of in 1863, but that, too, is another story). Bannack's heyday was short-lived: In 1865 the capital was moved to Virginia City after even bigger gold strikes were made in the Alder Gulch area. Still, the town persevered for many decades and mining didn't completely die out here until the 1940s.

Today tall sagebrush lines the dusty streets of Bannack ghost town, which encompasses some five-dozen old buildings, including the first frame house built in the Montana Territory (circa 1867). The adjacent campground can be a pleasant place to stay ... so long as you remembered to pack your mosquito repellent.

DAY 24 ROUTE

0.0 Continue south from Little Joe Campground, riding on blacktop.

8.6 Begin 4-mile descent.

12.3 Bear left. Elkhorn Hot Springs is to right.

18.8 Polaris Post Office.

25.4 Turn left onto County Road 278 and join the TransAmerica Bicycle Trail.

33.0 Turn right onto pavement toward Bannack State Park, leaving the TransAm Trail.

36.0 Leave route and ride 0.5 mile southeast to Bannack State Park, which includes a campground.

In Grand Teton National Park, the Great Divide route dishes up spectacular views.

CHAPTER 3

BANNACK STATE PARK, MONTANA, TO SWEETWATER RIVER CROSSING, WYOMING

514.9 MILES
Days 25 through 36 (twelve days)
Six Continental Divide crossings

Beginning at Bannack, this section of the Great Divide route first leads through the big-spread ranching country surrounding the Lewis and Clark National Historic Trail, then bumps up the Big Sheep Creek Back Country Byway, an official designation given the route by the BLM. Over the Medicine Lodge–Sheep Creek Divide you will go, along a portion of the historic supply route that linked the gold fields of southwest Montana with the Union Pacific railhead at Corinne, Utah. This sweep of empty country is visited by very few travelers, and after passing through you'll understand why you're lucky to count yourself among the few who have been there.

The isolated byway meets Interstate 15 near the tiny town of Dell. From there you'll parallel the interstate on a frontage road to Lima, then reenter a wild, dry terrain before pedaling into Red Rock Lakes National Wildlife Refuge, truly one of Montana's hidden gems. Chances are that here you'll see trumpeter swans, immense and beautifully white birds that nearly became extinct early in the twentieth century. You'll then ride over Red Rock Pass, an easy crossing of the Continental Divide, and drop into Island Park, Idaho, a summer haven for anglers and a winter mecca for snowmobilers and cross-country skiers. From near Big Springs, source of the legendary Henrys Fork, for 30 miles you'll negotiate the old grade of a Union Pacific spur line that ran from Ashton, Idaho, to West Yellowstone, Montana.

You'll leave the rail-trail at the pleasant Warm River Campground. From there the little-traveled Ashton–Flagg Ranch Road runs between Yellowstone and Grand Teton National Parks, delivering you along the upper Snake River at the north end of Jackson Hole. Nearly 70 miles of pavement follow, a necessary evil that route planners had to contend with in order to get through this section of wilderness areas, where mountain bikes are off-limits. It's not all bad, though, because the paved roads offer nonstop, jaw-dropping views of the Tetons and other mountain ranges. These roads also serve as a portion of the TransAmerica Bicycle Trail, so don't be surprised to meet fellow bicycle tourists equipped with Adventure Cycling maps. Watch also for elk, moose, bear, bison, and gray wolves.

Highlights down the road include Union Pass, a historic high place visited by explorer Wilson Price Hunt in 1811 and subsequently by a parade of beaver-seeking mountain men. Dropping from there into the drainage of the Green River, you'll enjoy a rarely seen perspective of the Wind Rivers, the highest range in all of mountain-filled Wyoming. You'll then visit Pinedale, one of the most authentic little cowtowns in the West (but a cowtown that's seeing major change, with a nearby energy boom underway). From there you'll find your way to Boulder, Wyoming, and onto the high desert spilling off the flanks of the southern Wind Rivers. You'll ride directly atop the Continental Divide in places as you visit this spectacularly high and lonely area, before the route takes you to South Pass City, a historically vital and well-renovated gold-mining outpost. The section ends about 15 miles south of there.

In many ways South Pass City is to Wyoming what Bannack is to Montana, so it is fitting indeed that Section 2 of the Great Divide route links these two ghost towns.

Day 25

BANNACK STATE PARK TO MORRISON LAKE TURN
46.4 miles

The first 16 miles of today's ride take you along a portion of the designated Lewis and Clark National Historic Trail (the first 12 miles over hard-packed gravel and the next 4 on pavement). At mile 10.3 you'll spin directly through the grounds of the Cross Ranch, a classic Montana cattle operation. At 16.1 miles you'll turn south to regain gravel and begin a big sweep through the southwestern-most corner of Montana along the exceedingly remote Big Sheep Creek Back Country Byway. Creek water is widely available throughout this otherwise service-less stretch of open country. The only established campground found on the entire 80 miles of the Great Divide route covered during Days 25 and 26, until the end of Day 26 in the town of Lima, is the Deadwood Gulch Recreation Area, at 68.5 miles (creek water only); however, camping is generally permitted anywhere on these BLM lands that aren't posted to the contrary or being actively grazed by cattle. Still, good campsites are at a premium. If, after already putting in 46.4 miles on today's ride, you can bear the thought of attacking a steep, 2-mile uphill, you will find some pleasant camping potential in the vicinity of Morrison Lake. Other than two relatively short passes—Bannack Bench and the Medicine Lodge–Big Sheep Creek Divide, which is quite steep in places—the terrain tackled today is moderate.

If you turned west off the route at mile 12.4, by following county and Forest Service roads you would, in 20 miles plus, arrive at Lemhi Pass, where the Corps of Discovery first set foot on the west side of the Continental Divide, in present-day Idaho. Meriwether Lewis was ecstatic, writing that he had found the "most distant fountain of the waters of the mighty Missouri. . . . I had accomplished one of those great objectives on which my mind had been unalterably fixed for many years." (The actual "most distant fountain," however, was later identified as a creek flowing through the upper Centennial Valley. You'll cross it on Day 28.)

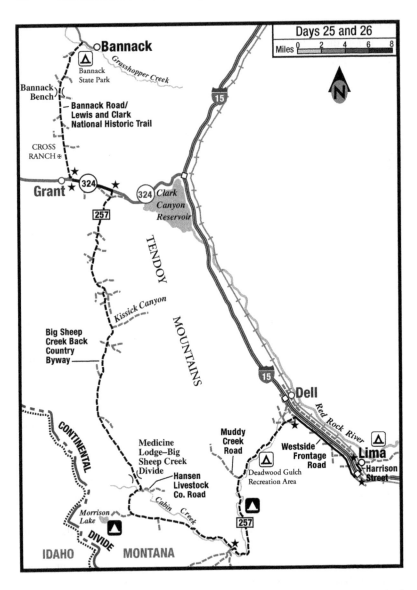

Or, if you were to continue straight off the route at mile 16.1, instead of turning south onto the Big Sheep Creek Back Country Byway, in approximately 3 miles you would arrive at Clark Canyon Reservoir, whose lapping waters cover the important Corps of Discovery site known as Camp Fortunate. Camp Fortunate marked the point at which navigation by canoe was no longer possible, where the Corps began their long, often arduous overland crossing by foot and horseback to northwestern Idaho. It was also

Fixing a flat tire on the road to the Medicine Lodge–Big Sheep Creek Divide. The photo does not show all the mosquitoes. (Michael Knip)

at Camp Fortunate that the party traded with Shoshone Indians, and where the most amazing coincidence of their entire journey took place. Back in the headwaters region (where the Jefferson, Gallatin, and Madison converge to become the Missouri River), Sacajawea had begun to recognize the countryside as that of her youth, where she'd lived before being kidnapped by Minataree Indians and taken to the Dakotas. Now, here at Camp Fortunate, she recognized one of the Shoshones, Chief Cameahwait, as her long-gone brother. The expedition's journals relate that Sacajawea "instantly jumped up, and ran and embraced him, throwing over him her blanket and weeping profusely." The fortuitous reunion certainly did nothing to hinder the horse trading that followed.

DAY 25 ROUTE

0.0 From where you left the route yesterday, ride south onto gravel toward Grant on the Lewis and Clark National Historic Trail.

0.2 Cross Grasshopper Creek.

5.1 Crest Bannack Bench.

10.3 Ride through Cross Ranch grounds.

12.4 Turn left at split in road; then, in 0.2 mile, turn left onto paved State Highway 324. (Grant, with extremely limited services, is 0.7 mile west off the route.)

16.1 Just before a power substation, turn right onto gravel road. You'll follow FR 257/Big Sheep Creek Back Country Byway for the next exceedingly remote 57 miles.

24.7 Continue straight where private road goes left up Kissick Canyon.

36.7 Use caution on the next 20 miles of unsurfaced road. It can be mucky if wet. You'll gain nearly 1,000 feet over the next 6 miles, the last mile-plus being steep.

42.5 Medicine Lodge–Big Sheep Creek Divide.

43.3 Bear right, away from Hansen Livestock Company road.

46.4 Road leaving route to right goes to Morrison Lake. Primitive camping at lake.

Day 26

MORRISON LAKE TURN TO LIMA

34.1 miles

On today's ride you'll continue along the Big Sheep Creek Back Country Byway, riding first along Cabin Creek, then along Big Sheep Creek. After 26 miles you'll exit the mouth of the canyon to meet up with Interstate 15. A wide, hard-surfaced frontage road will take you the rest of the way to Lima. You'll ride downstream along creeks for the majority of the ride, so surface water is abundant and the riding easy.

Yesterday at the Medicine Lodge–Big Sheep Creek Divide you may have noticed a sign marking the route as a portion of the Corinne–Bannack Road. Established in 1862, the year of Bannack's gold strike, the wagon supply road linked the gold fields of Montana with the Union Pacific railhead in Corinne, Utah. The barren, sprawling terrain you traverse on the Big Sheep Creek Back Country Byway is wild enough that it seems little has changed since the days of horse-drawn freight wagons storming through. The central parts of the byway are virtually uninhabited, although cattle companies do run seasonal operations in the area.

Keep your eyes peeled for pronghorns and golden eagles along the earlier wide-open stretches of the ride, and listen for the sweet song of the Western meadowlark, the state bird of Montana (and Wyoming). Once you enter the more protected canyon of Big Sheep Creek, watch for bighorn sheep and mule deer, especially at dawn and dusk. Good dispersed camping sites are found along the byway, in particular between miles 10 and 20. The established Deadwood Gulch BLM campground is at mile 22.1.

If you take a left at mile 26.7 and ride off route for 1.5 miles, you'll come to tiny Dell, home to one of southwest Montana's true dining treasures: Yesterday's Calf-A, housed in an old schoolhouse and serving up home-cooked fare—think hot beef sandwiches and cherry pie—to local stock growers, long-haul truckers out of Utah and Alberta, and two-wheeled wayfarers from around the world.

DAY 26 ROUTE

0.0 Morrison Lake turn; continue on main road.

5.7 Cross Cabin Creek.

9.9 Bear left at T-intersection, heading downstream.

16.7 Terrific camping spot on right beside stream, below big rock wall.

18.5 Continue straight; Muddy Creek Road goes left.

22.1 Deadwood Gulch Recreation Area on right. Primitive camping (pit toilet, picnic tables, fire rings, creek water only).

26.7 Turn right at T-intersection onto Westside Frontage Road, paralleling Interstate 15. (Dell is 1.5 miles to the left.)

33.9 Bear left to pass under the interstate.

34.1 Turn left opposite Exxon station onto Harrison Street in Lima; all services.

Some say you must be an animal to ride the Great Divide route—so what could possibly be a better fuel?

Day 27

LIMA TO UPPER LAKE CAMPGROUND

57.0 miles

Before setting out from Lima today, make sure you have enough groceries for one to two days. Surface, tap, and/or spring water are available intermittently throughout both today and tomorrow. After passing Lima Reservoir at approximately 14 miles you'll again penetrate a deserted countryside, riding first on hard-packed gravel, then on primitive dirt roads. Soon the big dry gives way to a wonderfully contrasting splash of mountain-surrounded wetlands encompassed by the Red Rock Lakes National Wildlife Refuge. The route through here follows narrow but high-quality all-weather roads. At about 53 miles you'll pass through Lakeview, where no services are available other than a guest ranch and a small visitor center operated by the U.S. Fish and Wildlife Service. Four miles later you'll arrive at the no-fee Upper Lake Campground, where camping is a real treat, particularly for bird lovers, and for water lovers, too—the spring water gushing forth at the site tastes better than most bottled waters. The day's mileage is high but the terrain is mostly flat. Moreover, if you don't feel up to tackling all 57 miles, there's decent dispersed camping elsewhere along the way.

If time permits, in tiny Lakeview swing into the grounds of the Red Rock Lakes NWR headquarters. Prior to the creation of the refuge in the mid-1930s, the Centennial Valley was an important sheep- and cattle-ranching basin that was home to several hundred humans, too. Monida, Montana, a town west of here on Interstate 15 that's almost in Idaho (*Mon*tana-*Ida*ho, hence the name Monida), was a major stock-shipping railhead; today, it's virtually a ghost town. The number of human residents in the area plummeted after the creation of Red Rock Lakes NWR, which removed thousands of acres of rich grazing lands from the hands of stockmen. In fact, Centennial Valley just might be the only major basin in western Montana whose population is smaller today than it was eighty years ago.

Red Rock Lakes NWR was created chiefly for the protection and hopeful propagation of the stunning trumpeter swan, whose numbers in the Yellowstone region—largely because of hunting and the draining of wetlands—had dwindled to fewer than a hundred birds by the early 1930s. And this was the only viable population remaining in the entire United States. Now, between 300 and 500 trumpeters live full-time on the refuge, and with the arrival of migratory birds from the north the greater Yellowstone population in winter swells to some 2,000 birds—big birds. Fully grown, a trumpeter swan can weigh as much as 30 pounds, attain a length of 4 feet, and boast a wingspan

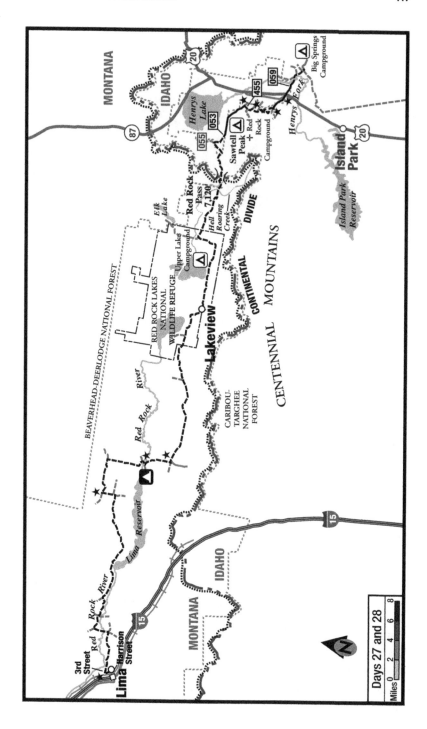

The Red Rock River flows out of Red Rock Lakes National Wildlife Refuge; swallows dart about from under a nearby bridge.

greater than 8 feet. Dozens of other bird species call the 42,525-acre refuge home at least part time, too, including bald eagles, great gray owls, willets, curlews, avocets, white pelicans, and great blue herons. Moose, elk, and pronghorns are some of the larger nonwinged critters you might spot around the refuge.

Upper Lake Campground is one of the best places to watch trumpeters and to listen for their loud honking. To avoid disturbing them you should not approach any closer than 400 yards—meaning binoculars are the only means you should use to "get close."

DAY 27 ROUTE

0.0 Proceed north on Harrison Street in Lima.

0.6 Turn right onto gravel 3rd Street.

6.4 Cross Red Rock River.

14.3 Pass Lima Reservoir dam and dam-keeper's house, then old ranch complex. Road becomes more rustic; muddy when wet.

24.1 Turn right at T-intersection onto higher-grade road. (Left goes toward Antone Station and Dillon.)

32.3 In wetlands area/river crossing, turn right/south, where a left goes toward Ruby Reservoir and Alder. Potential camping spots in this area (if flooding from spring runoff has subsided) with good bird-watching and mosquito slapping.

35.5 Turn left at T-intersection toward Lakeview.

44.6 Continue straight.

49.7 Continue straight.

52.8 Lakeview, home to Red Rock Lakes NWR headquarters.

57.0 Upper Lake Campground.

Day 28

UPPER LAKE CAMPGROUND TO BIG SPRINGS CAMPGROUND

32.5 miles plus 0.5 mile off route to Big Springs

Leaving Upper Lake Campground—where you likely will be awakened by a predawn cacophony of honks and calls coming from trumpeter swans, Canada geese, and a medley of songbirds—you'll continue riding eastward through Red Rock Lakes NWR on hard-packed gravel. With the high Centennial Mountains on your right and the wetlands of the refuge sprawling to the left, you'll soon cross Hell Roaring Creek, considered the most distant headwaters stream of the Missouri River. You'll subsequently make the easy climb to the Continental Divide at Red Rock Pass, elevation 7,120 feet, where again you will cross paths with the Continental Divide National Scenic Trail. Here you will also leave Montana and enter Idaho. If you think too hard about which way is which, you may become seriously discombobulated: Oddly, at this location you ride due east to go from the east to the west side of the Continental Divide, and to pass from Montana into Idaho—a state generally thought to lie west of Montana. Soon you'll snake up and over the eastern flank of Sawtell Peak, on a variety of roads ranging from good gravel to primitive two-track. At 28.9 miles, at the junction of U.S. Highway 20 and FR 059, is a collection of tourist services where you should stock up on food for two days (unless you plan to make the 12-mile off-route round-trip ride to the town of Ashton on Day 30, in which case you still should obtain provisions here for tonight and tomorrow). The day ends at Big Springs Campground, a pleasant, pine-shrouded Caribou-Targhee National Forest campground sitting adjacent to a bubbling spring. Today's ride is easy physically, and water is available.

Distinctive, typically snow-capped Sawtell Peak, elevation 9,866 feet, is a lonesome remnant of the rim of the Island Park caldera. Like several other natural features and businesses in the area, Sawtell Peak is a namesake of Gilman Sawtell, the first white man to settle in the area. In 1868 Sawtell set up home and shop on Henrys Lake, where he raised cattle and took fish from the lake's trout-prolific waters. Among his harvesting strategies was to spear monster lake trout. Much of his bounty Sawtell shipped north by horse-drawn wagon to sell in the Montana gold camps of Alder Gulch (Virginia City) and Last Chance Gulch (Helena).

Next comes Island Park, a flat, high-elevation basin approximately 18 miles wide by 25 miles long. The flats mark the floor of the Island Park caldera; this, along with the older Huckleberry Ridge and the younger Lava

Creek calderas, constitute what is collectively referred to as the "Yellowstone Caldera." Each of the three calderas exploded violently once during the last two million years, at intervals of roughly 600,000 years. The caldera explosions resulted from the North American continental plate moving across the Yellowstone hotspot, a plume of intense heat extending from the earth's core through the mantle. The hotspot is also responsible for the wondrous array of geothermal activity seen today in nearby Yellowstone.

DAY 28 ROUTE

0.0 Ride east from Upper Lake Campground, continuing up the Centennial Valley.

5.6 Bear right (a left-hand turn leads off route to Elk Lake Camp).

12.8 Cross Red Rock Pass and the Continental Divide (C.D. crossing #7), elevation 7,120 feet. Enter Idaho and the Caribou-Targhee National Forest, leaving Montana's Beaverhead-Deerlodge National Forest.

17.0 Turn right to follow FR 053 rather than heading straight onto FR 055.

22.6 Turn right onto FR 455; go around closed gate.

23.2 Bear left/straight onto the unsigned road rather than continuing along the more prominent road. Begin climbing onto the flank of Sawtell Peak.

24.9 Bear left, following a stream.

25.3 Pass through a gate, leaving it open or closed, just as you found it.

A cattle dog whose apparently pensive expression might be saying, "Have you heard from my herd?" (Ben Yandeau)

25.8 Ride across an earthen dam.

26.2 Road quality improves.

26.9 Stay right, following snowmobile trail.

27.1 Turn left onto the unsigned paved road.

28.9 Pedal directly across busy U.S. Highway 20 onto FR 059.

30.9 Cross bridge spanning Henrys Lake outlet and ride straight onto a wide gravel road.

32.5 Turn right onto the obvious old railroad bed. (To find Big Springs Campground, leave the route and continue on gravel for 0.5 mile.)

Day 29

BIG SPRINGS CAMPGROUND TO WARM RIVER CAMPGROUND

31.3 plus 0.5 mile returning to route from Big Springs

Today's ride of 31 miles plus is along the bed of the old Union Pacific spur line that ran between Ashton and West Yellowstone. Early on you'll cross a couple of bridges that lack guardrails, so ride with extra care. Flat rail-trails typically equate with easy cycling, but here that's not necessarily so. Some of the earlier stretches of the railroad bed are covered in deep, sand-like volcanic soil, making for tough riding conditions. (A tip: deflate your tires slightly for better flotation.) Other segments of the rail-trail are well compacted; even there, however, compression dents left by ties can create continuous, nagging bumps. If you tire of the rail-trail, note that nearby gravel roads roughly parallel most of today's route. The first 10 miles of the ride are pleasant, with several water crossings; the next 14 miles are more tedious; and the final 7 are downright stunning as you descend above the canyon of the Warm River. If you're carrying a fly rod, chances are it will not remain in its case today. No services are found on the route, but the day ends at one of the nicest Forest Service campgrounds you'll ever visit. (Note: After the main narrative below, an alternative, longer foothills route from Big Springs to Warm River Campground is described. It is more scenic than the main route and it avoids the soft volcanic soils of the rail-trail.)

A side trip beckons from Big Springs. By turning north rather than south onto the railroad grade at 0.0 mile in the mileage log, you could proceed over Reas Pass, then to West Yellowstone, over the course of approximately 15 miles. As you also do going south, you would trace a portion of the former spur of the Union Pacific Railroad, which began delivering tourists to Yellowstone's doorstep in 1908. For over three decades visitors had already been

Riding the route with a support vehicle permits you to bring along a few more items than when going self-supported.

filtering into Yellowstone at the location, but the town of West Yellowstone emerged only after the railroad arrived. And now the Yellowstone-curious could ride the rails all the way from Utah to the world's first national park. Trails advocates in the region hope one day to have the entire rail-trail from Victor, Idaho, to West Yellowstone—a distance of more than 100 miles— mapped and ready for riding.

Before leaving Big Springs, be sure to have a look around. It's a special spot. Huge rainbow trout can be seen swimming about in the impossibly clear water of the springs, which form the headwaters of the Henrys Fork of the Snake, a river owning a nearly mythical reputation among fly-fishers the world over. Gushing forth from the Yellowstone aquifer, Big Springs flows at the rate of more than 400 million gallons per day and at a constant, trout-friendly temperature of 52 degrees Fahrenheit.

On the far side of the springs you'll spot a tidy log cabin; beside that, looking like the lodge of a leprechaun, sits a pump house. The structures are the handiwork of Johnny Sack, who built his home here in 1932. After

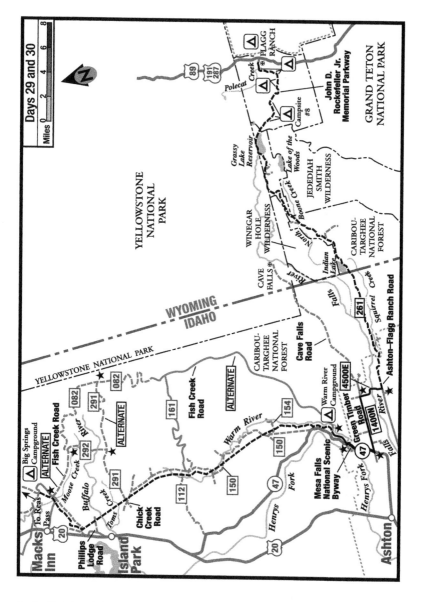

Sack died in 1957, the Forest Service proposed destroying the picturesque structures, but a groundswell of local protest led to congressional intervention and ultimately to the preservation of the buildings. Today, in addition to standing alongside Big Springs, Sack's structures reside on the National Register of Historic Places.

DAY 29 ROUTE

0.0 From where you left the route, ride south onto old railroad bed.

0.2 Bridge over Big Springs with no railing.

1.4 Ride over timber-deck bridge.

1.7 Ride across paved road.

5.2 Pass through wetlands area, then cross several dirt roads.

5.9 Pass through railroad cut with volcanic rocks bearing etched dates and names.

6.5 Cross Phillips Lodge Road.

7.0 Cross Buffalo River and enter a big meadow. Look for the Teton Range in the distance.

9.0 Cross Toms Creek on bridge.

9.8 Cross major gravel road (FR 291).

10.2 Just past old cattle-loading pens, cross Chick Creek Road.

14.5 Cross Warm River.

15.3 Cross FR 112.

18.2 Cross unsigned FR 150.

19.5 Cross FR 150 again (signed this time).

23.0 Cross FR 150 for third time.

24.2 Cross FR 154.

25.1 Pass through gate (leave it as you found it). Note "signature rock" just before gate. Superb views down to the foaming Warm River.

27.7 Walk around old 0.25-mile-long tunnel, which collapsed a few years ago.

31.3 Warm River Campground.

ALTERNATE ROUTE TO WARM RIVER CAMPGROUND:

0.0 Ride south from Big Springs Campground on pavement.

1.6 Turn left onto Fish Creek Road (wide, possibly washboard).

4.2 Turn right onto FR 292.

5.7 Come alongside beautiful Moose Creek.

8.4 Cross stream.

10.6 Turn left onto FR 291 toward Fish Creek Road (U.S. Highway 20 is 7 miles to right).

18.4 Turn right at T-intersection onto FR 082 (Fish Creek Road) toward sign reading "Warm River 30 miles." Wide gravel road.

24.7 Pavement begins.

26.1 Pass paved road going right.

48.1 Cross bridge; turn into Warm River Campground.

Day 30

WARM RIVER CAMPGROUND TO FLAGG RANCH

47.1 miles

Today's recommended ride is long, but 10 miles are paved and the next 15 are on a relatively flat gravel road—albeit a potentially dusty and washboarded gravel road. You'll climb out of the deep river notch formed by the confluence of the Warm River and the Henrys Fork (known also as North Fork of the Snake River), and—presto—just like that, you leave canyon country behind. Suddenly you're rolling through a wide-open terrain of grain and potato fields, a scene straight out of the Midwest ... were it not for the unmistakable profile of the Teton Range looming to the south-southeast. Not long after entering Wyoming, as it winds through the Caribou-Targhee National Forest, the Ashton–Flagg Ranch Road devolves into a narrow dirt track, bumpy, winding, hilly, and possibly dusty. If you'd prefer to shorten the ride and/or not spend the night at the industrial-strength camping scene of Flagg Ranch, opt instead for one of the eight primitive campgrounds found along the 6-mile stretch of route beginning at mile 39.6. These campgrounds, all within the John D. Rockefeller Jr. Memorial Parkway, feature from one to four tent sites each. They include pit toilets, fire rings, garbage cans, picnic

Ramsey Bentley of Laramie, Wyoming, enjoys a cold drink and a hot fire after a day of Great Divide riding in his home state.

tables, and bear-proof food-storage containers. Tonight, and on nights 31 and 32 as well, remain particularly bear-aware, for grizzlies are common in these portions of the greater Yellowstone ecosystem. Plenty of surface water is available on today's ride.

The Tetons may appear "backwards" from this perspective, for they're depicted far more often in paintings and photographs from the east. However, it was here on the west side of the range that the primary peaks were viewed and named Les Trois Tetons ("the three breasts") by Pierre Tivanitagon and other French-Iroquois trappers of the North West Company who were working the Teton River basin in the early nineteenth century. (Teton Valley, Idaho, a.k.a. Pierre's Hole, was named in honor of Tivanitagon.) The far more mundane title "Pilots Knobs" had been bestowed earlier by explorers viewing the peaks from the other side (see Day 33).

Before leaving the surroundings of fertile fields you'll pass the Cave Falls Road, which leads approximately 12 miles off the route to the Wyoming border and the relatively unknown Bechler Entrance of Yellowstone National Park. The road ends at the Bechler River Ranger Station, located in the part of Yellowstone known as "Cascade Corner" for its wealth of waterfalls and cascading streams. The big fires of 1988 missed this area for the most part. It's interesting to note that although the road dead-ends today, the long-gone "Marysville Road" of the 1880s through Cascade Corner was among the first wagon roads to reach into Jackson Hole, Wyoming. It was built by Mormon pioneers from Marysville (2 miles east of Ashton).

DAY 30 ROUTE

0.0 Leave Warm River Campground on paved road.

0.4 Turn left onto Mesa Falls National Scenic Byway/State Highway 47. Cross Warm River; road shoulder narrows as you climb out of the canyon into farm country, so ride with caution.

3.2 Turn left toward Cave Falls onto paved Green Timber Road/1400 North. (Ashton, with all services, is approximately 6 miles off the route from this point.)

8.0 Turn right onto paved 4500 East. (Straight goes to Yellowstone National Park's Bechler Entrance.)

9.4 Cross canal, then Falls River.

10.3 Turn left at the T-intersection onto Ashton–Flagg Ranch Road, which becomes gravel at this point (going west it's paved). Next 15 miles are wide and potentially dusty.

13.2 Enter Caribou-Targhee National Forest; road becomes FR 261.

15.0 Crest ridge to look down on Squirrel Creek and the spectacular Tetons.

20.8 Enter Wyoming.

22.0 Lily-pad-covered Indian Lake on the left.

22.4 Continue straight toward Grassy Lake Reservoir.

25.1 Continue straight on FR 261 toward Lake of the Woods/Grassy Lake. Road narrows.

28.0 Cross North Boone Creek.

31.0 Road becomes rough as it traverses the rocky northern flank of the Tetons.

33.6 Yellowstone National Park on left.

34.3 Yellowstone's Cascade Creek trailhead on left.

35.9 Grassy Lake Reservoir on right. Tough, rocky climb heading away from reservoir.

38.0 Enter John D. Rockefeller Jr. Memorial Parkway. Camping permitted only at designated sites over the next several miles.

39.6 Campsite #8. Campsites #7–#1 are distributed over the next 6 miles.

46.0 Hit pavement; cross Polecat Creek.

47.1 Flagg Ranch. Campground, cabins, restaurant, minimally stocked store.

Day 31

FLAGG RANCH TO TURPIN MEADOW CAMPGROUND
38.8 miles

Plan carefully for the next four days. Other than small stores at Flagg Ranch and at Colter Bay Village, 16 miles into today's ride you will find only one minimally stocked store (at Togwotee Mountain Lodge, mile 8.2 on Day 32) before reaching Pinedale, the recommended overnight on Day 34. Some restaurant possibilities do exist, including the pizzeria at Leeks Marina on Jackson Lake—a place lots of riders consider a must-stop. (See the service directory on the Adventure Cycling map for more dining options.) Today's ride includes 29 miles along busy highways, but they're 29 of the most beautiful highway miles in the world, as they skirt the dramatic east slope of the Teton Range. They're also coincidental with Adventure Cycling's TransAmerica Bicycle Trail. Next up are 10 additional paved miles on the low-traffic Buffalo Valley Road. The final 13 miles of the route involve a substantial amount of climbing. Surface water is available throughout the day's stretch.

Note: The Forest Service no longer permits tent camping at Turpin Meadow Campground due to the prevalence of grizzly bears. Riders should

The distinctive profile of Grand Teton National Park's Mount Moran, seen standing sentinel over the upper Snake River (Ben Yandeau)

be prepared to do a long day of 61–65 miles from Flagg Ranch to one of three other campgrounds: Pinnacles, Brooks Lake, or Falls. Alternatively, riders can break this section up into two shorter days by camping at Colter Bay (16 miles from Flagg Ranch) or Grand Teton Park RV Resort (at mile 29 from Flagg Ranch, then 2 miles east off the route).

Try to keep your eyes on the road, if that is possible in such dramatic surroundings. Pull off here and there to take in the spectacle of one of the world's most stunning mountain ranges.

The jagged, bereft-of-foothills Tetons present a compelling geological paradox: They are the youngest range in the Rocky Mountains, yet they are composed of some of the North American continent's oldest rock. At Colter Bay Village, for instance, you can look out across Jackson Lake at the massive hulk of 12,605-foot Mount Moran. Look closely at the crown of Mount Moran, and you can see, unless snow covers the summit, that the peak is capped in a layer of sandstone, a sedimentary rock much lighter in color than the granitic gneisses and schists making up most of the Tetons. The cap is a remnant of a layer of sandstone that geologists say once covered much of the region. When the Tetons began building a few million years ago, the sandstone layer fractured, and the cap worn by Moran now resides some 6,000 feet above the valley floor. But that's nothing: It's thought that the same layer lies buried under 24,000 feet of sediment beneath the floor of Jackson Hole, meaning that in this classic example of fault-block mountain building, the valley floor has sunk roughly four times as far as the mountains have risen.

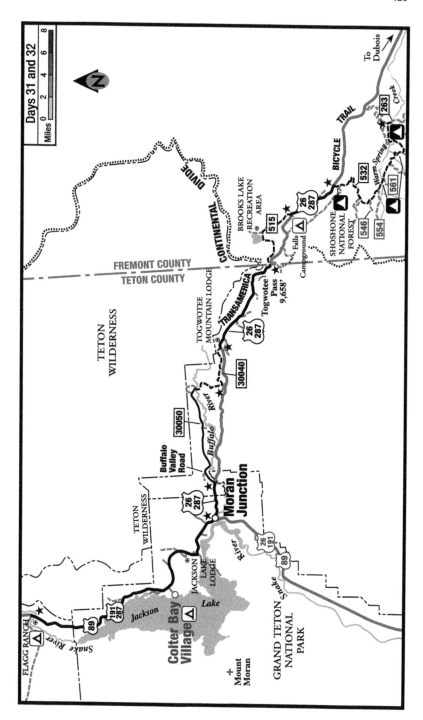

DAY 31 ROUTE

0.0 From Flagg Ranch, turn right onto U.S. Highway 191/287, which is rather narrow and can carry huge quantities of traffic. Traffic tends to travel slowly, but motorists are often looking at the mountains, or for moose and bears, and not for cyclists. Ride defensively.

0.7 Cross the Snake River.

8.4 Come in alongside Jackson Lake.

15.8 Colter Bay Village on right; all services, including camping.

20.3 Jackson Lake Lodge.

21.4 Go straight toward Moran Junction.

25.2 Grand Teton National Park entrance/exit station.

25.4 Turn left at Moran Junction toward Dubois.

27.5 Exit Grand Teton National Park; shoulder widens.

29.0 Turn left onto paved Buffalo Valley Road/FR 30050.

35.0 Great view down to the Buffalo River.

38.8 Turpin Meadow Campground to left.

Day 32

TURPIN MEADOW CAMPGROUND TO WARM SPRING CREEK AREA

56.1 miles

Early on today's ride you'll tackle a fun 4-mile climb on dirt roads running through the grounds of Togwotee (*TOE-guh-tee*) Mountain Lodge. The grizzly bear factor is palpable; make lots of noise. The ensuing ride comprises 22 miles on U.S. Highway 26/287, including a steady 9-mile climb to gain Togwotee Pass. At 39.2 miles you'll turn south onto 532 and begin climbing again in earnest to reach the high country. Once you turn back onto the Union Pass Road (FR 263) at mile 55.8 you'll find plenty of good dispersed camping available. There are also several nice dispersed sites along FR 532, should you opt to ride less than today's outlined 56.1 miles (and farther tomorrow than the recommended 39.4 miles).

As you approach Togwotee Pass be sure to survey your surroundings carefully, for you are passing through the domain of legendary Bear No. 203—or, more likely, the domain of his ghost. Nicknamed "Cowniverous" in a "Name That Cow-Killing Bear Contest" sponsored by the *Jackson Hole News* in the 1990s, Bear No. 203 was believed responsible for the deaths of dozens of cattle roaming grazing allotments in the Bridger-Teton National Forest. He was last heard from in 1997 when his radio-collar transmitter went dead.

The 13,770-foot Grand Teton, Wyoming's second-highest peak. Gannett Peak in the Wind River Range is about forty feet taller than the Grand. (John Blue Hannon)

Between 1994 and 1996 biologists conducted the "Blackrock Project," which documented nearly 200 cattle deaths over the course of three summers. About sixty of those were attributed to grizzly bears, and old Bear No. 203 did his fair share; he was credited with killing at least six head in just one of those summers. Bear No. 203 may be gone, but plenty of big bears still prowl the area. Plan and camp accordingly.

DAY 32 ROUTE

0.0 Cross Buffalo River and ride through Turpin Meadow Ranch. Start up the hill on gravel.

4.1 Turn left onto FR 30040 (may be impassable if wet, necessitating a detour to the highway).

4.8 Follow right fork.

7.5 Pass through gate.

8.0 Bear right into resort grounds.

8.2 Togwotee Mountain Lodge. Turn left onto U.S. Highway 26/287 and the TransAmerica Bicycle Trail.

17.2 Togwotee Pass, elevation 9,658 feet, and the Continental Divide (C.D. crossing #8).

24.3 Falls Campground on right.
24.7 At Wind River Lake Picnic Ground, turn left onto FR 515 toward Brooks Lake Recreation Area and historic Brooks Lake Lodge.
33.6 Turn left onto U.S. Highway 26/287.
39.2 Turn right onto FR 532.
39.5 Cross the Wind River.
40.2 Cross Sheridan Creek and begin 4-mile climb.
44.2 Crest the summit.
46.6 FR 554 goes right; in 0.1 mile, cross Warm Spring Creek.
51.4 Cross South Fork Warm Spring Creek.
55.8 Turn right onto FR 263.
56.1 Camp somewhere in this vicinity.

Day 33

WARM SPRING CREEK AREA TO WHISKEY GROVE CAMPGROUND

39.4 miles

You're confronted with a challenging climb right out of the gate this morning; once you get into the Union Pass high country, however, things flatten out, relatively speaking. You actually descend to cross 9,210-foot Union Pass at 8 miles. As you will vividly behold, Union Pass is a meeting place of mountains, with the Wind River, Absaroka (*Ab-SORE-uh-kuh*), and Gros Ventre (*Grow VONT*) ranges all converging in the area. From there you'll continue through agreeable subalpine terrain, roller-coastering along at around the 9,000-foot level. After several more miles amid timber, rocks, sagebrush, and, more than likely, cattle, at 31 miles you'll begin a 2-mile dive down a rough, gnarly, loose-surfaced hill, with plenty of angular, tire-threatening rocks in the way. The descent takes you out of the mountains and into the valley of the upper Green River. Whiskey Grove Campground offers a peaceful place to recover and repose, tucked as it is within a grove of trees lining the banks of the whispering upper Green. Surface water is abundant today, but no commercial services are encountered.

At Union Pass you cross the Continental Divide for the ninth time since setting out from Banff. Wilson Price Hunt, commanding an 1811 overland expedition of the Pacific Fur Company, was the first white man to cross through the pass, which he did by following game and Indian trails. From this area Hunt viewed the Teton Range some 50 miles to the northwest, giving them their first non-Indian name of "Pilots Knobs." It wasn't until seven

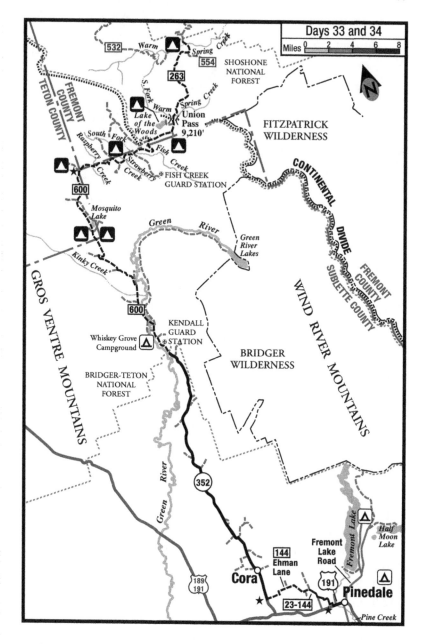

or eight years later that they received the name that stuck, after translation anyway—Les Trois Tetons (see Day 30).

Speaking of names, Union Pass was christened in 1860 by explorer Captain William F. Raynolds. He chose the name because the pass unites

A stormy sky backs an old log cabin and scattering of outbuildings marking a deserted homestead, a common sight on the Wyoming prairie. (Jerry Yeast)

a pair of major watersheds, that of the Green River (flowing west) and the Wind River (flowing east). Raynolds and his party, which consisted of some thirty infantrymen and seven scientists, had employed none other than Jim Bridger, the king of the mountain men, as their guide. The Raynolds military party had been sent West to explore "the headwaters of the Yellowstone and Missouri rivers, and ... the mountains in which they rise."

DAY 33 ROUTE

0.0 Continue riding uphill toward Union Pass.

0.1 Cross Warm Spring Creek.

0.3 Continue straight on FR 263 where FR 554 goes left.

4.1 The riding levels out after cattle guard. High, subalpine setting. Start descending toward Union Pass.

7.9 Cross bridge spanning South Fork Warm Spring Creek (high-country water source).

8.0 Union Pass, elevation 9,210 feet (C.D. crossing #9).

8.3 Pass road going right to Lake of the Woods. Good camping found along the route in this area.

9.1 Continue straight where FR 693 goes left

10.6 Piped spring on right side of road.

12.0 Bear left toward South Fork Fish Creek/Mosquito Lake/Green River.

12.8 Commence 1.5-mile downhill.

14.5 Cross South Fork Fish Creek (water source) and continue straight toward Mosquito Lake. Fish Creek Guard Station is located off the route about 1 mile to the left.

15.5 Nice dispersed campsite on right.

16.0 Cross Strawberry Creek.

17.6 Bear left where FR 637 forks right.

19.4 Curve hard right to cross Raspberry Creek and begin mile-long climb.

21.5 Go straight onto FR 600 toward Green River and Mosquito Lake. Cross cattle guard.

24.8 Cross cattle guard and continue straight. The towering Wind Rivers rise immediately ahead left.

26.7 Mosquito Lake on left.

27.2 Good camping on both sides of road.

30.9 Bear left downhill toward Pinedale (uphill heads toward Kinky Creek and Darwin Ranch). Rocky, loose descent into Green River drainage.

32.9 Bear left downhill to continue on FR 600.

35.4 Turn right downstream at T-intersection to continue on FR 600.

38.8 Cross bridge spanning the Green River.

39.0 Turn right at T-intersection to continue on FR 600. Left goes to Green River Lakes, 17 miles.

39.4 Whiskey Grove Campground to right.

Day 34

WHISKEY GROVE CAMPGROUND TO PINEDALE

35.1 miles

A couple of miles after leaving Whiskey Grove Campground you'll empty onto paved State Highway 352, which takes you most of the way to Pinedale. Of the 35.1 miles ridden today, 28.5 are paved and flat. Faded green pastures, willow-embraced water courses, herds of milling Herefords, and aspen-studded topographical blips create a pastoral frame for the wild Wind Rivers to the east and, to the distant west, the Wyoming and Salt River ranges. It's a classic Western scene with few peers, a Charlie Russell canvas come to life. The day ends at Pinedale, where you'll find all services, including a well-stocked sporting-goods store.

Pinedale is the major west-slope staging ground for trips into the Wind River Mountains, widely regarded as Wyoming's preeminent range for backpacking and horsepacking. Containing some 800 miles of trails and untold acres of trail-less exploring, the Winds are also the highest range in the state. Gannett Peak, elevation 13,804, is the loftiest of all, surpassing the Grand Teton by all of 33 feet. The Winds are similarly massive in breadth and length, reaching 100 miles from Union Pass at the northwest to South Pass at the southeast.

If Wyoming is the Cowboy State, Pinedale might be considered the Cowboy Town. It's the real thing, with plenty of dusty wranglers—spurs a-jangling and lower lips protruding with wads of chew—frequenting the eateries and bars lining the wide main downtown street. However, with energy development running rampant on the mesa south of town, Pinedale's nature has changed substantially in recent years, and it's not the quiet and quaint town it formerly was. Off that main street, up the hill bordering the east edge of town on the way to Fremont Lake, you'll find the Museum of the Mountain Man, a must-see while in town. Among the displays in the 15,000-square-foot facility is a rifle once owned by Jim Bridger (whose name is ever popping up in this area). If it happens to be early July when you're visiting, you might even take in the Green River Rendezvous, a lively and critically acclaimed re-creation of those brawling days of the 1830s when trappers, Indians, and fur buyers rendezvoused in the valley of the upper Green. Of sixteen major Rocky Mountain rendezvous held during the heyday of the beaver trapper, six happened in this valley, not far from the present site of Daniel, located 10 miles west of Pinedale.

Miles must be made, but you would be remiss not to linger a day in the Pinedale area. Journey up the Fremont Lake Road, perhaps camping for the night beside that long, deep glacial lake, or spending a day hiking the trails around the impressive Half Moon Lake.

An Adventure Cycling tour group on the Great Divide route not far from Pinedale, Wyoming (John Blue Hannon)

DAY 34 ROUTE

0.0 Leave Whiskey Grove Campground.

0.4 Kendall Guard Station on left.

2.4 Cross cattle guard onto pavement and leave the Bridger-Teton National Forest.

23.8 Cora Post Office located up road to left. (Still open as of 2012, but possibly on the U.S. Postal Service's future chopping block.)

26.6 Turn left onto County Road 144/Ehman Lane.

30.8 Road turns to pavement.

33.6 Turn left onto U.S. Highway 189/191.

34.8 Cross Pine Creek.

35.1 Downtown Pinedale: all services.

Day 35

PINEDALE TO LANDER CREEK CAMPSITE

49.8 miles

Before leaving Pinedale it is imperative to consider that you won't find another full-service grocery store until Rawlins, 220 miles and at least 4 days away. Stock up on supplies in Pinedale and start thinking like a serious backpacker. Top off all of your water bottles here and at every ensuing opportunity. From Boulder, where there's a convenience store, the route is still quite straightforward, as it follows smooth, all-weather paved and gravel roads traversing the transitional landscape that sweeps up to meet the Wind River Range. All sorts of legal two-tracks invite off-route exploring in the area. The day's mileage is long, at 49.8 miles, but 31.2 of those are paved. In fact, the going is quite easy in general—so long as you're not faced by one of Wyoming's infamous headwinds.

East of Boulder you'll curve southeastward to parallel the southern Wind Rivers; as you do, look high into that world of crags, pinnacles, and snowfields. You're looking at the Bridger Wilderness. Encompassing nearly half a million acres, the Bridger—named for Jim Bridger, naturally—holds more than two dozen glaciers, 1,200 lakes, 500 miles of trails . . . and, during a normally damp summer, billions of mosquitoes.

The wild and remote nature of the countryside encountered during the next few days will be inspirational to some Great Divide route cyclists and unsettling to others. Just imagine traversing it in a horse-drawn covered wagon—not a hard thing to imagine, really, when traveling slowly and quietly by mountain bike. You're nearing some of our country's most important

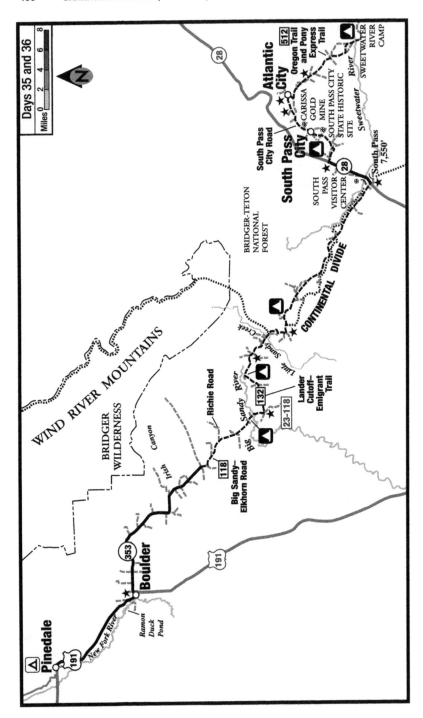

The author met this heavily loaded rider from Holland on the Great Divide route somewhere south of Pinedale.

historic trails as you approach South Pass, which served as a vital crossing point of the Continental Divide for nineteenth-century explorers and emigrants. Fifteen miles before day's end, beside hillsides revealing rainbows of erosion, you'll come down to a crossing of the Big Sandy River. The spot has been known as Buckskin Crossing since the 1860s when, so goes the story, a trapper named Buckskin Joe lived here with his wife and daughter. Earlier the crossing had been utilized by beaver-seeking mountain men, and the Lander Cut-off of the Oregon Trail also forded the river at this point. Look around and you'll find emigrant graves nearby.

DAY 35 ROUTE

0.0 Leave Pinedale on U.S. Highway 191.

11.7 Boulder; minimal services. Turn left onto paved State Highway 353.

18.7 Fremont Butte interpretive sign on right.

29.6 Continue straight where another road goes left up Irish Canyon.

29.9 Pavement ends.

30.6 Bear left at house, continuing straight onto Big Sandy–Elkhorn Road/ County Road 118.

30.8 Skirt ranch yard.

33.5 Richie Road goes left. Keep straight.

37.6 Continue straight where road goes right into Buckskin Crossing Ranch.

38.4 Cross Big Sandy River at Buckskin Crossing (water source). Good campsite.

39.4 At four-way junction turn on FR 132/Lander Cutoff–Emigrant Trail toward Big Sandy Campground.

43.8 Top out, then bear right on main road toward Big Sandy Lodge/Big Sandy Campground.

46.5 Turn right at T toward Sweetwater Guard Station.

49.8 Cross Little Sandy Creek (water source).

53.8 Camping allowed alongside Lander Creek.

Day 36

LANDER CREEK CAMPSITE TO SWEETWATER RIVER CROSSING

47.3 miles

Portions of today's ride wind directly atop the Continental Divide, providing some of the emptiest, biggest, most dramatic views imaginable, spreading out below both left and right. You "officially" cross the divide three times, but you may well imperceptibly cross it more times than that. Where the Wind Rivers start fading out you'll cross South Pass, barely noticeable as a climb in the direction you're traveling. At 37 miles, as you make the steep ascent out of Atlantic City, bid a fond farewell to the trees growing at road's edge, for you'll see few others, if any, before Rawlins, 135 miles distant. Today's mileage is high, but the terrain and riding surfaces are such that it's easy to gobble up the miles (keeping in mind that caveat mentioned yesterday concerning Wyoming headwinds). Several water sources are found, including ones at 22.5 miles (South Pass Visitor Center/rest area) and at day's end on the Sweetwater River.

Unlike nearby South Pass City, which is a ghost town (and a state park), Atlantic City claims some current activity and human denizens.

With hundreds of miles of thirsty desert leading to barrier mountains to the south, and the wall of the Wind Rivers and other ranges to the north, you will understand why South Pass became the place to wrangle horse-, mule-, and ox-drawn wagons across the Continental Divide. South Pass was, in fact, the most important travel gap in the entire chain of the Rocky Mountains during the nineteenth century. The pass offered overland travelers a broad, gentle, and relatively water-abundant corridor linking the Atlantic and the Pacific watersheds. First Indians, then mountain men, followed by Oregon and Mormon Trail emigrants, Pony Express riders, and prospective gold miners all learned in turn about the worth of this gateway straddling the Continental Divide.

Set aside an hour or two to wander around old South Pass City, now a Wyoming State Historic Site. The town didn't emerge until 1867, but had those gold-hungry California forty-niners known what lies hidden in the hills here—gold, that is—they might have put a quick halt to their westward travel. It was in South Pass City where Wyoming earned its nickname "The Equality State," after the territorial legislature in 1869 passed the first bill of any state or territory giving women the rights to vote and hold office. Shortly thereafter Esther Hobart Morris was named justice of the peace, becoming the first female judge in America.

Turn off at mile 40.9 for a recommended side trip leading to the Willie's Handcart Disaster Site. Here you can earn a poignant and vivid impression of just how hard life and death could be for emigrants, and why the Oregon-Mormon Trails have been referred to as "the longest graveyard in America."

At this spot, in 1856, seventy-seven Mormon pioneers, all members of the 400-member Willie Handcart Company, died of exposure and/or starvation after being trapped in a ferocious October snowstorm. Their dream of reaching the promised land of Utah remained forever that—just a dream. Today, there is camping, with water and restrooms, at the site.

DAY 36 ROUTE

0.0 Leave Little Sandy Creek campsite.

2.1 Crest Continental Divide (C.D. crossing #10). At three-way junction, turn left toward Sweetwater Guard Station/State Highway 28.

6.7 Continue straight toward State Highway 28.

12.4 Begin 1.5-mile stretch of riding along Continental Divide.

15.2 Cross Continental Divide (C.D. crossing #11).

21.7 Turn left onto paved State Highway 28. Continental Divide (C.D. crossing #12).

22.5 Cross Sweetwater River. South Pass Visitor Center/rest area, with water and interpretive information.

27.1 Turn right onto improved gravel road.

28.5 Bear left on main road.

32.2 Pass old cemetery.

32.6 Drop into South Pass City. South Pass City State Historic Site is a fee area open May 15 through September 30. Continue out of town toward Atlantic City.

33.1 Carissa Gold Mine. Bear right.

35.1 Continue straight through four-way intersection.

35.5 Turn right at stop sign onto higher-grade road.

37.0 Atlantic City. At Miner's Delight Inn (lodging available), turn right toward sign reading "Willie Hand Cart 7.8 miles."

37.7 Top out, then curve left at the junction.

40.9 Continue straight toward "Sweetwater Bridge Crossing 7." To take an optional side trip to the Willie's Handcart Disaster Site, turn left here, and proceed 4 miles to the site.

43.9 Junction of Oregon Trail and Pony Express Trail, as marked with concrete monument.

47.3 Sweetwater River. On the south side of the river, after crossing the cattle guard, follow the two-track east along fence line to a meadow and primitive camping area on BLM lands. (The north side of the river is private property, so camping is trespassing.) This site provides access to the river, which is the last reliable water source for many miles.

The Oregon-California Trail's Seminoe Cutoff, a historic travelway north of Rawlins

CHAPTER 4

SWEETWATER RIVER CROSSING, WYOMING, TO DILLON RESERVOIR, COLORADO

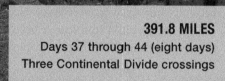

391.8 MILES
Days 37 through 44 (eight days)
Three Continental Divide crossings

T his section of the Great Divide Mountain Bike Route encompasses the Great Divide Basin, a 3,600-square-mile geographic conundrum where waters drain neither west to the Pacific nor east to the Atlantic. Rather, they drain inward to evaporate or settle into temporary lakes. It is one of the emptiest, driest long stretches of the Great Divide route (the other being the segment between Cuba and Grants, New Mexico). Here you will encounter herds of pronghorns and wild horses, and ride amid endless sweeps of sage-brush and saltbrush. In this big wide-open you will also continue tracing segments of some of our country's most important historic trails.

From Rawlins—which may appear a rather drab place to motorists speeding along Interstate 80 but will look like heaven to you after miles of solitude—the route climbs southerly into the high Sierra Madre. Next up: Colorado, where the first full-service town you'll come upon is the fun-hog haven of Steamboat Springs. The route skirts Howelsen Hill, breeding and training grounds over the years for a slate of American ski jumpers and Nordic combined athletes, including 2010 Olympic silver medalist and Steamboat native Johnny Spillane. From Steamboat you'll trace parts of the Yampa River Trail system before beginning the climb up Lynx Pass. From there you'll progress through the subalpine chill of lush high-country meadows and forests before commencing an unforgettable descent to the Colorado River at Radium.

In Kremmling you'll see just how plain and down-home a Colorado mountain town can be if there's no alpine ski resort in close proximity. After another stretch of broad basin country, it's up and over Ute Pass, into Summit County, and down to State Highway 9. This busy road, which you follow for roughly 12 miles, will remind you of what it is you've come to love about the gravel and dirt byways along the Great Divide route. And don't despair, because many, many more miles of those kinds of roads remain.

At Dillon you'll spin onto a separated bikeway that passes directly through the Heaton Bay Campground, where Section 3 ends.

Day 37
SWEETWATER RIVER CROSSING TO A & M RESERVOIR
68.6 miles plus 1 mile off route

Plan on an early start today, because the mileage is big and all on dirt and gravel roads. But be sure to take the time to fill up on water before setting out, and then top off your water-carrying capacity again at Diagnus Well, mile 11.5. (Here a pipe provides flowing water. Use stile to climb over the fence

The Sweetwater River cuts a verdant, life-providing path through the otherwise arid high desert of south-central Wyoming.

to access the water. Please close the gate. Camping is permitted outside the fenced area.) After Diagnus, there's a good chance that you won't find water again until reaching camp, 57 miles away. And even at that camp, at A & M Reservoir, some riders in the past have found water lacking. However, in 2006 the BLM received a $6,000 donation from Pacific Power to purchase and install a new pump at the reservoir, which serves as an important water source not only for humans traveling the Great Divide Mountain Bike Route and the Continental Divide hiking trail, but also for elk, wild horses, and pronghorns. Other nearby water options include Crooks Creek, along the Crooks Gap Road (approximately 3 miles north off the route from mile 51.3 on today's ride), or the Hadsell Spring drainage (about 2 miles east of A & M Reservoir toward Bairoil). Another possible water source is the intermittent Arapahoe Creek, which you'll cross at mile 47.3. Also, according to the BLM, recent range-improvement efforts have caused the creek to continue flowing later into the summer than before. To get an update of the water situation at A & M Reservoir and elsewhere, call the BLM in Lander (307-332-8420).

Four officially designated National Historic Trails—the Oregon, Mormon Pioneer, California, and Pony Express—converge in what is known as the Sweetwater corridor of central Wyoming. Mountain biking through this quiet, broad-shouldered country is a humbling yet inspiring experience. More than anywhere else along these historic trails the landscape remains largely unchanged from the nineteenth century. True, in some places the trail corridor has been swallowed by highways or improved into gravel or two-track roads; in others, though, actual segments of the original trails can be seen, wagon ruts and all.

If you listen hard enough as you pedal through you might detect—in addition to the sounds of the wind and your own rubber tires snapping across gravel—the faint echoes of creaking wagon wheels. Or you might hear the grunts and groans of Mormon men toiling to pull their families' worldly belongings in heavily laden hand carts . . . or the labored breathing of a Pony Express mount whose rider is whipping him to go even faster, wanting to make time through these hauntingly empty spaces separating St. Joseph and Sacramento.

Some 50 miles into the day's ride, to the left you'll see Green Mountain, a dark hulk lying between you and U.S. Highway 287 and the sometimes-boom, sometimes-bust town of Jeffrey City, originally known as Home on the Range, Wyoming. (During the uranium boom of the late 1970s Jeffrey City boasted some 4,000 residents; today, fewer than 100.) Green Mountain, along with its neighbor to the east, Whiskey Peak, and that to the west, Crooks Mountain, make up a minor subrange of the Rocky Mountains. Unlike most others, this range has no solid-rock core; rather, it is composed of sediments that eroded off the much older Granite Mountains to the north.

Green Mountain is a verdant island in a desert sea. Administered by the BLM, the mountain is noteworthy as home to the only developed recreational facilities in a subalpine environment (the Cottonwood Campground and the Wild Horse Point picnic area) found inside an area of hundreds of thousands of acres. There's also stream fishing for brook trout, rock-hounding, and mountain biking on the Green Mountain loop, a 31-mile route designated by the BLM.

DAY 37 ROUTE

0.0 Sweetwater River camp.

2.2 Cross cattle guard; bear right along fenceline.

2.4 Join California Trail–Seminoe Cut-off.

5.6 Stay right to follow main road (unsigned County Road 2317). California Trail–Seminoe Cut-off leaves route, following a two-track east. (This offers a potential alternative route; request information at the BLM office in Rawlins.)

11.5 Diagnus Well to right. Water source.

13.1 Continue straight on County Road 2317. (Another water source and informal camping at Picket Lake, 2 miles off route to south.)

28.5 Veer left at Y.

30.1 Curve left/north to stay on County Road 2317.

32.7 Turn right onto slightly rougher surface to continue on County Road 2317. Sweetwater Station on U.S. Highway 287 is 15 miles north off route from this point on CR 3221/Bison Basin Road.

35.2 Veer right at Y away from cow camp.

37.0 Curve right, staying on main road.

40.3 Bear right. In another 0.3 mile two roads simultaneously join the main route.

45.3 Cross Continental Divide (C.D. crossing #13), entering the Great Divide Basin.

47.3 Cross through the bed of Arapahoe Creek (intermittent flow).

48.1 Continue straight as another road comes in from behind right. Road becomes wider.

51.3 Go straight onto Crooks Gap Road, which curves right in 0.25 mile. Jeffrey City on U.S. Highway 287 is approximately 14 miles north off route from this point.

54.9 Enter Sweetwater County. Road becomes County Road 23.

57.6 Turn left onto County Road 22 toward sign reading "Bairoil 20."

68.6 Junction with Sooner Road 3215, a gravel road winding through flatter country. To find A & M Reservoir, the recommended campsite, continue straight (east) off route for 1 mile.

Day 38

A & M RESERVOIR TO RAWLINS

56.4 miles plus 1 mile returning to route

Today's ride is largely more of the same: wide-open, unpopulated country. After 39.5 miles of dirt and gravel, though, the final 17 miles are along U.S. Highway 287. This road's moderate to heavy traffic might make you feel as though you've pedaled onto the Ventura Freeway, after the deserted country you've just come from. No water is available today, other than by way of flagging down a motorist once you reach the highway. Rawlins is a relatively large, full-service town, home to the Wyoming State Penitentiary. The Old Frontier Prison, which housed convicted Wyoming lawbreakers—including the likes of Martha "Calamity Jane" Canary—from the turn of the century until 1982, makes for an intriguing visit while in town. Rawlins also has some good restaurants, including Mexican and Thai cuisine.

In this land of emigrant trails, oil wells, and infamous outlaws, chances are you will encounter herds of speeding pronghorns. The critter is commonly called an antelope, but that's a misnomer; the true antelope is an animal that lives only in the Old World. In fact, pronghorns are not closely related to any other animal living on earth today. They do share various traits with an array of animals, including goats, sheep, and giraffes, but pronghorns are

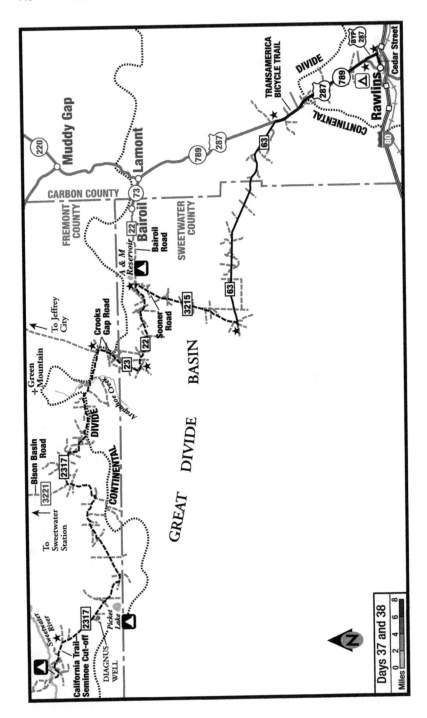

actually the lone remnant of an unusual family of animals. Rather than antlers, which are shed yearly, they have a horn composed of a permanent bony core that's covered with a horny sheath. As if to underscore their uniqueness, the horny sheath is shed yearly, making pronghorns the only animal in the world exhibiting this trait.

Don't try racing a pronghorn on your bike and expect to win, even on the steepest of downhills. They can maintain a pace of 30–40 mph for several miles and can hit 60 mph over short distances. Their speed and telescope-like vision are both adaptations for avoiding predators in the wide-open spaces they favor. There's approximately the same number of pronghorns (between 400,000 and 500,000) in Wyoming today as there are human residents.

Pronghorns are native to the Great Plains, where they've lived for thousands of years. Wild horses, another animal you'll likely encounter out here, aren't native, although they are managed as if they were. The Wild Free-Roaming Horse and Burro Act of 1971 stated, "Congress finds and declares that wild free roaming horses and burros are living symbols of the historic & pioneer spirit of the West; that they contribute to the diversity of lifeforms within the nation and enrich the lives of the American people." In view of this declaration, the numbers of horses using various ranges are controlled—or attempted to be controlled—by federal land managers in efforts to maintain the health of the ranges and of the herds.

One rider works at fixing a flat tire in the Great Divide Basin while others help by watching and supervising.

Some of the wild horses roaming the West are descendants of equines that escaped and/or were released from farms and ranches in relatively recent times; others are thought to descend directly from horses brought to the New World by Spanish Conquistadors in the 1500s. The results of the most recent wild-horse census indicate that the estimated population of the Great Divide Basin herd was around 1,700, or nearly three times what land managers consider to be the optimum "appropriate management level" of around 600 animals.

By the way, keep a close eye out for "stud piles" on the roads of the area. You definitely do not want to crash into one of these monumental deposits of manure, which wild stallions employ to mark their territories.

DAY 38 ROUTE

0.0   From where you left the route, ride south on Sooner Road 3215.

13.7 Turn left onto paved County Road 63. Very little traffic.

39.5 Turn right onto U.S. Highway 287/State Highway 789, joining the TransAmerica Bicycle Trail. This is a potentially busy road with a small shoulder, so ride with care.

45.5 Cross Continental Divide (C.D. crossing #14), leaving the Great Divide Basin and riding onto the east slope.

52.9 Turn left onto U.S. Highway 287 Bypass.

54.4 Bear right, following U.S. Highway 287 Bypass, which becomes Cedar Street.

56.4 Rawlins business district.

Day 39
RAWLINS TO CAMPSITE BEFORE ASPEN ALLEY

52.9 miles

It's important to know that upon leaving Rawlins you won't encounter another grocery store until Steamboat Springs, three days and 135 miles away via the main route. Heading south from Rawlins you'll continue through an expansive landscape largely devoid of timber. It doesn't last too long, though; after the pavement ends at 25 miles you'll find yourself climbing, first into the foothills and then into the timber of the Sierra Madre Range of the Medicine Bow National Forest. Today's mileage is high and much of the riding is rigorous—particularly the steep uphill of almost 6 miles required to gain Middlewood Hill and Continental Divide crossing number 15. Regarding water, you should be okay as long as you stock up before leaving Rawlins, since you'll encounter several streams along the later parts of the ride.

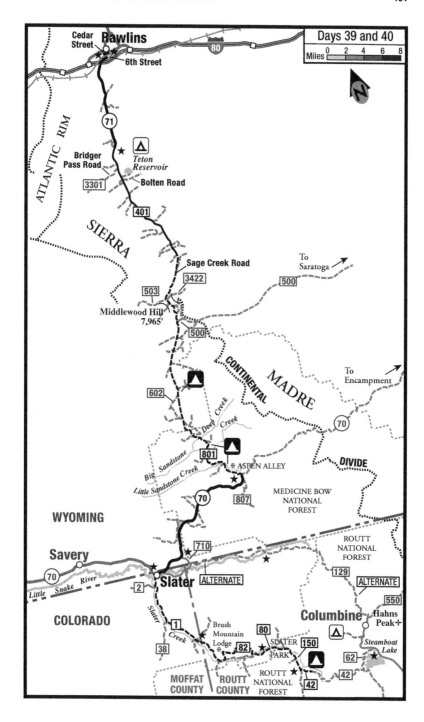

You won't find a wild columbine near Rawlins, but chances increase as you climb into the Medicine Bow National Forest.

The Sierra Madre, not to be confused with the mountains of Mexico where Humphrey Bogart's movie character scratched for treasure, encompasses a particularly enticing corner of the Cowboy State. These mountains hide the remains of numerous mines and mining camps, as well as a pair of small, relatively unknown wilderness areas: the Huston Park and Encampment River wildernesses. The narrow canyon of the Encampment River, with its locally legendary fishing, is the centerpiece of the latter.

About 27 miles into the day's ride you'll climb past a string of beaver ponds, which are quite a common sight throughout the well-watered Sierra Madre. Beavers have lived on the North American continent for hundreds of thousands of years, and cumulatively they have modified the landscape more than we can ever know. It's commonly said that only humans have a greater capacity than beavers to alter their natural surroundings. A series of beaver dams will break up the flow of sections of a stream, making it overflow its banks and creating a chain of wetlands. The resultant placid waters provide a home for a host of new flora and fauna, from the smallest of microorganisms and insects to moose, the world's largest antlered animal.

The activities of beavers may be for the most part environmentally beneficial, but their motives are not altruistic: By building dams and creating ponds, the beavers fashion havens in which to construct their lodges, as well as creating relatively safe, underwater routes to their streamside feeding grounds. There they gnaw down trees to get at the succulent leaves and twigs of the canopy. Felling streamside trees has the spin-off benefit of letting in sunlight, which promotes the growth of trees and shrubs like willow, the beaver's favorite food. When the food stores run out, the beavers move on to a new stretch of stream. Old dams go unrepaired and begin leaking; eventually the pond drains, becoming a marsh and, finally, a meadow.

DAY 39 ROUTE

0.0 Ride west on Cedar Street.

0.2 Turn left onto 6th Street and pass over railroad tracks.

0.7 At stop sign turn right onto State Highway 71.

1.4 Pass under Interstate 80. As you proceed south, the major geographic feature to the west is Atlantic Rim, which forms the Continental Divide.

11.0 State highway ends; road becomes County Road 401.

13.5 Pass ranch road going right, then pass Bridger Pass Road 3301.

14.7 Road going left to Teton Reservoir (camping).

24.8 Pavement ends. Begin climbing steeply.

30.2 County Road 503 goes right.

30.4 Crest Middlewood Hill (C.D. crossing #15), returning to the west slope. BLM Road 3422 goes left here.

33.1 Pass County Road 500, which leads to Saratoga.

41.5 County Road 602 goes right.

45.3 Enter Medicine Bow National Forest. Road becomes FR 801, turning narrower and rougher.

47.3 Pass over Deep Creek.

48.0 Go straight at major junction toward State Highway 70 and the town of Encampment.

49.0 Cross Big Sandstone Creek.

52.6 Cross Little Sandstone Creek.

52.9 Good campsite on left, with outhouse.

Day 40

CAMPSITE BEFORE ASPEN ALLEY TO FR 42 DISPERSED CAMP

45.1 miles

Today you'll begin by riding 2.5 miles on gravel, then follow a ribbon of pavement known as State Highway 70 for 17 miles before commencing the climb up Slater Creek into a wild terrain covered in scrub oak and largely lacking in human intruders. (Alternatively, at mile 15.7, you can opt to leave the main route by going southeast on County Road 710, which leads to Steamboat Springs via Columbine, Colorado. Wider and potentially busier than the main route, it is no second choice in terms of gorgeous scenery; moreover, unlike on the main route, you'll find limited services at the settlement of Columbine. Directions for this option follow the main route description below.) The only services encountered on the main route today are the camping and bed-and-breakfast-style accommodations available at Brush Mountain Lodge (mile 33.1). The route has plenty of water available.

Aspen Alley, a popular tourist attraction in the region when the fall colors are at their peak

Where you turn south in Slater, Colorado, you're at the upper end of the valley of the Little Snake River, which is no relation to the better-known Snake River that you crossed in northwest Wyoming. In fact, the Little Snake flows into the Green-Colorado Rivers system, while the more famous Snake meanders its way northwestward to the Columbia.

The quaking aspen, whose leaves dance in the sunlight even in the slightest of breezes, is a favorite tree of the middle and southern Rockies. You'll be accompanied by millions of them as you make your way to northern New Mexico. Here in the Sierra Madre the slopes are alive with "quakies," largely a legacy of the fires that stormed through during the mining days. A little over a mile into today's ride, for nearly a mile, you'll pedal beneath a particularly gorgeous canopy of *Populus tremuloides*, known locally as "Aspen Alley." It's quite the tourist attraction come fall, when the foliage colors are at their peak (usually sometime in September).

Aspens do multiply by dispersing their seeds, but that is not their chief mode of reproduction. The seeds are extremely sensitive, and they remain fertile for only a few days after falling. Unless conditions are perfect during that brief period, the seeds simply dry up and die. More commonly, aspens multiply by sprouting suckers from the roots of existing trees, a process that is enhanced when trees are felled or when fire sweeps through a stand. Trees sharing a root system in a given stand are technically part of the same organism, or clones of one another. This is why an apparently independent tree in a grove resembles its neighbors in configuration and, come autumn, in the color of its leaves. Those colors can vary greatly from those of aspens in other nearby groves, whose trees are genetically distinct.

DAY 40 ROUTE

0.0 Continue riding south on FR 801.

1.4 Road narrows into "Aspen Alley."

2.5 Turn right onto paved State Highway 70.

15.7 For easier alternative to the main route: Turn left onto County Road 710 toward Steamboat Springs and Columbine. (See description below.)

18.9 Enter Colorado.

19.6 One-quarter mile past the Slater, Colorado, post office (housed in a trailer) on the right, turn left onto gravel road to drop through ranch grounds.

20.7 Cross Slater Creek on narrow bridge.

21.0 Bear left across bridge to cross Slater Creek again and continue on County Road 1 (County Road 2 goes right).

23.7 Pass ranch on right, continuing up Slater Creek.

25.4 Pass County Road 38 going right; start climbing more steeply.

28.7 Begin steep 0.5-mile-long hill.

30.9 Cross cattle guard onto private ranchlands. No camping for next 10 miles.

33.1 At private Brush Mountain Lodge, go straight onto County Road 82 toward Slater Park and California Park.

33.8 Bear left, following main road.

38.3 Cross creek on a bridge. Road turns more primitive.

40.4 Route changes designation from County Road 82 to County Road 80.

41.0 Cross cattle guard and enter Routt National Forest; road becomes FR 150 and improves a bit.

45.0 Road going left into Smith Ranch.

45.1 Turn left onto FR 42 toward Hahns Peak Basin. Plenty of nice, timbered, dispersed campsites.

ALTERNATE ROUTE FROM MILE 15.7 ABOVE:

0.0 Turn left onto paved County Road 710 toward Steamboat Springs and Columbine.

1.8 Little Snake River joins in on right; begin riding upstream alongside it.

2.0 Road turns to gravel.

2.3 U Lazy C 2-Bar Ranch on right.

9.9 Curve right at Focus Ranch.

10.1 Cross river and begin climbing.

10.8 Road becomes County Road 129.

16.2 Entrance to the imposing Three Forks Ranch headquarters.

17.5 Enter Routt National Forest.

20.3 Cross Tennessee Creek.

26.8 Guard Station.

28.9 Go straight toward Steamboat Springs where FR 550 goes left. Begin pavement.

29.5 Columbine, with cabins and general store. Begin downhill.

30.6 Pass right-hand turn to Hahns Peak Campground (USFS; 2.5 miles off route).

33.0 Turn right onto gravel County Road 62 toward marina just before Steamboat Lake Visitor Center. (Go to visitor center for camping permit and information.)

36.2 Pass FR 42 going right. Rejoin main route at mile 10.8, Day 41.

Day 41

FR 42 DISPERSED CAMP TO STEAMBOAT SPRINGS

37.8 miles

The day begins with a gnarly, eye-opening 4-mile ascent—the last 1.6 miles of which are particularly grueling—to the watershed divide separating the Slater Creek and Mill Creek drainages. The climb is followed by an equally rugged descent toward Steamboat Lake State Park. After another 8.5 miles along all-weather gravel roads winding through rolling terrain, you'll make contact with the Elk River at 19 miles. From there it's 18 smooth, mostly paved miles to Steamboat Springs, along a narrow road with intermittent shoulders and possible traffic, but which is widely used by recreational cyclists. If you stock up on water before leaving Slater Park this morning, you should be well set to make it at least as far as the Clark Store (mile 19.3), where for once you can procure something other than water to drink. If it's

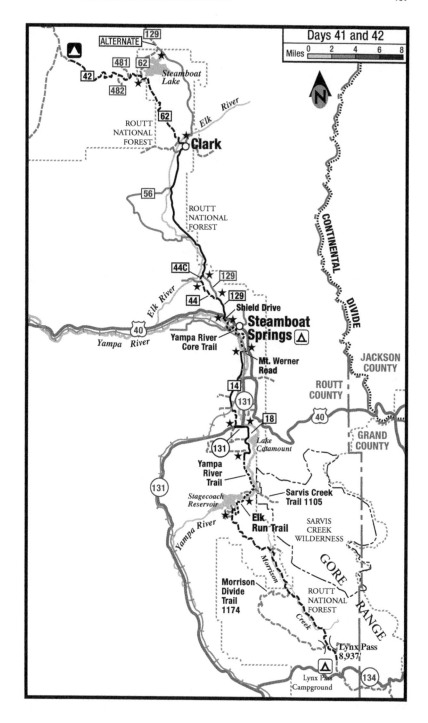

Remember the photo caption on page 152? Now you're getting into wild columbine country.

a beer you're craving, hold off until day's end at Steamboat Springs, where you can recover at the excellent brew pub located smack in the middle of downtown.

Steamboat Springs (Steamboat for short) provides an auspicious introduction to Colorado. Arguably, more than any other ski town in the state, Steamboat offers an appealing mix of the new and old. Because it was a town of substance before skiing grew into business locally, the town retains a degree of old-fashioned authenticity, even with its burgeoning number of boutiques and real-estate brokers. Downtown you might see old, beat-up four-wheel-drive pickups vying with Land Rovers for parking spaces, and cowboys in pointy-toed boots and dusty blue jeans sharing the sidewalks with mountain bikers or skiers.

Steamboat's Howelsen Hill is the longest continually running ski area in Colorado. Ski jumping became a surprisingly popular activity in the ranching and mining community after Norwegian Nordic ski champion Carl Howelsen moved to town in 1913. Howelsen, who soon organized the town's first winter carnival, impressed and inspired locals with the huge air he attained on jumps. Jumping groomed the way for downhill skiing, which grew popular among residents by the early 1940s; by late in that decade and in the 1950s Steamboat was America's leading producer of Olympic alpine skiers. When the Steamboat Ski Area opened in 1963 on nearby Storm Peak, the town was well on its way to becoming a world-class destination resort. (After local ski legend Buddy Werner died in a 1964 avalanche in Switzerland, the peak was renamed Mount Werner in his honor.)

For camping here, the private Steamboat Campground, with a special tenting area, is located 2 miles west of town on U.S. Highway 40. If you don't need to go into town (you probably will), you can avoid backtracking by turning right onto U.S. Highway 40 at mile 36.4.

DAY 41 ROUTE

0.0 Ride east up FR 42.

1.2 Continue straight as FR 49 goes left.

1.6 Continue straight as FR 48 goes left. Road turns rougher.

2.5 Begin extremely steep and rocky 1.5-mile uphill.

3.2 Pass through gate.

4.1 Watershed divide; bear right downhill on FR 42. Nice primitive campsite at top. Striking vistas of Hahns Peak and other mountains as you descend several miles of rough road.

9.1 Continue on FR 42 as FR 482 goes right.

10.2 Ride through gate; road improves as you enter area of rural homes.

10.8 Turn right at T-intersection onto County Road 62.

14.2 Switchback right and begin long descent.

17.9 Curve left (Indian Rocks subdivision is to right).

18.7 Curve left at T-intersection.

19.0 Cross Elk River.

19.3 Turn right at T-intersection onto pavement at Clark Store.

21.3 Shoulder begins.

25.1 Shoulder ends.

32.1 Turn right onto gravel County Road 44C.

32.6 Fork left at Y onto County Road 44.

34.8 Veer right back onto main paved road.

36.4 Cross U.S. Highway 40.

36.5 Turn left onto Shield Drive.

36.7 At "No Motor Vehicles" sign, turn left.

36.9 Ride straight onto Yampa River Core Trail.

37.3 Bear right and cross Yampa River.

37.8 Ride through parking area. Turn left onto 13th Street, crossing Yampa River. Turn right into parking area. Yampa River Core Trail continues.

Day 42

STEAMBOAT SPRINGS TO LYNX PASS CAMPGROUND

39.3 miles

Before striking out from Steamboat Springs stock up on grub for at least a couple of days, as you won't encounter another store close to the route until Kremmling, at the end of Day 43. Surface water is abundant, however, as you'll be along a river, stream, or lake most of the way. Today's riding encompasses a wide variety of surfaces, including separated bikeway, hard-packed gravel road, chip seal, dirt, and the crush-covered Elk Run Trail. The going is relatively flat until around 22 miles, where you'll begin a steady but gentle 4-mile climb, soon followed by another climb of approximately 8 miles to Lynx Pass.

Skiing may be what Steamboat Springs is best known for, but even during the snowless months this area is a recreational mecca, offering top-notch hiking, horseback riding, and mountain biking. Steamboat is a community of trails. The heralded Yampa River Trail is a 4-mile paved trail that connects town with the newer ski-resort community; and the ski hill boasts miles of trails tailored for mountain bikes (highly recommended for a "rest" day—you can, after all, ride the lifts up). Moreover, a network of dirt roads, four-wheel-drive tracks, and single-track trails webbing the surrounding lands of the Routt National Forest offers endless opportunities.

In fact, heading south from town you'll get to sample a stretch of the Yampa River Trail. Beginning at the town of Yampa, in southern Routt County, then passing through Steamboat Springs and Craig, the trail terminates at Dinosaur National Monument, which straddles the Colorado-Utah border. Much like the Great Divide route, the Yampa River Trail pieces together existing trails and roads, taking advantage of public lands as well as public rights-of-way across private lands.

DAY 42 ROUTE

0.0 From where you left the route in parking area, ride onto the Yampa River Trail.

0.4 Ride over Yampa River, then under the railroad tracks through Howelsen Tunnel (below river grade).

0.9 Ride under railroad tracks, then over river.

1.0 Cross river; bear right at Y.

1.4 Turn right onto Trafalgar Drive; follow it to the end, then ride straight back onto the Yampa River Core Trail.

3.1 Turn right onto Mt. Werner Road.

3.6 Bear left onto County Road 14.

Don't be surprised if, somewhere in Montana, Wyoming, or Colorado, you find yourself surrounded by cattle or stuck in a "lamb jam" such as this. (Etienne Theroux)

5.5 At T-intersection and yield sign, turn right.

8.4 Bear left onto gravel and cross railroad tracks—carefully, as they're at a hazardous angle—to continue on County Road 14.

9.1 Turn left onto State Highway 131.

10.9 As road completes left-hand curve, turn right toward Lake Catamount onto County Road 18.

14.4 Go left at Y past rustic log house.

15.5 End of county maintenance; road narrows.

15.7 Pass through gate and ride onto the Yampa River Trail system. The road is narrow and brushed-in; keep an eye out for hard-to-spot drainage ditches and for traffic coming around blind corners.

16.8 Ride onto BLM land.

17.4 Leave BLM land.

17.5 Crest a rise and bear right over two cattle guards. Left goes down to trailhead for Sarvis Creek Trail 1105. (It soon leads into the Sarvis Creek Wilderness, off-limits to bikes.)

19.1 Cross cattle guard and enter Blacktail Conservation Easement.

19.7 Turn left into second entrance to state-park trailhead. Walk across dam and ride onto the Elk Run Trail.

21.5 Ride into a parking area and turn left uphill, leaving the trail.

21.6 Turn right at the T-intersection.

22.6 Continue straight toward High Meadows; do not go right onto County Road 16. The road is wide at the start, as it begins a steady 4-mile climb.

31.4 Cross creek and begin climbing again.

32.5 Morrison Divide Trail 1174 goes right.

34.9 Cross North Fork Morrison Creek as you ride through a scattering of rural homes.

37.3 Enter Routt National Forest.

38.9 Lynx Pass, elevation 8,937 feet. Work center on left.

39.3 Lynx Pass Campground (USFS) on the right.

Day 43

LYNX PASS CAMPGROUND TO KREMMLING

37.5 miles plus 2 miles off route

Today's ride is a study in the striking difference several hundred feet of elevation and a few inches of precipitation can make. Early in the day, at mile 4.8, you'll encounter a stream ford. If it's too high to be safely crossed—a possibility at the height of spring runoff—then simply return to State Highway 134 (crossed at 2.9 miles) and follow it to the southerly turn onto FR 212 (mile 7.7 below). Speaking of alternative routes, you could choose simply to follow State Highway 134 over Gore Pass to its junction with U.S. Highway 40, then take 40 into Kremmling. It's a substantially easier way to go, but be forewarned: You will miss out on some gorgeous country and one of the great downhills of the entire Great Divide Mountain Bike Route. Losing nearly 2,000 feet of elevation in a matter of a few miles, you instantly go from forests of spruce and aspen to baked hillsides cloaked in piñon and juniper. You'll finally bottom out at the Colorado River along a stretch of the legendary river that is popular for fly-fishing and boating. If the weather is warm you'll no doubt see a bustle of activity at the BLM put-in outside Radium. A 4-mile uphill greets you on leaving Radium, followed by—after a short hiatus of downhill and level riding—several more miles of climbing. After about 0.5 mile along paved State Highway 9 you'll continue off the

Colorado may be best known as a skier's paradise, but it's also home to acres of beautiful backcountry and expansive ranching spreads. (Etienne Theroux)

route into Kremmling if you choose to overnight there. No services are found today until Kremmling, but you will come across plenty of surface water.

Kremmling, a plain-brown-wrapper of a town that sits amid a gorgeous setting in Middle Park, is itself known for nothing remarkable. Historically, in fact, Kremmling was better known for where it was than for what it was: Well after the railroad had come to town in 1905 and the town was well established, mail regularly came to Kremmling residents addressed "118 miles west of Denver." You'll end the day by riding along yet another stretch of the TransAmerica Bicycle Trail, the cross-country route developed in 1974–75 by the Adventure Cycling Association (then called Bikecentennial). Here's an interesting piece of trivia: As you're learning, the Great Divide route encompasses relatively little pavement. Yet the TransAmerica Bicycle Trail shares itself with the Great Divide Mountain Bike Route in seven different places and in three states, for a grand total of nearly 115 miles.

DAY 43 ROUTE

0.0 Lynx Pass Campground.

2.4 Bear hard left where FR 275 goes right to Toponas Campground (USFS).

2.9 Ride straight across State Highway 134 toward Long Park on FR 206, a rough-surfaced road that will be muddy if wet.

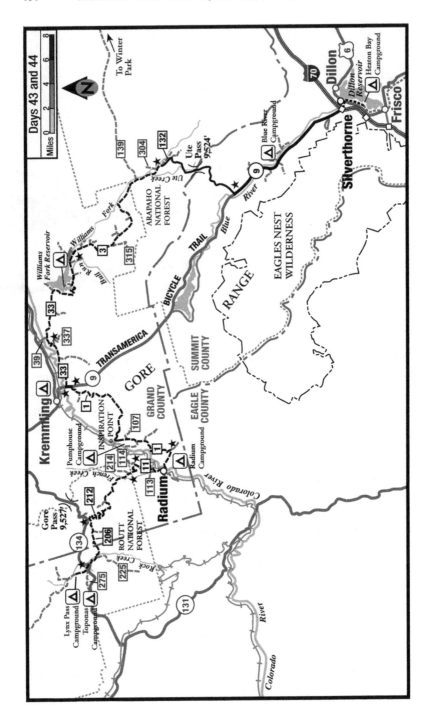

3.7 Cross cattle guard and continue straight/left on FR 206 as FR 225 goes right.

4.8 Ford Rock Creek. Warning: If this creek is too deep to safely cross, backtrack to the highway and turn east.

5.7 Continue straight where FR 209 goes right.

6.7 Continue straight where FR 210 goes right.

7.7 Turn right onto FR 212 toward Radium.

11.4 Bear right/continue straight on FR 218. Several short, 0.25- to 0.5-mile ups and downs over the next 3 miles.

13.0 Cross French Creek. Water source and possible camping.

13.1 Leave Routt National Forest and enter Radium Blacktail Unit State Wildlife Area.

13.7 Bear right downhill at saddle where FR 214 goes left. Commence long descent, keeping your speed in check. Some hazardous corners lie ahead.

15.6 Bear right to continue on County Road 11, where County Road 114 comes in from behind left.

16.8 Private ranch home on right.

18.0 Go straight where County Road 113 joins in from behind right.

19.4 Radium. No services. Turn left at stop sign to cross railroad tracks, then ride over the Colorado River bridge.

19.6 BLM recreation area/river put-in just down road to right. Start upward grade.

20.6 Primitive Radium Campground immediately beside road.

22.0 Turn left at T-intersection onto County Road 1 toward Kremmling, turning off County Road 11. Start steep uphill.

23.9 High point, with stupendous canyon views.

26.5 Off route 1.3 miles to left on County Road 106 is Pumphouse BLM Recreation Area and Campground, situated 200 feet below on the Colorado River.

27.0 County Road 107 comes in on right.

28.1 Begin pavement; uphill steepens.

28.4 Inspiration Point. Gore Canyon, route of the Denver & Río Grande Railroad.

29.4 Road reverts to dirt.

30.8 Watershed divide; start down.

36.3 Cross river/irrigation ditch.

37.1 Turn left onto State Highway 9/TransAmerica Bicycle Trail.

37.5 The route turns right onto County Road 33. Kremmling, with all services, is 2 miles off route north on State Highway 9.

Day 44

KREMMLING
TO HEATON BAY CAMPGROUND ON DILLON RESERVOIR

54.2 miles plus 2 miles returning to route

From Kremmling you'll strike out along the Colorado River, then meander up the broad basin of the Williams Fork before entering the Arapaho National Forest. After climbing over 9,524-foot Ute Pass and entering Summit County, you'll zip down a paved byway to State Highway 9, with a mind-boggling panorama of the Gore Range, home to the Eagles Nest Wilderness, unfolding across the Blue River Valley. Several miles of busy highway with a good shoulder then take you to and through Silverthorne (where you should pick up supplies for the night) and to Dillon Reservoir, where you'll hop onto the car-free Dillon Dam Bikeway. The bike path leads right into Heaton Bay Campground, a great place for a Summit County overnight. Today's distance of 54.2 miles is considerable, but nearly half of it is paved and the rest is over hard-surfaced gravel. Moreover, other than the 4-mile climb to Ute Pass, the terrain is quite moderate, although the potential for headwinds does exist, particularly along the earlier stretches. Water is plentiful.

The bike path by Dillon Reservoir which, although it lies on the opposite side of the Continental Divide from Denver, feeds water to the city via a tunnel (Etienne Theroux)

At mile 25.8, were you to go off route to the left rather than continuing straight, you'd wind up in the resort of Winter Park in about 20 miles. Don't do it if you're pressed for time, for it may take a while to get back to the business of the Great Divide route. The self-proclaimed "Mountain Bike Capital USA," Winter Park and the greater Fraser River Valley encompass some 600 miles of signed and unsigned mountain biking routes, ranging from old logging roads and two-tracks to several dozen miles of single-track trails accessed by chairlifts on a trio of ski mountains.

Dillon Reservoir, which lies on the west side of the Continental Divide, provides water to the city of Denver, which is on the east slope. In a classic example of humans fooling with Mother Nature, the water is pumped more than 20 miles through a tunnel that was bored and blasted through the bowels of the Front Range.

DAY 44 ROUTE

0.0 From where you left the route, ride onto County Road 33, which rollercoasters along beside the Colorado River.

4.3 County Road 337 goes right.

4.6 Bear right uphill on County Road 33, as County Road 39 drops left to cross river. Start climbing through an open, arid basin.

6.3 Cross over stream and start up.

9.1 Come in beside Williams Fork Reservoir.

12.1 Campground on left.

13.2 Pass County Road 37, which goes up Copper Creek.

14.2 County Road 331 goes right up Bull Run Creek.

14.3 Curve right, staying on level, as unsigned road goes straight ahead, dropping toward inlet.

15.4 Ride straight onto County Road 3, leaving County Road 33 as the former comes in from behind left.

18.6 Stay on County Road 3 as County Road 315 drops to the right.

24.2 Morgan Gulch Ranch on left.

25.3 Enter Arapaho National Forest.

25.8 Continue straight on County Road 3 where FR 139 goes left toward Winter Park.

26.9 Cross Ute Creek. See dam and mine ahead.

27.8 Start upward grade.

28.2 County Road 304 goes left.

28.5 Bear right at junction toward Ute Pass; the road turns to pavement and the grade steepens.

29.5 Bear right toward Ute Pass.

32.3 Ute Pass, elevation 9,524 feet. Enter Summit County and begin descending.

37.8 Turn left onto State Highway 9/TransAmerica Bicycle Trail.

42.8 Blue River Campground (USFS) on left.

47.5 Silverthorne city limit.

50.5 Pass under Interstate 70.

51.4 Ride onto bike path and turn right toward Frisco onto the trail leading over the dam.

54.2 Cross road into Heaton Bay Campground (USFS). Some sections of the campground are set aside for reserved camping, while others are first-come, first-served.

The Rocky Mountain columbine was elected
Colorado state flower in a popular vote in 1899.

CHAPTER 5

DILLON RESERVOIR TO SOUTH OF PLATORO, COLORADO

335.4 MILES
Days 45 through 53 (nine days)
Three Continental Divide crossings

This section includes both the Great Divide route's loftiest Continental Divide crossing (Boreas Pass, elevation 11,482 feet) and its highest pass of all, Indiana Pass, 11,910 feet—which, as it happens, is not on the Continental Divide.

The section starts out on Summit County's Blue River Bikeway, a blacktopped recreational path that leads to the mining-town-turned-ski-boomtown of Breckenridge. (In case you're interested, by going right rather than left at the trail junction in Frisco you can take a side trip to Vail on the Vail Pass Trail.) From Breckenridge the route follows the route of the historic narrow-gauge Denver, South Park & Pacific Railroad over Boreas Pass, before traversing a succession of high, mountain-ringed valleys, or parks. The ensuing descent into Salida dishes up a spectacle of several of Colorado's famous 14,000-foot-plus peaks, including the Fourteeners of higher learning known as Princeton, Yale, Harvard, and Columbia—the Collegiate Peaks.

Marshall Pass, southwest of alluring Salida, is the meeting place of three primary mountain ranges: the Sawatch Range, Sangre de Cristo Range, and Cochetopa Hills. Here the Great Divide route junctures with the Continental Divide National Scenic Trail and the Colorado Trail, a 470-mile footpath stretching from near Denver to just outside Durango. (The trail is open to mountain bikes, with detours identified around wilderness areas.) Marshall Pass is also the southern terminus of the Monarch Crest Trail, much of which is coincidental with the Colorado and Continental Divide trails. This 12-mile single-track running south from Monarch Pass is regarded as one of the top trail rides in Colorado, a state crisscrossed with great rides.

Spots on or near the route encountered beyond Marshall Pass include Sargents, Doyleville, and La Garita. Then, from the relative metropolis of Del Norte you'll climb more than 4,000 vertical feet in 23 miles to the Great Divide Mountain Bike Route's high point at Indiana Pass. From the apex of the route it is *not* downhill all the way to the Mexico border. It's not even downhill all the way to the end of this section, which you'll reach south of Platoro, 48 miles after cresting Indiana Pass.

Day 45

HEATON BAY CAMPGROUND TO SELKIRK CAMPGROUND

27.0 miles plus 1 mile off route

A couple of miles after leaving Heaton Bay Campground you'll enter Frisco, where you'll wind for a mile down residential streets to find your way back to

Just another day in paradise—a.k.a. the Colorado high country

the Blue River Bikeway, which continues for another 9 miles to Breckenridge. (Alternatively, if you're up for a strenuous, technical single-track ride, rather than following the mellow bikeway from Frisco you can take the popular and demanding Peaks Trail, which emerges from the woods at the base of the big ski hill above Breckenridge.) You'll want to obtain enough provisions here to get you to Hartsel, tomorrow's destination. After spinning through downtown Breckenridge—one of the few places directly along the Great Divide route where you can obtain gourmet meals and similar civilized niceties—you'll turn onto the Boreas Pass Road, which turns to gravel after about 4 miles. Considering that Boreas, elevation 11,482 feet, is the second-highest pass on the entire route, the ride to get there is surprisingly easy; Breckenridge's lofty base elevation of 9,603 feet has a lot to do with that. From the pass it's a downhill ride of about 5 miles to Selkirk Campground.

Breckenridge is one of several Colorado one-time mining towns that have evolved into ski towns. It is, in fact, one of the oldest continuously inhabited towns in the state, with origins dating to an 1859 gold strike on the Blue River. Like Aspen and Crested Butte, communities sharing similar pasts and presents, Breckenridge boasts a bevy of alluring old Victorian homes that have been spruced up to serve as colorful residences and businesses of various sorts. Not surprisingly, plenty of newer condominiums and trophy homes are scattered about the landscape, too.

Beware of getting splashed with cappuccino as you roll along buffed and boutiqued Main Street in Breckenridge, off of which you turn southeasterly to begin up a path of history. The well-graded road leading to the Continental

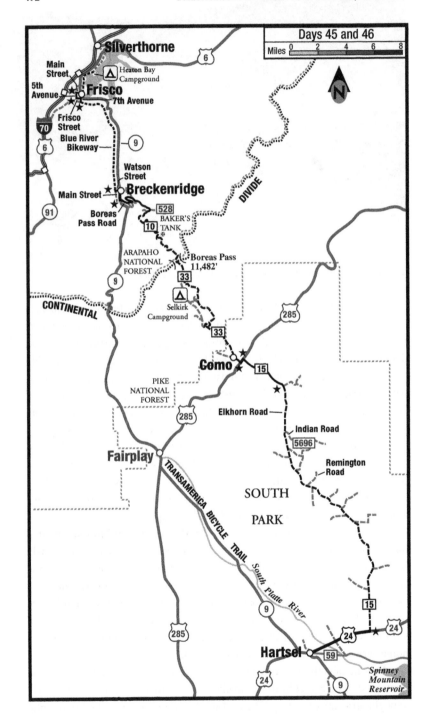

Divide at 11,482-foot Boreas Pass was the route of the narrow-gauge Denver, South Park & Pacific Railroad, which linked Breckenridge to the outside world after the rails reached town in 1882. Narrow-gauge tracks, which were often employed in steep, rough country, featured rails that were just 3 feet apart instead of the more common 4 feet 8 inches.

The grade leading to the top may seem relatively tame by today's mountain biking standards, but it wasn't tame by those of the locomotives that tackled it. In fact, only three cars at a time could usually be pulled up the big hill. According to local lore, P. T. Barnum's circus train was once on its way up Boreas Pass en route to a show in Breckenridge, when it stalled on the steep grade. No big deal: They simply let the elephants out of the cars and utilized their pushing power to boost the train over the pass.

At 19.7 miles you'll pass Baker's Tank, a wooden cistern that served to restock coal-fed steam locomotives with water. Tanks such as this were situated below natural streams, where water could be gravity-fed into them. When full, Baker's Tank held 9,305 gallons of water. (The tank at the location today was moved here in 1910 to replace the original, which wound up being too small for the task.) On Boreas Pass proper you'll find structural remains of Boreas Station, as well as tree stumps remaining from timber felled in the late 1800s to construct various buildings at the site. Once quite the thriving place, at the turn of the twentieth century Boreas Station boasted the highest post office in the United States. It is a striking, otherworldly alpine setting for any sort of settlement.

DAY 45 ROUTE

0.0 Leave Heaton Bay Campground to continue following bike path.

0.4 Cross access road.

1.5 Turn right onto road, then ride back onto the bikeway. Path swings left to parallel highway.

2.3 Go to other side of State Highway 9 at School Road (use crossing signal).

2.4 Go straight where a bikeway branch forks right to a park.

2.6 Turn right onto Main Street in Frisco.

2.8 Turn left onto 5th Avenue.

2.9 Turn left onto Frisco Street; begin following blue-and-white bikeway signs.

3.0 Turn right onto 7th Avenue.

3.5 Turn left toward Breckenridge at the T-intersection onto the signed bikeway (right goes to Vail-Copper Mountain).

8.8 Cross the Colorado Trail.

12.1 Turn left off bikeway onto Watson Street.

12.2 Turn right at stop sign onto Main Street to pass through downtown Breckenridge.

12.9 Turn left onto paved Boreas Pass Road.

14.0 Illinois Gulch Road on right.

16.0 Illinois Gulch Road rejoins on right.

16.2 Bear right on Boreas Pass Road; Road 528 goes left.

16.5 Enter Arapaho National Forest; road turns to gravel and becomes narrow and bumpy as it winds through big rock outcrops. See ski area in distance to the right.

19.7 Baker's Tank.

22.8 Boreas Pass, elevation 11,482 feet (C.D. crossing #16). Road becomes County Road 33.

24.6 Windy Point.

27.0 Leave route, turning west toward sign reading "N. Tarryall Cr. & Selkirk Campground 1 Mile."

Day 46

SELKIRK CAMPGROUND TO HARTSEL

35.9 miles plus 1 mile returning to route plus 2 miles off route

About 6 miles into today's ride you'll pass through Como, named by early Italian settlers for a town and lake in their home country. The limited services here include a restaurant/B&B. From there it's into wide-open South Park, which bears little if any resemblance to the South Park, Colorado, of television notoriety. This broad, mountain-rimmed basin appears to be a piece of Colorado that for some reason has been overlooked, practically the polar opposite of adjacent Summit County. South Park is void of ski areas; in fact, it's virtually void of tourism development altogether. Located almost smack in the middle of Colorado, it's as if development is trying to reach South Park from every direction, but hasn't quite gotten there yet. It's arid country, too, so be sure to stock up on water before leaving Como. Today's mileage and terrain are moderate and the gravel roads hard-surfaced; save for a possible headwind, you should find the effort a breeze. The last 4.5 miles into Hartsel are along potentially busy U.S. Highway 24.

The route over Boreas Pass began as a simple foot and pack trail leading in from the south. That was improved into a wagon road in the early 1860s, twenty years before the arrival of the Denver, South Park & Pacific Railroad—additional evidence of which you'll see on your trip down Boreas Pass. Certain reminders are vivid, others subtle. An example of the latter

True, Montana is rightly known as "Big Sky Country," but it doesn't have a monopoly on infinite blue skies.

are the big stands of aspen sweeping away from the roadsides, the result of huge forest fires ignited by sparks from locomotives on several occasions in the late 1800s. One of the more obvious reminders is the beautiful old stone roundhouse located on the edge of Como. (It used to be even bigger, but the wooden sections burned early in the twentieth century.)

The history of humans in South Park is long, storied, and colorful. Ute Indians, who hunted elk and bison here, were followed by Spanish explorers, beaver trappers, and gold prospectors. Many of the Anglos early on the scene knew South Park as Bayou Salado owing to its wealth of natural salt springs. In 1864 the Colorado Salt Works began evaporating brine into salt at a location near present Antero Junction, producing as much as two tons per day to be used domestically and in refining gold ore.

Between Como and Hartsel you can't help but notice that intermittent winds of change are blowing. You'll zip past deserted road after deserted road, many of them laid out in grid patterns. Some are even marked by street signs that look like someone's idea of a joke. They're obviously subdivision roads, but mostly overgrown and lacking houses. At 26.1 miles there's even an abandoned playground and baseball diamond. Rest assured, though, that freshly painted "Real Estate for Sale" signs adorn storefronts in Hartsel, where you shall again—for the last time on the Great Divide route—come in contact with the TransAmerica Bicycle Trail.

Camping and cabin rentals are available at Hartsel Springs Ranch Guest Lodge, 2 miles east of town on County Road 59. There are no other known accommodations in the Hartsel area at this time.

DAY 46 ROUTE

0.0   From where you left the route, continue riding southeasterly.

3.3   Turn left at T-intersection following County Road 33.

6.2   Cross cattle guard into historic Como; road turns to pavement. Services include a restaurant/B&B.

6.5   Curve left to stay on pavement.

7.1   Turn left at T-intersection onto U.S. Highway 285 and proceed through open country.

7.5   Turn right onto paved County Road 15 toward Indian Mountain. Flat, open, and mountain-surrounded.

11.1   Bear right onto gravel Elkhorn Road, as the road going left leads to Indian Mountain. Road is wide and potentially washboarded.

12.0   Cross cattle guard and head down into drainage.

14.1   Continue on Elkhorn Road, as Indian Road 5696 goes left.

16.1   Cattle guard.

18.9   Continue straight uphill where Remington Road goes left to Elkhorn Ranch.

19.3   Cross low watershed divide.

26.1   Wildwood Recreation Area on left.

31.4   Turn right at T-intersection onto U.S. Highway 24. Commence narrow and potentially busy 4.5-mile stretch of highway.

34.6   Cross South Platte River.

35.9   Hartsel.

Day 47
HARTSEL TO SALIDA

46.6 miles plus 2 miles returning to route

Upon leaving Hartsel, after a couple of miles on State Highway 9 you'll turn south onto gravel to continue past another progression of apparently abandoned subdivision roads. Soon you'll penetrate a high basin that looks rather like a misplaced piece of Alaskan tundra; a high-lonesome stretch of terrain rising toward the mountains of the San Isabel National Forest. At 27.7 miles you'll ford a small creek that offers an easy opportunity to replenish your water. From there you'll climb for about 7 miles, the last 2 of them quite steep, to the high watershed divide that serves as the border between Fremont and Chaffee counties. Some nice dispersed campsites are found near the top, in case you'd prefer to spend the night on high. If not, you'll commence a long descent through surroundings that turn ever more arid the

Tending a fire on a cool Colorado evening after a warm, windy day of riding in the high grassland basin known as South Park

lower you get. Try to keep your eyes on the road during the descent—it's a tall order, with the stunning crags of the Collegiate Peaks of the Sawatch Range looming high above the deliciously green Arkansas River Valley. The downhill bottoms out at the outskirts of Salida.

The procession of Collegiate Peaks includes 14,420-foot Mount Harvard, 14,073-foot Mount Columbia, 14,196-foot Mount Yale, and 14,197-foot Mount Princeton. The southernmost Fourteener in the Sawatch, 14,229-foot Shavano Peak, is named not after an Ivy League school but for a chief of the Tabeguache band of Utes. As the snowfields on the slopes of Shavano melt away in summer, fissures still filled with snow assume the form of an angel with outstretched arms. Legend has it that it's the annual return of the angel who visited Chief Shavano as he prayed for his dying friend, Jim Beckwourth, the mountain man, trader, and founder of the city of Pueblo.

If you're ready for a respite when you hit Salida—and it's a great place for a layover—consider taking a guided float trip on the Arkansas River. It's one of the foremost rafting and kayaking rivers of the West, offering a wide range of waters, from stretches calm enough even for the hydrophobic among us, to wild rides that can test the mettle of the most experienced river rat. A slate of outfitters in Salida (*Suh-LIE-duh*) and Buena Vista (*BYOO-nuh-VIS-tuh*) are at your beck and call, waiting to make all the arrangements for you.

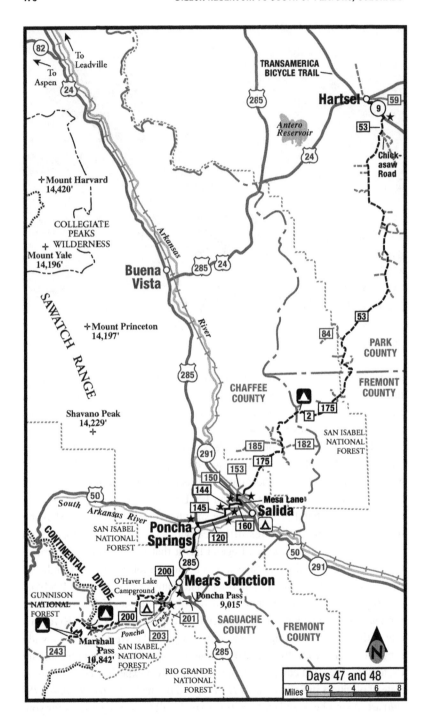

Salida—quaint and historic, yet modern and vigorous—has received votes as "favorite town on the Great Divide route" by a lot of those who've ridden the route. Downtown Salida comprises one of the largest historic districts in Colorado, boasting a collection of red-brick beauties that once housed bars, bordellos, and other businesses vital to the rip-roaring Wild West railroad town that Salida was. Today the same structures are more likely to hold bakeries, good restaurants, bike shops, and art galleries.

DAY 47 ROUTE

0.0 In Hartsel, turn left toward Canyon City onto State Highway 9/ TransAmerica Bicycle Trail.

2.0 Turn right onto County Road 53, which starts off as a wide, well-graded road with very little traffic.

3.3 Chickasaw Road on left.

11.5 Cross low divide.

15.9 Bear right, as a slightly lower-grade road goes left.

19.1 Pass through another little gap, continuing into a dry basin encircled by a bulk of dark mountains.

23.9 Continue straight on County Road 53 at unsigned junction, as County Road 84 goes uphill to right. Route soon turns narrower.

26.2 Cross cattle guard; road turns more primitive.

27.7 Ford small creek.

27.8 Enter Fremont County, leaving Park County and riding toward a higher basin. Road becomes County Road 2/FR 175.

30.3 At the junction at a powerline, continue straight rather than turning left. Enter San Isabel National Forest.

30.6 Continue straight on County Road 175, as another road goes right to Cable Gulch and Herring Park.

32.6 Start climbing quite steeply toward the high ridge, amid aspen groves and rock outcrops.

34.5 Cross cattle guard at watershed divide. As you descend you'll see the spectacular 14ers of the Sawatch Range; the Continental Divide runs along their spine.

37.0 Round bend and look far down on valley.

39.0 Continue downhill straight on County Road 175 at junction, as County Road 185 goes right to Turret and Aspen Ridge.

39.5 Pass County Road 182 going left.

40.0 Pass under powerline where unsigned road goes left.

42.5 Leave San Isabel National Forest.

44.4 Road surface turns to chip seal.

46.1 Cautiously cross two sets of railroad tracks at stop sign.

46.3 Turn left at T-intersection to continue on County Road 175, as County Road 153 goes right. Immediately after turning, go straight to cross river, where County Road 150 goes right.

46.5 Turn left onto State Highway 291 toward Salida.

46.6 Route goes right onto Mesa Lane. Leave route to ride into Salida, which has all services.

`Day 48`

SALIDA
TO CAMPSITE 6.2 MILES WEST OF MARSHALL PASS

`32.6 miles`

Stock your larder before saying goodbye to Salida, because it's 4 days and 153 miles to Del Norte, the next town of any size. Other than services in Poncha Springs, just 5.5 miles into today's ride, you'll find only extremely limited services on this stretch, including a minimally stocked store in Sargents (mile 10.3 on Day 49) and another small store in La Garita, 2 miles off the route 14.4 miles into your ride on Day 51. Today's adventure begins with 11 miles of pavement, including a climb of more than 4 miles toward Poncha Pass on U.S. Highway 285. Before reaching that pass you'll turn to begin an even longer ascent on gravel to Marshall Pass, elevation 10,842 feet, and

South of Salida the route alternates between classic high country like this and lower-elevation terrain that evokes the Southwest. (Andrew Sufficool)

your seventeenth crossing of the Continental Divide since setting out from Canada. (The first 4 miles are quite level; the real climbing is from 13.9 to 26.4 miles.) An alternative to the main route, beginning at mile 13.9 in the description below, will also take you to Marshall Pass, in just over half the distance of the main route (7.1 compared to 12.5 miles). And that does mean it's a proportionally steeper ride—very steep, in fact. Its good points include a greater amount of shade and water than the main route, a fine selection of private, dispersed campsites, and little or no vehicle traffic. Regardless of which route you take to Marshall Pass, from there it's a quick, 6-mile zip on gravel to the recommended overnighting spot.

If on a layover day in the Salida area you'd rather go for a mountain-bike ride than a river trip, as was suggested in yesterday's route summary, it's good to know that in addition to being Colorado's number-one river-running hotspot, the Salida–Buena Vista area owns a reputation as a fat-tire mecca. The Monarch Crest Trail, whose southern terminus you'll skirt at Marshall Pass, has garnered a distinction as one of the top-ten single-track rides in the Rocky Mountain West. The trail meanders up and down along the Continental Divide for 12 miles, at elevations ranging between 12,000 and 11,000 feet. (If you do the ride you'll want to set out at the other, northern end.) Other popular local rides include Tenderfoot Mountain, Bear Creek–Methodist Mountain, and the old Midland railroad grade, a designated Forest Service mountain-bike trail ending in Buena Vista. Area bike shops can provide detailed information on these and other rides.

Speaking of railroad grades, the main route over Marshall Pass follows a former grade of the Denver & Río Grande Railroad. A toll road over Marshall Pass, which had evolved into an important connection between the Gunnison and Arkansas valleys, was completed in 1880, and a year later the Denver & Río Grande laid tracks through the pass.

DAY 48 ROUTE

0.0 From where you left the route, turn west onto Mesa Lane.

0.2 Turn right at T-intersection onto County Road 160.

1.0 Turn left onto County Road 144 rather than going straight down the hill.

1.7 Turn right at T-intersection (signed bike route goes left).

2.2 Turn left onto County Road 145.

2.9 Turn right at stop sign onto County Road 120.

5.5 Turn left at stop sign onto U.S. Highway 285. Poncha Springs has services, including a convenience store.

5.7 Bear right toward Monte Vista on U.S. Highway 285 and begin climbing toward Poncha Pass.

10.9 Mears Junction. Turn right onto gravel County Road 200 toward Marshall Pass.

13.2 At anglers' parking area go straight rather than turning right toward Marshall Pass.

13.3 Turn right onto FR 200 (FR 201 goes straight).

13.9 Cross Poncha Creek on old bridge, then bear right on FR 200. (For tougher alternate route: Turn left onto FR 203 and proceed up Poncha Creek. You'll reach Marshall Pass in 7.1 miles.)

14.6 Begin uphill.

15.8 Cross FR 202 and continue on FR 200 past O'Haver Lake Campground (0.5 mile to left on FR 202).

17.6 Continue straight toward Marshall Pass.

19.9 Dispersed camping areas along both sides of road.

25.6 More dispersed camping sites.

26.1 Hutchison-Barrett Cow Camp cabin up rough road to right.

26.2 Toilets, information kiosk. Meeting place of Continental Divide National Scenic Trail, Colorado Trail, and the Great Divide Mountain Bike Route.

26.4 Marshall Pass, elevation 10,842 feet (C.D. crossing #17). (Alternate route rejoins main route.) Enter Gunnison National Forest. Road becomes FR 243.

30.9 Campsite on right.

32.6 Campsite on right.

Day 49

CAMPSITE 6.2 MILES WEST OF MARSHALL PASS TO LUDERS CREEK CAMPGROUND

58.8 miles

On today's ride you'll begin by continuing downstream along Marshall Creek for 10 miles on gravel to Sargents, Colorado, whose right-to-the-point greeting sign reads "Elevation High, Population Few." From there you'll pedal along U.S. Highway 50 for about 13 miles on a shoulder with a surface alternating between gravel and blacktop. At the dot on the map called Doyleville you'll turn south onto gravel to begin spinning through another high, dry, mountain-ringed basin of the sort you're beginning to recognize as typical of Colorado. After the wide gash of Cochetopa Canyon comes into view at roughly 36 miles, you'll ride for a little over a mile on State Highway 114, then begin the gentle climb up Cochetopa Creek to the Continental Divide at Cochetopa Pass. Luders Creek Campground, a designated Forest Service site, is found a couple of miles on the other side of the pass. Surface water is available on much of the route today.

Cochetopa Pass, elevation 10,032 feet, evolved from an important passage over the Continental Divide for early Ute Indians (Cochetopa is a Ute word meaning "buffalo crossing") into a toll-road route for an 1870s stage road built by Otto Mears and Enos Hotchkiss. John C. Fremont and his party had crossed the divide here earlier during their exploratory mission to identify a transcontinental railroad route. Unfortunately, Fremont's "guide" got the group severely lost and nearly a third of the thirty-five men died in a blizzard. In 1868, the year before the toll road was completed, the Los Pinos Indian Agency was set up on the west slope of the pass, serving for years thereafter as the primary outpost of dealings between the U.S. Government and the Utes. In 1914, after internal-combustion-driven vehicles came into being, the roadway was improved and opened to cars.

No doubt you're sensing that the farther south into Colorado you go, the more "Southwestern" your surroundings seem, both in terms of landscape and place names. Tomorrow and the next day those feelings will intensify, as you skirt the western edge of the flat San Luis Valley, the only true desert within the Colorado Rockies (it gets less than 8 inches of precipitation per year). Also one of the most beautiful and least populated, yet longest settled, basins of the West, San Luis Valley is like a part of Mexico surviving in Colorado.

DAY 49 ROUTE

0.0   Leave campsite, riding southwest on Forest Road 243.

5.2   Junction. Continue low left/straight on FR 243 where another road comes down from behind right.

5.6   Enter Marshall Pass State Trust Wildlife Management Area.

6.1   Continue straight where Indian Creek Road goes right.

10.3   Sargents. Turn left onto U.S. Highway 50 to begin 12.8-mile stretch of pavement.

18.0   Enter Gunnison County.

23.1   Doyleville. Turn left onto County Road 45. Starts out as wide, flat gravel ranch road ribboning across barren BLM lands.

24.0   Bear right uphill; County Road 46 goes left to Needle Creek Reservoir.

25.1   Reenter Saguache County; road designation changes to County Road 14PP.

25.7   Cattle guard; begin climbing more steeply. Continue straight uphill as County Road 18VV forks right.

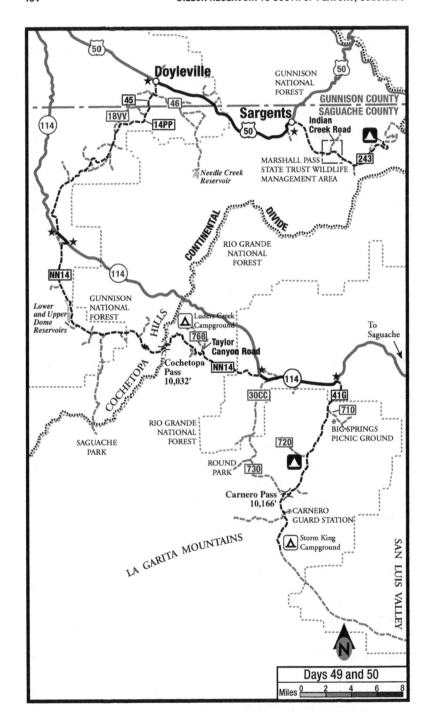

26.6 Start down into wide-open basin with huge bulk of mountains looming to west.

29.5 County Road 18VV goes right.

37.9 Road curves left and starts dropping steeply.

39.7 Turn left at stop sign onto State Highway 114.

41.0 Turn right onto County Road NN14 toward sign reading "National Forest Access/Old Agency Work Center."

44.5 Go straight toward Cochetopa Pass.

46.5 Lower Dome Reservoir on right.

48.1 Continue straight where another road goes right toward Eddieville Trailhead and Stuart Creek.

49.4 Continue straight on County Road NN14.

50.5 Pass a road going right to Saguache Park and La Garita Wilderness.

52.1 Enter Gunnison National Forest.

56.9 Cochetopa Pass, elevation 10,032 feet (C.D. crossing #18). Enter Río Grande National Forest.

58.8 Luders Creek Campground on left.

Colorado classic: A close-up of a columbine flower backed by lofty mountains still snowcapped in mid-summer (Kyle Karlson)

Day 50

LUDERS CREEK CAMPGROUND
TO STORM KING CAMPGROUND

29.7 miles

Early on during today's ride you'll descend past an array of colorful rock outcrops, which may lead you to suspect that you're leaving the Rockies behind and entering Southwest canyon country. Never fear: Plenty of Rockies remain! In about 9 miles you'll turn onto the generally low-traffic State Highway 114 to parallel Saguache Creek downstream for 6 miles before riding south onto gravel to reenter the Río Grande National Forest. After cresting Carnero Pass at 25.9 miles you'll descend southeasterly along Carnero Creek for 4 miles, to the night's destination of Storm King Campground. Stream water is readily accessible throughout much of the day.

Today's and tomorrow's rides are both relatively short and easy; no doubt with the fitness you've attained by this point in your adventure you could link them together into one long day. But it would be a shame to rush through country as quiet and fine as this. If you're compelled to tackle additional mileage, consider instead taking a side trip east to the fascinating little town of Saguache. To find south-of-the-border-like Saguache (*Suh-WATCH*, Ute

Leaving the Rockies behind? Not yet—there are still plenty of mountains to climb and descents to enjoy. (John Beck)

for "blue earth"), simply continue straight on State Highway 114 at mile 14.9, rather than turning right onto FR 41G. After approximately 17 miles you'll roll into town, where you'll find one of the niftiest little community museums in Colorado. Helping to make the village's history more arresting than that of many small towns are its ties to cannibalism, one of the grisliest stories to emerge from the nineteenth-century Rocky Mountain West.

Components of the legend vary depending on which account you read, but it is generally agreed that it was into Saguache that a robust-appearing Alfred G. "Alferd" Packer wandered in April 1874 after spending a hard, cold winter trapped in the San Juan Mountains. Evidently not the smartest cannibal in world history, Packer aroused suspicion by going on a drinking binge at a Saguache saloon, where he spent large amounts of money that he took from a number of different wallets. Meanwhile, the five fellow prospectors with whom Packer had forged ahead into the mountains the previous January, against the better advice of some Ute Indians, were nowhere to be seen. Under suspicion of murder, Packer was contained in the Saguache jail (he soon escaped), despite his insistence that four of his companions had killed one another while feuding and that he, Packer, had shot the other in self-defense. The next summer their five bodies were found a few miles outside of Lake City. Four had died from axe blows to the head and the other from a gunshot, and all had strips of flesh cut from their thighs and chests.

If, instead of learning about the Wild West past of Saguache and surroundings, you'd rather explore more of the attractive La Garita Mountains by mountain bike, designated Forest Service bike trails are found in the vicinities of both Luders Creek Campground, at the day's beginning, and Storm King Campground, at day's end.

DAY 50 ROUTE

0.0 Continue riding southeast from Luders Creek Campground.

3.2 Taylor Canyon Road 768 goes left.

7.1 Leave Río Grande National Forest.

7.7 Drop through a red-rock canyon, peppered with stands of piñon and juniper.

8.8 Turn right onto State Highway 114.

9.4 Pass County Road 30CC going right to Round Park/Squaw Creek (this offers a tougher alternative to the main route).

14.9 Turn right onto FR 41G toward La Garita and Carnero Pass.

16.9 Enter Río Grande National Forest.

17.7 Pass FR 710 going left toward Big Springs picnic grounds.

18.8 Start climbing into aspens.

21.5 FR 720 goes right. Good dispersed campsites in the area.

24.8   Continue straight toward Carnero Pass.

25.9   Carnero Pass, elevation 10,166 feet.

27.4   Road going left into Carnero Guard Station. Beautiful surroundings of boulders and hoodoos.

29.7   Storm King Campground on left. Water available.

Day 51

STORM KING CAMPGROUND TO DEL NORTE

33.7 miles

From Storm King Campground you'll continue downstream along Carnero Creek, skirting Coolbroth Canyon, then passing through an intriguing "gates of the mountains" formation of columnar basalt. At 14.4 miles you'll see the left-hand turn to La Garita, a miniscule village located about 0.5 mile off the route that boasts a mercantile and a beautiful hilltop Spanish-style church. It's worth pedaling the extra miles just to capture the scene with your eyes and/or your camera. At 15.2 miles you'll pass the westerly turn up La Garita Creek and Penitente Canyon. Then, soon after turning west onto Old Woman's Creek Road at 18.7 miles, you'll begin a stretch of rather tricky routefinding to follow a back-door route into Del Norte. (If you're in a rush, rather than turning right onto FR 660 at 18.7 miles, simply continue straight on County Road 38A to its junction with State Highway 112. A right turn at that point leads into Del Norte. This route is not a bad second choice, because it skirts the unusual Elephant Rocks formation.) Other than two stretches of pavement totaling 5.5 miles, all of today's route follows either high-grade gravel or rustic dirt roads traversing gentle terrain.

You'll have access to another couple of short, noteworthy side trips in addition to the one to La Garita. The first goes to Penitente Canyon (mentioned above), where at a point approximately 1.5 miles off the route you can see ruts carved into rock, the legacy of horse-drawn wagons. The canyon is a namesake of Los Hermanos Penitentes (the Penitent Brothers), a branch of Catholics whose sect began in thirteenth-century Europe and was brought to New Mexico in 1598 by Don Juan de Onate. In the early 1800s the Penitentes began branching out from their remote villages in northern New Mexico, with a fair share of them landing in southern Colorado. The men of the sect would meet at their lodges, or *moradas*, where, among other rituals, they practiced torture and self-flagellation. During Holy Week they would reenact the capture and crucifixion of Christ—to the extent, by some accounts, of nailing or tying one of the members to a cross and leaving him

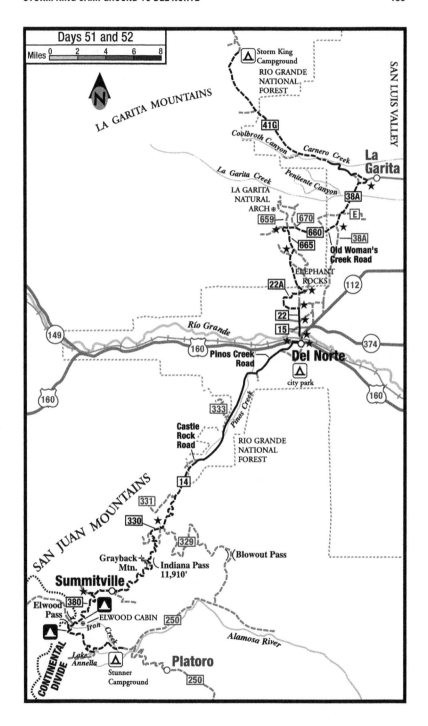

there until he passed out. The Catholic Church ultimately outlawed these practices, but the Penitentes surreptitiously continued them well into the twentieth century. Even to this day, abandoned *moradas* can be seen in the San Luis Valley and around Hispanic villages elsewhere in southern Colorado and northern New Mexico.

Side trip number two goes to La Garita Natural Arch, known also as Del Norte Window or La Ventana. The arch, located about 2 miles off the route up FR 659 (the turn is at 22.7 miles in the narrative below), is formed by an immense hole that eroded through a volcanic dike. This part of Colorado became volcanically active around 30 million years ago when the San Juan Mountains began forming, and La Garita Natural Arch is one of numerous dikes and plugs found in the region. Wildlife is abundant, too: You may see pronghorns in the rolling scrublands of this area, and on and around the arch itself there's a good chance of spotting bighorn sheep.

DAY 51 ROUTE

0.0   Continue riding south from Storm King Campground.

4.2   Cross cattle guard and leave Río Grande National Forest. With rustic homestead on right, bear left/straight on County Road 41G toward sign reading "Hwy. 285—15 Miles."

8.2   Coolbroth Canyon to right.

10.9   Cross cattle guard and ride onto pavement.

14.4   Turn hard right off County Road 41G onto County Road 38A, a gravel road leading toward Del Norte and Penitente Canyon. La Garita is located 0.6 mile east off the route from this point.

At the intersection of the Great Divide route and the Del Norte Municipal and County Airport, riders are urged to stay off the runway. (Kyle Karlson)

15.2 Penitente Canyon is 1.5 miles off route to the west.

17.5 Continue straight/right on County Road 38A where Road E goes left.

18.7 Turn right onto FR 660/Old Woman's Creek Road toward La Garita Natural Arch.

21.9 Pass FR 670 going right to La Garita Creek.

22.7 Continue straight where FR 659 goes right to La Garita Natural Arch.

23.0 Turn left onto FR 665, heading due south for Del Norte. Primitive road next 5.6 miles.

23.8 Road makes abrupt curve east to get around head of drainage.

25.2 Cross drainage.

25.7 Continue straight where another road goes right.

26.0 Where signed FR 665 goes left, bear right down unsigned road to cross drainage.

26.9 See house on left.

27.4 Pass through obvious gap.

28.4 Drop into wash bottom where another road forks away. Beware of sharp rocks, sand, and washouts.

28.6 Ride onto wide gravel road.

28.9 Pass another road going left.

29.1 Turn right onto unsigned County Road 22A, following it through a series of right and left turns.

30.9 Landing strip on left.

32.0 At stop sign, turn right onto unsigned County Road 22 (paved).

32.5 Continue straight on pavement off County Road 22 onto County Road 15. Cross canal.

33.3 Turn right at stop sign onto State Highway 112 and cross river.

33.7 Turn right at stop sign into Del Norte; all services, including camping at city park with permission of police.

Day 52
DEL NORTE TO STUNNER CAMPGROUND

42.5 miles

This is it, The Big Day, particularly for individuals fond of "biggests" and "bests." Less than 24 miles after leaving Del Norte you'll hit the high point of the Great Divide route, Indiana Pass, elevation 11,910 feet above sea level. Fittingly, getting to Indiana Pass is no picnic. After all, it would be rather anticlimactic if climbing to the apex of the route was a breeze—as easy as, say, Boreas Pass outside Breckenridge. To put the ensuing climb in perspective, consider that the elevation of Del Norte is 7,874 feet, meaning that you'll gain 4,036 feet of elevation over 23.5 miles. The math-savvy may contend that although that is a lot of climbing, it's an average grade of only 3.25 percent, not bad at all. However, over the first half of those miles you'll gain relatively little elevation as you parallel Pinos Creek on paved Pinos Creek Road. Where the pavement ends, the real climbing begins, and... suffice it to say that you won't soon forget the final 12 miles to Indiana Pass.

The next few days are tricky in terms of finding things to eat. There's not a reasonably well-stocked store until El Rito or Abiquiu, New Mexico (Day 56), 173 and 190 miles, respectively, from Del Norte. Operational cafés will probably be found at Platoro, 49 miles from Del Norte, and at the State Highway 17 junction, 72 miles from Del Norte, although you should call ahead to verify operation if you'll be depending on them. (The phone numbers are listed on the Adventure Cycling maps.) One way or the other, you'll need to stock up in Del Norte and commence thinking like a backpacker. Also stock up on enough water in Del Norte for the entire day: After crossing Indiana Pass you'll skirt the Summitville Mine EPA Superfund Site, where the surrounding surface water is too contaminated to be safely ingested even after filtering. Not far from there you'll spin through some of the prettiest subalpine basins on the entire Great Divide route, made particularly striking due to their proximity to bombed-out Summitville. The suggested overnight, Stunner Campground, elevation 9,800 feet above sea level, is pleasantly situated among aspen groves and has potable well water. It is indeed a stunner.

Also know that at 33.8 miles, on Shinzel Flats, you'll pass the Elwood Cabin. It is available to rent from the Forest Service, but advance reservations must be made (719-274-8971).

DAY 52 ROUTE

0.0 From where you left route, ride through downtown Del Norte.

0.5 Turn left onto paved Pinos Creek Road toward Summitville.

4.9 Cross creek as you continue through mountain-ringed ranch country.

9.5 Valley narrows considerably.

11.7 Just past the right-hand turn to Castle Rock Road, cross bridge and ride onto gravel. Commence climbing on FR 14.

12.2 Enter Río Grande National Forest.

13.4 Burro Creek Trail on left.

14.5 Go straight toward sign reading "Summitville—14" where FR 331 goes right toward Bear Creek.

17.0 Cross over to right side of ridge, passing under powerline. Dirt tracks over next couple of miles lead to potential dispersed camping sites.

Hitting the high point of the Great Divide route: Indiana Pass, elevation 11,910—more than 4,000 feet higher than Del Norte, just 23.5 miles back. (Julie Wilson)

18.3 Turn right onto FR 330 toward Summitville at four-way junction; FR 329 goes left toward Blowout Pass and straight ahead dead-ends.

19.8 Bear left to continue on FR 330 toward Grayback Mountain/ Summitville.

22.9 Cross trickle of a stream.

23.5 Indiana Pass, elevation 11,910 feet. High point of Great Divide Mountain Bike Route! Continue straight downhill on FR 330 toward Summitville.

27.6 Continue straight on FR 330 toward Summitville.

27.9 Summitville. No services.

28.1 Start climbing away from Summitville.

30.6 Turn hard left onto FR 380 toward Elwood Pass; FR 330 ends.

33.4 Nice primitive campsite on left.

33.8 Pass Elwood Cabin.

34.1 Go straight on FR 380 toward Platoro.

38.4 Private Lake Annella (no camping). Continue straight toward Stunner and Platoro.

38.5 Pass a second private lake.

40.0 Cross colorfully toxic-looking Iron Creek.

42.5 Turn into Stunner Campground.

Day 53

STUNNER CAMPGROUND
TO ELK CREEK CAMPGROUND

28.6 miles plus approximately 2 miles off route

After climbing over Stunner Pass at 3.5 miles, you'll descend into the drainage of the Conejos (Spanish for "rabbits") River, a popular fishing stream that flows from Platoro Reservoir southeasterly to join the Río Grande not far from Alamosa, Colorado. You'll follow the Conejos south past Platoro, a collection of cabins and other services for tourists, a large share of whom, you may notice, drive cars sporting Texas license plates. You'll subsequently pass a string of nice riverside Forest Service campgrounds, as well as several hiking/horsepacking trailheads for the nearby South San Juan Wilderness. One of the lesser-visited of Colorado's numerous wildland parcels, the South San Juan comprises 127,000 acres of subalpine and alpine terrain, with elevations ranging from 8,000 to over 13,000 feet. Sprawling grasslands, forests of aspen and spruce, and tundra and rocky areas are all parts of the package. The wilderness is home to a plentiful assortment of wildlife, too, including elk, bighorn sheep, mule deer, black bear, and wild turkeys.

At lower elevations, you definitely know when you're getting into the great American Southwest. (Joanna Muirhead)

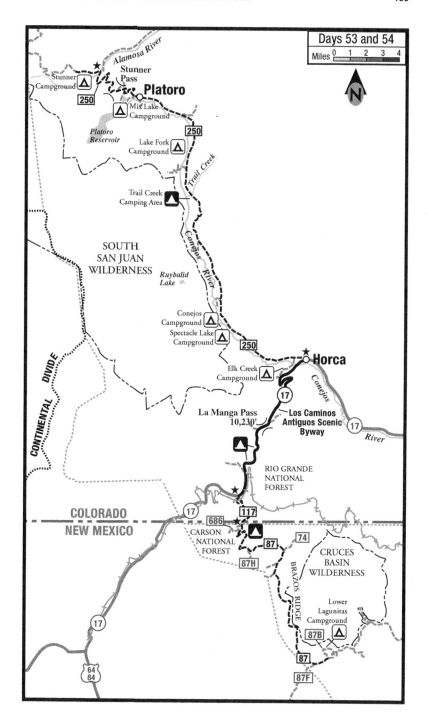

Tonight's recommended campground, Elk Creek, is located up a road that leaves the route 0.5 mile before the junction with State Highway 17. (Any one of the previously encountered, route-side campgrounds would make for a fine overnight as well.) In addition to those found at Platoro, seasonal tourist services are located at the junction with State Highway 17. Today's ride is generally easy, and good surface water is readily available after crossing Stunner Pass.

State Highway 17 in Colorado is a component of the 170-mile Los Caminos Antiguos ("the ancient roads") Scenic Byway. The name derives from the route's winding path through the San Luis Valley, where Native American, Hispanic, and Anglo peoples have commingled through the centuries, resulting in an unusually rich cultural mix. Also be aware that the route between Antonito, Colorado, and Chama, New Mexico, along Highway 17 constitutes one of the truly great road rides of the American Southwest, should you get the itch for a pavement interlude. (Day 54 of the Great Divide route follows the highway for 11.6 miles, so you'll get to sample it one way or the other.) Chama and Antonito are also connected by the narrow-gauge Cumbres & Toltec Scenic Railroad (see Day 54), making it feasible to pedal in one direction and take the train the other.

DAY 53 ROUTE

0.0 Continue riding southeasterly from Stunner Campground.

0.3 Turn right onto FR 250 toward Platoro. River water contaminated (see sign).

0.5 Cross Alamosa River and begin climb to Stunner Pass.

1.1 Cross Globe Creek.

3.5 Stunner Pass.

4.7 Turn left toward Mix Lake Campground and Platoro.

5.8 Mix Lake Campground is located up road to the right.

6.2 Pass right-hand turn leading into cabin-filled Platoro. Begin paralleling the Conejos River.

11.7 Lake Fork Campground on right.

14.9 Trail Creek Camping Area to right (designated dispersed camping).

17.9 Wilderness trailhead on right.

21.4 Pass road going right to Ruybalid Lake Trailhead.

22.6 Conejos Campground on right. Pleasant setting along river.

22.9 Spectacle Lake Campground on right.

28.6 Route continues straight on FR 250; Elk Creek Campground is up road to right.

El Malpais National Monument is home to La Ventana Natural Arch. (Etienne Theroux)

CHAPTER 6

SOUTH OF PLATORO, COLORADO, TO PIE TOWN, NEW MEXICO

408.2 MILES
Days 54 through 63 (ten days)
Three Continental Divide crossings

This section begins in Colorado but remains in that state for only 15 miles before entering New Mexico. Guaranteed to delight, New Mexico contains 701 miles of the Great Divide Mountain Bike Route—just 9 miles fewer than state-mileage leader Montana claims. Arguably, New Mexico is also the most diverse of the five states encountered, with landscapes ranging from the high-elevation, subalpine mountains of the north, to the low-lying, cactus-filled Chihuahuan Desert at the southern end—and with plenty of surprises in between.

From the highlands of the San Juan and Tusas mountains of the Río Grande and Carson national forests, the route wends southward through a panorama of public lands administered by the BLM, the Santa Fe and Cibola national forests, and the National Park Service, as well as through short stretches of private and Acoma Indian tribal lands. Towns, few and far between, include places such as Vallecitos, El Rito, and Abiquiu, villages as appealing to the eye as their names are poetic. The towns and their surroundings are like dynamic works of art, making it easy to understand why

Tour Divide racer Jay Petervary's bike at a New Mexico cattleguard, no doubt enjoying a rare moment of repose (Jay Petervary)

spiritual seekers and artists both unknown and renowned, such as Georgia O'Keeffe, have been attracted to the area through the decades.

From Abiquiu the Great Divide route climbs, seemingly forever, up Polvadera Mesa to the lofty forests of the Santa Fe National Forest. From there it's down to Cuba, then up and down through one of the most remote and fantastically eroded regions you'll ever encounter. In Grants you'll cross paths with Route 66, the legendary Mother Road of American story and song—and the focus of a mapped Adventure Cycling road route—then traverse the volcanic terrain of El Malpais National Monument. The section ends at Pie Town, not your common New Mexico town name by any means, but a very New Mexican place in that the community and its eclectic collection of residents defy stereotyping.

Incidentally, if it seems that the following route descriptions concentrate more on the surrounding soils and rocks than do those of the previous sections, it is not your imagination. In New Mexico the scenery is so ever-changing, and the innards of the earth so often bared and void of vegetation, that one cannot help but wonder about its geologic history.

Day 54
ELK CREEK CAMPGROUND TO LOWER LAGUNITAS CAMPGROUND

29.8 miles plus approximately 2 miles returning to route from Elk Creek Campground and 1 mile off route to Lower Lagunitas Campground

Today's ride, beginning with 12 miles of paved highway, leads from Colorado's Río Grande National Forest into the Carson National Forest of New Mexico, by way of lofty La Manga Pass and Brazos Ridge (see map on page 195). For more than 14 miles—beginning at mile 20.7 today and continuing to mile 5.3 tomorrow—you'll make a broad curve around the circular-shaped Cruces Basin Wilderness of the Carson National Forest. Stream water is abundant throughout the area. This region of New Mexico is one of the wildest and most stunning stretches of the entire Great Divide route, boasting landscapes that are about as far as one can imagine from the standard image of what New Mexico should look like. Unfortunately, many sections of unimproved dirt roads in the area also are impassable during wet weather. So, if you land here during a rainy period, you might be wise to plan on detouring through Chama, then to Abiquiu via U.S. Highway 84.

About 0.5 mile after turning from State Highway 17 onto FR 117 you'll bump across the curiously narrow tracks of the Cumbres & Toltec Scenic

Railroad, the "Pride of the Rockies." Time it right, whether by accident or by design, and you'll see and hear pulsing up the high valley a vision straight out of the old West: an iron horse, chugging, belching black coal smoke, and letting loose a high-pitched, spine-tingling whistle that resounds through the lofty basin, evoking visions of train robbers on speeding horses and freights of gold.

The tracks of the Cumbres & Toltec were originally laid in 1880 by the Denver & Río Grande Railroad, which wanted ready access to the rich gold and silver camps of southwestern Colorado. As the mining dwindled and finally died out, so did the need for the train. During the 1960s a group of railroad/history buffs from the two-state area organized and began refurbishing the line. The train started running again in the early 1970s, filled this time with a freight of tourists rather than minerals. The longest and highest narrow-gauge railroad in the country, the Cumbres & Toltec, when traveling westbound, winds for 64 miles, first up the valley of the Río Los Pinos and over Cumbres Pass, where in the sixteenth century Spanish explorers entered the future Colorado. It then descends along State Highway 17 at a 4 percent grade (steep, by train standards) toward Chama. The tourist train is co-owned by the states of Colorado and New Mexico—appropriately so, since the tracks cross from one state to the other a total of seven times.

DAY 54 ROUTE

0.0 From where you left the route for Elk Creek Campground, continue southeast on FR 250.

0.6 Horca. Pass collection of tourist services, then turn right onto State Highway 17, Los Caminos Antiguos Scenic Byway, a pleasant, uncrowded and well-shouldered road.

0.9 Cross the Conejos River and begin climbing.

3.7 Terrific views of the valley below from where you have come.

6.5 Road goes left to Spruce Hole.

6.7 La Manga Pass, elevation 10,230 feet. Nice campsites available over the next few rolling miles.

12.2 Turn left onto gravel FR 117 and head down switchback.

12.7 Cross narrow-gauge railroad tracks.

13.5 Cross over creek, continuing downhill.

13.6 Stay right as another road veers left to private cabins.

13.9 Stay right as two-track goes left.

15.2 Enter New Mexico, leaving the Río Grande National Forest and entering the Carson National Forest.

15.4 Bear left at Y onto FR 87; FR 686 goes straight.

17.8 Continue climbing on FR 87; 87H goes right.

18.0 Bear left at Y toward Lagunitas.

18.2 Cross cattle guard. Road is rocky and steep.

18.7 Pass FR 87 sign on high plateau. Begin long descent with awesome views.

20.7 Continue right, following FR 87. FR 74 goes left.

22.1 Bear left on FR 87; two-track goes right.

22.7 Cross cattle guard and encounter 0.5-mile stretch steep uphill (probably unrideable).

24.3 Signed Brazos Ridge overlook, with views into the Cruces Basin Wilderness.

29.0 FR 87F goes right.

29.8 Leave the route, turning left toward Lower Lagunitas Campground on FR 87B.

Day 55

LOWER LAGUNITAS CAMPGROUND TO HOPEWELL LAKE CAMPGROUND

35.1 miles plus 1 mile returning to route from Upper/Lower Lagunitas

Today's ride continues through a mountainous highland that is sometimes rolling and other times very hilly, a part of the state that is more like a wedge of Colorado than like the majority of New Mexico. At 5.3 miles you'll ride from unimproved road onto a higher-grade gravel surface, then at 10 miles commence a long downhill slicing through stands of aspen interrupted by undulating grasslands. Good water sources include the Río San Antonio, crossed at 15.7 miles, and Little Tusas Creek, which you'll begin descending alongside at about 27.5 miles. At just past 30 miles you'll turn westerly onto U.S. Highway 64 and begin a 5-mile climb to the turn to Hopewell Lake, the day's destination. Here you'll find a pleasant, pack-it-in/pack-it-out Forest Service campground.

You'll have a good chance of spotting pronghorns in the grasslands of Cisneros Park, and of seeing beaver signs along Little Tusas Creek and other streams. Not surprisingly this very country was the haunt of mountain men during the early nineteenth century. The beaver-rich region of yore, where you'll be until around Abiquiu, is bounded roughly by Chama to the west, Santa Fe and Las Vegas to the south, and Raton to the east, with Taos almost smack in the middle. For some reason—probably because fur was not in style in the warm climates of Spain as it was elsewhere in Europe—the Spaniards who settled New Mexico in the sixteenth through eighteenth centuries

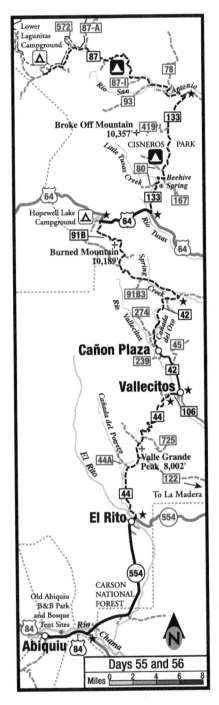

Days 55 and 56

failed to capitalize on the bounty of beaver that awaited harvest in this mountainous region. Rather, it took Anglo trappers of the 1820s to take advantage of the abundance of *Castor canadensis*. The Spanish provincial government of New Mexico was adamantly against the idea of trade with Americans, but the native Pueblo and other tribes were open to the prospect. In the early 1820s a Ute Indian purportedly told a U.S. trapper-trader, "Come over among us, and you shall have as many beaver skins as you wish." Spain released its hold on New Mexico when Mexico gained independence in September 1821, and outsiders were suddenly welcome, as long as they paid their taxes—as well as the often-expected bribes—on goods extracted.

Back in St. Louis, General William H. Ashley and Major Andrew Henry formed the Rocky Mountain Fur Company, posting notice in 1822 in the *Missouri Republican* that they were looking for "one-hundred young men to ascend the Missouri River to its source, there to be employed for one, two, or three years...." Legendary mountain men like Jim Bridger and Jedediah Smith headed west at this time, where they worked streams of the northern Rockies. A party of approximately fifty men also headed to Santa Fe that year, from

Bare rock and timber, a vision characteristic of northern New Mexico

which point they branched into the stream-rich mountains of north-central New Mexico. The most famous New Mexico mountain man—arriving from his native Kentucky in 1826—was Kit Carson, who after several years as a trapper went on to make his marks as a guide, Mexican War courier, Taos-area rancher, Indian agent, and Indian fighter. It's said that Carson never learned to read or write English, yet he came to speak not only that language, but Spanish, French, and several Indian dialects.

DAY 55 ROUTE

0.0 From where you left the route, continue on FR 87, which soon turns smoother.

4.5 Pass FR 572, which goes left into a corridor gap in the Cruces Basin Wilderness.

5.3 Continue straight uphill on FR 87 rather than left turning onto FR 87-A. Ride onto good gravel surface.

10.0 Start long downhill through aspen groves.

10.6 Nice dispersed campsites.

13.1 Pass FR 87-I going right.

14.3 Curve left toward U.S. Highway 285 across cattle guard. Remain on main road where FR 93 goes right. (Good campsites on the left before the river.)

15.6 Bear right, continuing on FR 87 where FR 78 goes left toward Chino Peak. Cross Río San Antonio.

18.0 Turn right onto lower-grade FR 133 rather than continuing straight on FR 87. (Potentially mucky road; if it's raining, consider continuing on FR 87 to highway.)

20.5 Pass FR 419 going right toward Broke Off Mountain.

25.3 Cisneros Park. Great view of southern Colorado mountains to left.

25.7 Good primitive campsites on right.

25.8 Pass FR 80 going right.

26.2 Turn right to continue on FR 133, rather than going straight onto FR 167. Begin descent.

27.1 Beehive Spring on left (possibly dry).

27.7 FR 80 loops back in on right; continue straight on FR 133, descending along Little Tusas Creek.

30.2 Turn right onto U.S. Highway 64 and begin climbing.

35.0 Turn left off U.S. Highway 64 onto FR 91B, toward Hopewell Lake Campground (picnic area has piped water).

35.1 Ride onto dirt and make right-hand turn into Hopewell Lake Campground.

Day 56

HOPEWELL LAKE CAMPGROUND TO ABIQUIU

57.4 miles

Today's long ride begins in mountains and ranchlands still very Colorado-like in nature, but ends by winding through a series of villages evocative of old Mexico, where you'll sense that you really are in New Mexico at last. As characterizes so much of the Great Divide route, you'll usually find yourself riding either uphill or downhill, and rarely on the level. You'll begin by pedaling through the rolling uplands of the Tusas Mountains, where Pleistocene glaciers shaped the terrain, reaching with their icy fingers down into the surrounding mountain canyons to elevations as low as 8,000 feet. Like a geological goulash, the Tusas Mountains are a convoluted mix of Precambrian igneous and metamorphic rocks, capped with newer volcanic tuff of Tertiary age and bisected by numerous faults. Surface water is encountered frequently today, but no services are found until El Rito, mile 40.2. Approximately 23 miles of today's route are paved; the rest alternate between hardened gravel and unimproved dirt. The latter, when saturated with rain, transform into an awful, wheel-sucking gumbo, so if the weather is wet you'll want to detour on U.S. Highway 64/84 all the way from Hopewell Lake to Abiquiu (*AB-uh-kyoo*).

At 19.4 and 23.8 miles, respectively, you'll pass through the tiny villages of Cañon Plaza and Vallecitos. Both are farming communities settled in the 1770s during the Spanish colonial days, and the Spanish influence is still strong. Sixteen miles beyond Vallecitos is El Rito, a somewhat larger and newer town, settled early in the nineteenth century by Spanish ranchers.

From your destination of Abiquiu, if you've any miles left in your legs, you may opt to detour off the route approximately 7 miles to the northwest, to the Corps of Engineers campground on Abiquiu Reservoir. The view over the surrounding countryside is remarkable, encompassing Mogote Ridge, the gash of the Chama River Canyon Wilderness, and the distinctive profile of Cerro Pedernal, which you may recognize from Georgia O'Keeffe paintings. You'll long remember the way the vivid colors of the desert—red beds of Triassic sediments backed by cliffs of Jurassic sandstone—blend as one with the darker hues of a mountainous backdrop, as the sun goes down on the Land of Enchantment.

DAY 56 ROUTE

0.0 Continue riding south on FR 91B.

0.9 Stay on main road.

3.2 Burned Mountain, elevation 10,189 feet. Start down.

4.5 Pass two-track dropping left into wetlands. Pass several more two-tracks over next couple of miles.

8.2 Pass FR 91B3 going right.

8.6 Saddle; start down narrow road along Spring Creek, paralleling a ranch inholding.

9.3 Pass old cabin on left, then cross spring.

12.3 Turn sharp right uphill onto FR 42 toward Cañon Plaza.

13.5 Continue straight on FR 42 toward Cañon Plaza, starting down.

16.8 Cross stream (Cañada del Oso) and start up amid stands of aspen and pine.

18.5 Ride straight onto pavement where FR 274 goes right.

19.4 Cañon Plaza.

20.0 County Road 239 goes right.

21.1 FR 45 goes left.

23.8 Turn right toward sign reading "Canjilon" at Vallecitos Post Office (no other services).

23.9 Cross Río Vallecitos.

24.0 County Road 251 goes left.

24.2 Ride onto gravel.

24.9 Turn left off FR 106 toward Valle Grande Peak onto rougher FR 44 (very muddy if wet).

26.6   Veer left downhill, following FR 44.

30.8   High point; start down.

31.8   Continue down FR 44 where FR 725 goes left.

32.0   Go straight toward El Rito.

32.3   Valle Grande Springs.

33.6   Head uphill on FR 44 where FR 122 goes left toward La Madera.

36.0   Pass FR 44A going right to Cañada del Potrero.

39.8   Ride straight onto pavement, State Highway 554, leaving County Road 247/FR 44, rather than turning left onto pavement.

40.2   El Rito.

49.6   Leave Carson National Forest, continuing south on State Highway 554.

53.6   Cross Río Chama.

54.2   Turn right onto U.S. Highway 84.

57.4   Abiquiu. Services include a mercantile and the Abiquiu Inn, with accommodations and restaurant. (A couple of miles before town you'll pass a B&B and cyclists-only lodging/camping at Old Abiquiu B&B Park and Bosque Tent Sites, 505-685-4784.)

Someone obviously drove this road when it was muddy (probably with chains), but you definitely don't want to try riding it when it's that way. (Jim Blodgett)

Day 57

ABIQUIU TO POLVADERA MESA CAMPSITE

23.2 miles

Today's mileage may appear short, but the effort expended to make those 23.2 miles will be considerable. You'll want to stock up on food for a couple of days before heading south from Abiquiu; replenish your water to the max, too, for much of both days is spent on a dry ridge, and tonight's camp will probably be dry. The ride out of town is rather mellow for the first few miles, but soon the climbing intensifies. The unmistakable profile of 9,860-foot Cerro Pedernal comes into view at around 7 miles, and for the next few miles you'll wind through an extraordinarily empty rural countryside, where Santa Fe National Forest inholdings are marked by venerable yucca-pole fence lines. After approximately 16 miles you'll start the long, steadily steep grind up Polvadera Mesa, a volcanic ramp to the sky. You won't reach the top of it until 5.3 miles into tomorrow's ride. It's considered by many the toughest extended climb on the entire Great Divide route.

First things first, however. If you bothered pedaling all the way to Abiquiu Reservoir yesterday afternoon, consider killing a day by wandering even farther off the route, first continuing several miles north up U.S. Highway 84 to the Ghost Ranch Living Museum. It's a terrific place to get oriented to the unique and varied natural history of this high-desert region. About a mile north of the museum, on the opposite side of the highway, begins FR 151, a dirt road leading 12 or 13 miles up the wilderness-surrounded Río Chama Canyon. It makes for a great ride, ending at the surprising Monastery of Christ in the Desert, whose Benedictine monks, believe it or not, were the subject of a 2006 television reality show broadcast on The Learning Channel. Visitors are welcome.

The Abiquiu area is considered by those who know about such things as a primary center of universal energy; it's long been a gathering place for the magical, mystical, spiritual, and artistic. In early times sacred Pueblo Indian traditions mixed with the Catholic beliefs of the Spanish settlers, while more recently all sorts of religious practitioners, from New Age to Islam, have been attracted to Abiquiu. For example, high on the bluff above town on the north side of the Río Chama, you'll see a beautiful and immense white structure that from below appears to be a Spanish-style mansion. But it's actually the Dar Al-Islam mosque, the centerpiece of some 9,000 church-owned acres of prime New Mexican desert and mesa land. Here, too, visitors are welcome.

Abiquiu was settled in the mid-1700s by Spanish colonialists, and soon thereafter became an important launching point for travels on the Old Spanish

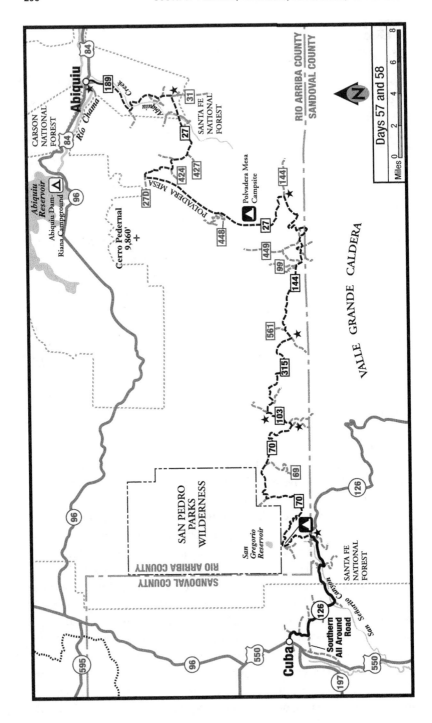

Border dreams: You're less than two weeks away from this lonely stretch of New Mexico State Highway 81, which leads to the Mexican border. (Etienne Theroux)

Trail of the late eighteenth and early nineteenth centuries. The pack-mule trail, which traversed 1,200 miles of impossibly rugged, arid, and empty country, was established to link Los Angeles and other California missions with the colonial settlements of New Mexico, both as a trade route and as a "statement" by Spain, letting it be known that this was their empire. It is said that from the beginning, Catholic priests sent to attend to the spiritual needs of the growing population of Abiquiu found themselves submerged in a place of sin, lethargy, and witchcraft, leading some historians to refer to Abiquiu as a high-desert counterpart to Salem, Massachusetts.

DAY 57 ROUTE

0.0 Continue riding west through Abiquiu.

0.8 Turn left (south) onto paved County Road 189 and ride onto the lands of the Abiquiu Grant. No camping permitted over the next 10 miles.

2.7 Cross cattle guard and ride onto gravel.

3.9 Cross Abiquiu Creek.

4.5 Recross creek.

4.7 Two-tracks going left and right as you cross stream. Climb steeply onto ridge to be greeted with splendid views.

5.5 Top of plateau, with its peppering of piñon and juniper trees.

8.3 Turn right onto FR 27 as FR 31 continues straight.

9.7 Pass two-tracks going left and right.

10.8 Enter Santa Fe National Forest; FR 27 deteriorates some (muddy when wet).

11.7 Two-track going left; enter a canyon.

12.6   Continue straight on FR 27; start descending.

13.7   Cross cattle guard and bear left to continue on FR 27.

14.3   Continue on FR 27 where FR 424 drops left.

15.3   Swing around fence marking private lands.

16.4   Continue up rough hill on FR 27 where FR 27D goes right; begin ascending Polvadera Mesa.

19.0   Continue riding on surface of tuff "slickrock" amid a forest of aspen and ponderosa pine.

21.7   Continue uphill on FR 27 where FR 448 drops right.

23.2   Polvadera Mesa campsite on left. Nice primitive camping.

Day 58

POLVADERA MESA CAMPSITE TO CUBA

56.0 miles

Today's recommended ride is long; however, several good dispersed camp-sites can be found along the way, should you choose to divide the distance into a 2-day ride. Except for the last 10 miles, during which you'll descend toward Cuba (*COO-ba*), the route is largely through cool, forested high country, where sightings of black bear, elk, and other wildlife are not uncommon. Stream water is abundant over the second half of the day's ride. The final 10 miles are paved; the rest are on dirt or gravel.

Occasionally, between areas of darker and older volcanic rocks, you may notice deposits of lighter-colored volcanics that are pale or pinkish in color. Known as Bandelier tuff—it's named for the famous nineteenth century archaeologist, Adolf Bandelier—the rock covers large areas within the rough triangle formed by drawing lines between the towns of Los Alamos, Jemez Springs, and Cuba. The Bandelier tuff is particularly dramatically displayed at Bandelier National Monument, where prehistoric Anasazis occupied naturally occurring caves in the soft rock. (Located off the route, Bandelier National Monument is best accessed by going southeast from Abiquiu on U.S. Highway 84, then following secondary roads from Española.)

Bandelier tuff originated from the second of two immense volcanic erup-tions of about a million years ago that formed the Jemez Mountains. In its two eruptions the volcano spewed colossal quantities of ash and other materials, estimated to be 100 times the amount released by the 1980 Mount St. Helens eruption. Purged of its support of underlying magma, the volcano—thought to have been about the size of pre-1980 Mount St. Helens—collapsed into its magma chamber, almost like a deflated balloon, leaving a circular valley that

These ruins are evidence that in New Mexico, as elsewhere, early structures were often constructed out of their surroundings. (Etienne Theroux)

is 14 miles across and known today as the Valle Grande Caldera. One of the most impressive volcanic craters in the world, Valle Grande is mostly under private ownership and almost pancake flat—except for several lava domes that rise from its floor—in startling contrast to the surrounding Jemez Mountains.

You'll be virtually on the north rim of the caldera as you negotiate the route through the Santa Fe National Forest, and at mile 38.3 you'll pass a viewpoint offering a vista that encompasses part of the rim, as well as the distant Sandia Mountains—and, on a clear day, even the Gila Mountains way to the south.

DAY 58 ROUTE

0.0 Continue uphill from Polvadera Mesa campsite.

2.8 Continue straight on FR 27.

4.0 Pass two-track going left as you swing right up a steep climb.

4.5 Pass two-track going left.

5.3 Top of the world. Veer right onto unsigned FR 144.

9.9 Pass FR 144-01 going right.

10.7 Pass FR 144-11 on left.

11.9 Continue straight as FR 449 drops to the right.

13.7 Cross cattle guard and ride onto rocky and steep surface.

14.1 Go straight onto the more rugged four-wheel-drive road at unsigned junction, where high-grade FR 99 drops to right and another, lesser road goes left to a quarry. Start descending. Note: This turn is easy to miss, but don't miss it.

15.2 Pass two-track going left.

18.7 Swing left rather than turning right onto unsigned FR 561.

19.6 Cross cattle guard onto better road; then, in about 100 yards turn right onto FR 315, leaving FR 144.

26.3 Turn left at the T-intersection onto FR 103 and ride into the Cuba Ranger District.

27.0 Open park with several private cabins.

28.2 Turn right onto FR 70.

33.2 Continue straight on FR 70 where FR 69 goes south.

38.3 Viewpoint on left, where you can see the rim of Valle Grande Caldera, as well as distant mountains.

43.2 Good dispersed camping on left, just past Trail 51.

45.5 More dispersed campsites in this area.

45.9 Turn right at T-intersection off FR 70 onto main road, State Highway 126.

46.2 Cross cattle guard onto pavement and start down.

50.7 Leave Santa Fe National Forest.

55.5 Curve left into Cuba.

56.0 Turn left onto U.S. Highway 550 at stop sign in Cuba; all services.

Day 59

CUBA TO DESIGNATED HUNTERS' CAMP

46.6 miles

The 115 miles separating Cuba and Grants constitute one of the wildest and least watered segments of the entire route, rivaling the 135-mile stretch between Atlantic City and Rawlins, Wyoming. As you're well aware if you pedaled that portion of the route, careful planning and loading up on water and provisions are mandatory, and one should not venture into such unforgiving country on anything even faintly resembling a lark. (This three-day ride has been successfully divided into two long days by quite a few Great Divide route tourers, with the break point coming at 62 miles at the BLM wildlife exclosure mentioned in the Day 60 description, mile 15.4. That leaves 54 miles to go to Grants on the next day.) After starting with 11 miles of pavement, the rest of today's route winds amid sage- and piñon-covered plateau country, over hard-packed sandy roads, so you don't get to the really rough stuff until Day 60.

While you may be wishing you'd find more water to drink along this stretch, you'd better also hope that none falls from the sky. Don't head into

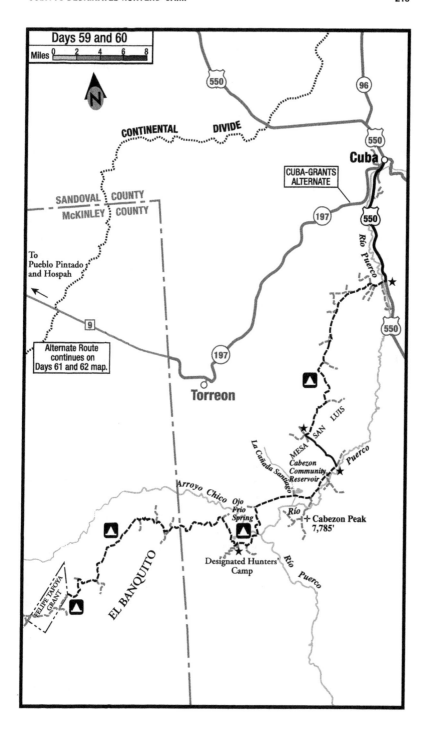

it if it looks like an extended period of wet weather, for the rugged, unsurfaced roads of the area will become impassable, as is the case in so much of northern and central New Mexico. (Afternoon thundershowers—in contrast to prolonged rains—may make the roads temporarily impassable, but the roads tend to dry out quickly and generally will be negotiable again by morning.) Stories have come back from Great Divide route riders who had to temporarily abandon their bikes on this stretch, after the bikes became mired in mud. Moreover, on Day 60 and much of Day 61 the route traverses a seemingly endless rollercoaster of arroyo crossings, where flash floods are a very real danger. An alternative route from Cuba to Grants, entirely on pavement, is detailed below the main route description for today's ride. It meanders through an area that is not part of the Navajo Indian Reservation proper, but in which Navajo lands are checkerboarded among lands under other jurisdictions. The route also passes a string of Navajo settlements, including Torreon, White Horse, and Hospah. Finding a place to camp is the primary challenge; previous riders have had luck securing camping spots adjacent to a couple of the small markets located along the way. Because the roads are all paved, you should be able to make the 120 miles to Grants in just two days, limiting the need to find a campsite to only one night. (Continental Divide crossing-baggers take note: This route crests the C.D. several times, compared to zero times for the dirt Cuba-to-Grants route.)

Students of archaeology may choose to take the paved route even if the weather is exquisite, for it provides access to the ruins of Chaco Culture National Historical Park, one of the most remarkable and remote prehistoric sites in North America. Chaco Culture NHP, which in 1987 was named a World Heritage Site, holds the remains of what is thought to be the highest level of civilization reached by any prehistoric American Indians north of Mexico. The most impressive ruins at Chaco Canyon are those of Pueblo Bonito ("beautiful town"), a five-story structure that encompassed some 800 rooms. This area was occupied for more than 300 years, from approximately from AD 850 through AD 1200. Today the park has a National Park Service campground but no other services.

Just northeast and northwest of Pueblo Pintado (53 miles from Cuba on the alternative route) are a pair of satellite ruins of Chaco Culture NHP. Scattered about the San Juan Basin of the Four Corners region are numerous other outlier ruins, all associated with a series of ancient "roads" that appear to radiate from Chaco Canyon. To this day archaeologists debate their significance—were they actually routes used for travel and trade, or were they built to serve more spiritual and less pragmatic needs in the lives of the Anasazi?

DAY 59 ROUTE

0.0 From where you left the route, continue south through Cuba.

0.9 Continue following U.S. Highway 550, a wide road with good shoulders.

10.9 Turn right off highway onto dirt road and cross bridge over Río Puerco.

13.7 Pass two-tracks going left and right at top of climb.

14.8 Turn left and cross a cattle guard as you're going up a little hill (first major left-hand turn since topping the hill a mile back).

16.4 Continue straight as another road goes right.

17.4 Concrete-block building on right.

23.3 Two-track leading behind right to potential camping spots.

24.4 Top out in saddle and begin down.

25.2 Curve right to stay on main road.

28.3 Pass under powerline.

28.6 Turn left to begin 4-mile descent on pavement.

32.4 Turn right at T-intersection onto gravel road.

33.6 Continue straight as another road goes right.

35.0 Pass under large powerline.

36.2 Bear right on main road as another road goes left toward Cabezon Peak.

37.5 Pass Cabezon Community Reservoir, then continue on main road as another road goes right up La Cañada Santiago.

41.1 Continue on main road where another road goes right.

44.1 Cross Arroyo Chico on big bridge and ride onto BLM lands.

45.5 Stay on main road where another road goes left. Begin climbing. (A deep artesian well is located approximately 0.7 mile up the road to the left. This a better option for water than Ojo Frio Spring, located 1 mile into tomorrow's ride.)

46.6 Turn right onto road skirting designated "hunters' camp"—although nonhunters are welcome too. Water available at Ojo Frio Spring, a mile farther up the route. (If you already have water for tonight, be sure to fill up at Ojo Frio in the morning.)

PAVED ALTERNATE ROUTE FROM CUBA TO GRANTS:

0.0 At south end of Cuba, turn right off State Highway 44 onto State Highway 197.

19.6 Road to Torreon goes left. Route becomes Reservation Road 9.

46.3 Convenience store on right.

46.6 Pueblo Pintado.

59.1 Turn left onto State Highway 509 at White Horse toward Hospah. (To visit Chaco Culture National Historical Park, continue 10 miles west on Reservation Road 9, then go 20 miles north on unpaved Reservation Road 14.)

64.7 Hospah community on left.

73.4 Road going right follows the Continental Divide to Borrega Pass.

88.9 The prominent profile of Mount Taylor comes into view ahead left.

95.0 Turn right at T-intersection onto State Highway 605.

108.8 Turn left onto Route 66/State Highway 117.

109.8 Milan.

110.9 Grants; all services.

112.4 Rejoin main route at mile 2.7, Day 62.

A desert break between the mountains east of Cuba and the mountains southwest of Cuba (Kyle Karlson)

Day 60

DESIGNATED HUNTERS' CAMP
TO FELIPE TAFOYA GRANT BOUNDARY

24.4 miles

Today's recommended short distance is dictated by the fact that at 24.4 miles you will encounter the boundary of the Felipe Tafoya Grant, where for the next approximately 20 miles—across that land grant, as well as the Bartolome Fernandez Grant—travel is not permitted off the main road, meaning no camping, either. At Ojo Frio Spring (or at the artesian well mentioned yesterday, 0.7 mile off the route from mile 45.5) stock up on enough water to get you through today, tonight, and tomorrow as far as San Mateo Spring, 25.6 miles into the 44.6-mile day.

Another way to divide up the mileage—one that would deliver you tonight to a substantially more hospitable place to camp—is to continue for 25.9 miles to the "beautiful pine- and aspen-surrounded park with good dispersed camping potential" mentioned in tomorrow's route summary. This would translate to a distance ridden today of 50.3 miles, leaving just 18.7 mostly downhill miles to ride tomorrow to Grants.

The eerily eroded, sculpted badlands you'll penetrate today and tomorrow are partly the result of natural conditions; the handiwork of a singular blend of geography, soil type, and weather. They're also no doubt due in part to unnatural conditions: years of overgrazing by stock. Keep your eyes peeled for the ghostly remains of hardscrabble livestock-and-farming operations, and just imagine what it must have been like for homesteaders trying to scrape a livelihood out here in this hard, exceedingly remote land. Not surprisingly, their structures were typically constructed of materials at hand—rock slabs—and those remaining often appear more like part of the native landscape than something manmade.

Dominating the already impressive, variegated landscape is a series of volcanic necks located just south of the route. They stick out like throbbing thumbs above the sedimentary rocks encompassing them. Perhaps the most striking of all is 7,785-foot Cabezon Peak, which you passed late in yesterday's ride. The necks, which are of the Tertiary geologic period, are actually hardened lava that once filled the conduits of volcanoes, the less resistant rock of the volcanoes having long since eroded away. In the eastern distance, on the other side of State Highway 44, you can make out the southern tip of the Sierra Nacimiento, noteworthy because the range is one of the two southernmost extensions of the Rocky Mountains. That's right,

The 115 miles between Cuba and Grants are some of the most remote and waterless of the entire Great Divide route. (Andrew Sufficool)

you are leaving the Rockies behind after an intimate affair with them that has lasted well over 2,000 miles.

DAY 60 ROUTE

0.0 Continue riding northwest from designated hunters' camp.

1.0 Ojo Frio Spring along road to right, at the base of Cerro del Ojo Frio.

1.2 Cross cattle guard.

3.3 Cross cattle guard.

5.1 Drop into deep arroyo.

5.5 Cross cattle guard.

5.8 Cross cattle guard; pass through arroyo several times over next couple of miles.

8.5 Pass minor road going right.

9.3 Cross cattle guard.

9.6 Bear left away from road dropping right toward private structures.

10.4 Bear right where closed two-track leads left to El Banquito. Road surface deteriorates; you'll encounter some serious erosional problems over the next few miles.

11.2 Pass through very deep arroyo.

12.0 Pass two-track going right.

12.8 Cross cattle guard and descend into arroyo.

13.2 Continue straight; gated road on left.

15.4 BLM wildlife exclosure on right.

20.0 Ride through deep arroyo.

22.7 Open gate; pass through and close it. Ride through arroyo several times in close succession.

24.4 Gate to the Felipe Tafoya Grant. No trespassing off route or camping approximately next 20 miles. Camp before passing through gate, or continue for 25.9 miles to the dispersed camping area mentioned in the Day 61 Route.

Day 61

FELIPE TAFOYA GRANT BOUNDARY TO GRANTS

44.6 miles

Today's ride continues southwesterly through desert scrublands, above which El Dado and other volcanic necks loom like rock-solid sentinels. In the 8- to 13-mile range you'll face some fairly tricky routefinding, but if you've managed to make it this far from Cuba you probably won't get too lost. The route soon swings to the southeast, then curves west to climb for approximately 5 miles to surmount the northern flank of the San Mateo Mountains and pass through a portion of the Mount Taylor Ranger District of the Cibola National Forest. Cool, verdant forests of aspen and pine—with good drinking water available at San Mateo Spring, mile 25.6—will make a distant dream of where you were only 15 miles previously. At just under 28 miles begins the long descent into Grants, population around 10,000. It's the biggest town you've visited on the Great Divide route since Rawlins, Wyoming—coincidentally, the community that marks the southern end of the route's other unforgettably long, dry stretch. Fifteen of today's 44.6 miles are paved, including nearly 11 miles of the final approach to Grants; the rest are mostly hardened gravel.

Through downtown Grants runs historic Route 66, the focus of Adventure Cycling's aptly named Bicycle Route 66. In its day, the "Mother Road" offered an American odyssey not entirely unlike that provided by the Great Divide Mountain Bike Route today...the fact that it was tackled by car rather than bicycle notwithstanding. Completed in 1926, Route 66 opened the West to tourism, at a time when travel by car was still a real adventure. The character of the road, like that of the Great Divide route, compelled those traveling it to stop often and look around. It forced them to get acquainted with the towns and people dotting the wide-open spaces between the corner of Michigan Avenue and Jackson Boulevard in Chicago, Illinois, and the Pacific Ocean waterfront in Santa Monica, California.

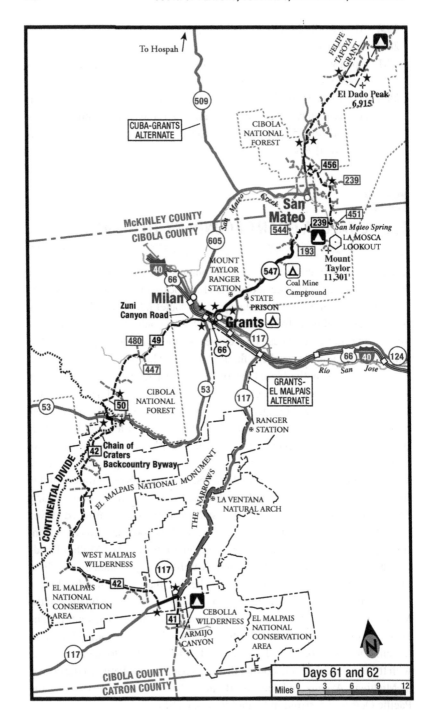

Route 66 was the antithesis of Interstate 40, which has replaced the historic road as the primary east-west highway crossing New Mexico. I-40, like other interstates, bypasses cities and towns, permitting travelers to get to their destinations fast, perhaps leaving the route only long enough to fill up on gas and grab a burger that tastes no different than the one they had 1,000 miles back. Route 66, in contrast, not only ran through towns, but in many cases served as the main downtown street. Unique diners and motor courts encouraged travelers to spend time (and dollars) in small towns. Indian trading posts in places like Grants, Gallup, and Albuquerque beckoned. Just as for those riding the Great Divide route (hopefully!), the journey was as important as—if not more important than—the destination.

If you spend time in Grants, don't miss the excellent New Mexico Museum of Mining, located at 100 Iron Street. The mining of uranium is largely responsible for the existence of the on-again, off-again boomtown, and this museum does a good job of replicating an underground uranium mine.

DAY 61 ROUTE

0.0 Open gate; pass through and close it. Ride onto Felipe Tafoya Grant. No trespassing off route approximately the next 20 miles.

1.4 Curve right into rocky canyon where another road curves left toward private holding.

1.8 Pass through gate, leaving it as you found it (open or closed). Ride through draw, noting the old names carved in rock.

2.6 Impressive old homestead. Gate (leave as you found it).

4.0 Curve left where another road drops right toward sign reading "Robert L. Bayliss Oil Field."

4.4 Cross cattle guard.

5.0 Pass under small powerline.

7.5 Gate.

8.3 Stay on main road where another road forks right. El Dado Peak towers to the left.

9.1 Cross cattle guard. Water tank on right should have water available.

10.2 Cross super-wide haul road.

10.9 Bear left as another road goes right.

11.2 Pass track going right.

12.2 Bear left, then immediately turn right at T-intersection.

12.4 Turn left onto paved road toward San Mateo. Caution: truck traffic.

16.6 Cross cattle guard, then turn left onto gravel FR 456 to commence long climb.

20.1 Resume climbing.

20.8 Turn right onto FR 239 and continue uphill.

22.7 Stay on FR 239.

25.2 Turn right at T-intersection toward Grants to continue on FR 239; left is FR 451 to La Mosca Lookout.

25.6 San Mateo Spring on left.

25.9 Beautiful pine- and aspen-surrounded park with good dispersed camping.

27.6 Begin long descent into Grants.

30.5 Pass road going left to Mount Taylor and La Mosca Lookout.

33.9 Pedal onto pavement where FR 193 goes left and FR 544 goes right.

36.2 Coal Mine Campground (USFS) on left.

42.0 Leave Cibola National Forest.

43.2 Prison on left.

44.6 To continue on route, turn left onto the paved road. (If you pass the Mount Taylor Ranger Station on the right, you've gone 0.2 mile too far.) For downtown Grants, continue straight off the route for 1.2 miles, turning right at major junction onto unsigned Roosevelt; in another 0.3 mile turn left onto one-way Second Street and continue for a mile. Grants has all services.

A New Mexico panorama: Brush, sand, and low, shrub-covered mesas (Kyle Karlson)

Day 62

GRANTS TO ARMIJO CANYON

63.0 miles (43.7 miles via paved alternate route)

Before leaving Grants, carefully plan your schedule for the next few days, for logistics are tricky. The distance from Grants to Silver City is more than 260 miles, or six riding days as suggested herein, although riders have made it in fewer days. The only commercial food source found along this extended section of the route is a small café in Pie Town, which marks the end of Day 63. The enterprise—known for its scrumptious pies, of all things—may also have a small selection of groceries on hand, but call ahead to check. Another possibility is to mail supplies ahead from Grants to the Pie Town post office, to yourself in care of general delivery; again, call ahead for information, because the Pie Town post office keeps limited hours. (Note: Groceries are also available at Top of the World General Store, located 3 miles off route west of Pie Town on U.S. 60.)

Today's ride is a long and potentially hot 63 miles if you follow the main route; your distance and effort can be reduced substantially by following the mostly paved, 43.7-mile alternate route. The main route, composed of gravel and dirt roads, includes the Chain of Craters Backcountry Byway, which may be impassable if wet. At the point where you pick up the backcountry byway at mile 25.0, the El Malpais Information Center is off route 4.7 miles east on State Highway 53. Open daily 8:00 AM to 4:30 PM, the center has water and bathrooms.

Regardless of which route you choose, today's ride will take you into a new and strange world known as El Malpais ("the badlands"). The 114,000-acre El Malpais National Monument, which straddles the east slope of the Continental Divide, is sandwiched within the larger El Malpais National Conservation Area. Also adjacent to the monument in various directions are the West Malpais Wilderness and the Cebolla Wilderness. Together these constitute one huge chunk of contiguous, protected federal lands that are extremely diverse in character.

Within the present national monument's boundaries, a number of small volcanoes have spewed lava across the land over the centuries, most recently fewer than 1,000 years ago. Local Indian lore relates a story about the "fire rock" that buried certain ancestral tribal homelands; it is widely believed that the legend is steeped in truth and refers to El Malpais. Among the features you can witness here are youthful lavascapes of hardened, ropy, gas-bubble-filled lava; pine-studded bluffs of light-colored sandstone; and lava-tube

The black basalt landscape of El Malpais was fashioned by molten lava from scores of eruptions flowing over the desert. (Etienne Theroux)

caves, including the remarkable Ice Cave, which maintains its deep deposits of blue-green ice even during the hottest, 100-plus-degree days of summer.

DAY 62 ROUTE

0.0 From where you left the route, turn south onto the paved road located 0.2 mile northeast of the Mount Taylor Ranger Station.

0.9 Four-way stop.

1.4 Stop sign adjacent to playing fields; continue straight.

1.9 Cross Camino del Coyote.

2.4 New Mexico State Women's Correctional Facility on left.

2.7 Turn right onto Santa Fe Avenue/U.S. Highway 66/State Highway 117. (Go left for the Grants–El Malpais Alternate; see below.)

4.1 Turn left onto State Highway 53.

4.6 Turn right onto paved Zuni Canyon Road/FR 49.

8.8 Enter Cibola National Forest. Road becomes gravel.

14.2 Bear right to continue on FR 49; dirt FR 447 goes left.

14.9 Bear left to continue on FR 49; FR 480 goes right.

20.2 Ride straight onto FR 50.

22.0 Continental Divide (C.D. crossing #19).

24.3 Turn left onto State Highway 53.

25.0 Turn right onto County Road 42/Chain of Craters Backcountry Byway (may be impassable if wet).

25.8 Continental Divide (C.D. crossing #20).

30.4 Continental Divide National Scenic Trail trailhead.

32.2 Bear left at Y as another road of equal quality goes right.

35.6 Bear left at Y following CR 42.

37.7 Bear left at Y following CR 42.

39.8 Continue straight as another road goes right.

42.5 Pass livestock tank on right; may have water.

43.7 Bear left at Y.

44.8 Continue straight as another road goes right.

46.9 Continental Divide National Scenic Trail trailhead.

51.6 Pass windmill on right; may have water.

54.2 Road from Hole-in-the-Wall joins from behind left.

56.5 Turn left onto State Highway 117.

59.0 Turn right onto gravel County Road 41.

63.0 Armijo Canyon on left (BLM primitive camping).

GRANTS–EL MALPAIS ALTERNATE:

0.0 From where you left the route, turn south onto the paved road located 0.2 mile northeast of the Mount Taylor Ranger Station.

0.9 Four-way stop.

1.4 Stop sign adjacent to playing fields; continue straight.

1.9 Cross Camino del Coyote.

2.4 New Mexico State Women's Correctional Facility on left.

2.7 Turn left onto State Highway 117.

7.4 Ride south across I-40 and continue along this shoulderless paved road that typically carries little traffic.

14.2 Enter El Malpais National Monument.

16.5 Ranger station on left.

25.4 La Ventana parking area and hiking trail to left.

29.4 The Narrows on right.

39.7 Rejoin main route; turn left onto dirt County Road 41 toward Pie Town.

43.7 Armijo Canyon on left (BLM primitive camping).

Day 63

ARMIJO CANYON TO PIE TOWN

28.1 miles

You'll continue south today, bumping along gravel and dirt roads that take you through open grasslands and forests of piñon pine and juniper. The relatively short distance of 28.1 miles will probably come as a relief, particularly if you pedaled the longer option yesterday. From here on out you'll encounter quite a number of windmills adjacent to the route. These same contraptions that make it possible to raise a cow in these thirsty climes also make it feasible to obtain good drinking water fairly often, provided they're actually running and pumping water through the spigot. Simply because a windmill is mentioned here does not necessarily mean you'll be able to get water, however; sometimes you will and sometimes you won't, so fully replenish your water supplies at every opportunity. This evening's destination of Pie Town marks the end of this section and the beginning of the end of the Great Divide Mountain Bike Route—the beginning of the final section, that is.

Taking aim at Pie Town, you'll ease into a setting of sprawling grasslands interspersed with rolling, piñon-covered hills. You'll see the Datil Mountains rising front left, the Mangas Mountains to the south, and Escondido Mountain ahead right. The Datils, which abut the Sawtooth and Crosby subranges, contain a bonanza of potential mountain-bike rides; take a look at the visitor map for the Cibola National Forest's Magdalena Ranger District, and you'll begin getting the picture. The lower slopes of the Datils are cloaked

This rider is heading the right way for taste-bud fulfillment: Pie Town is known for its... can you guess? (Candee Pearson)

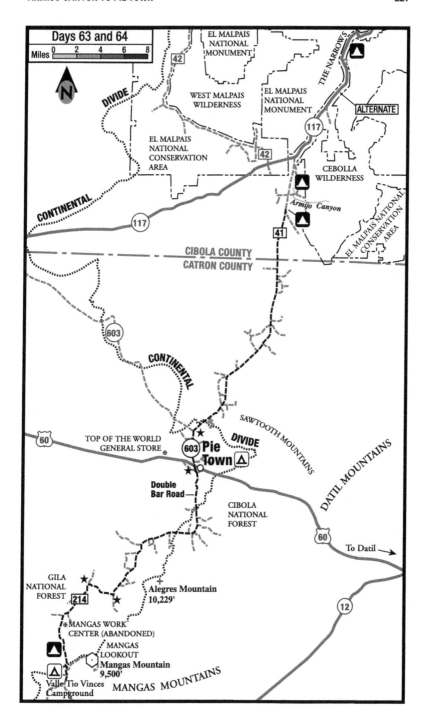

in grasses and bursts of piñon-juniper, while the upper slopes, topping out at 9,585-foot Madre Mountain, hold stands of ponderosa pine and Gambel oak. Rocky Mountain elk, wild turkeys, black bears, and cougars are among the critters you might spot while exploring there. The range is easily accessed from Pie Town by following U.S. Highway 60 a few miles to the southeast.

Pie Town, sitting near the Continental Divide at almost a mile and a half above sea level, like Truth or Consequences, is a New Mexico town that implores the visitor to get to the bottom of how its name came to be. In Pie Town's case, it is fairly straightforward: The settlement began as a service station run by a fellow with a mining claim nearby. After opening an associated eatery, the proprietor posted roadside signs bragging about his house specialty, pie. This led to the settlement being nicknamed Pie Town, a name that eventually received the official stamp of approval from the U.S. Postal Service. (Truth or Consequences, incidentally—or "T or C," as it's known locally and which is located well off the route northeast of Silver City—received its moniker in a publicity stunt for the radio show of the same name. After its citizenry voted to okay the change, the town of Hot Springs was branded with its new name when host Ralph Edwards broadcasted *Truth or Consequences* live from there on April Fools' Day, 1950.)

DAY 63 ROUTE

0.0 Leave camp, heading south toward Pie Town.

3.3 Cross cattle guard; windmill on right.

14.3 Pass road going 0.25 mile right to windmill; route is rising toward piñon-juniper forest.

14.8 Cemetery on left. Road turns rougher (mucky when wet).

8.6 Enter public lands; open to camping for next mile.

9.6 Cross cattle guard onto private lands.

12.0 Pass old cabin on right. You may find water in blue container in back.

14.3 Pass old rock, slab, and mortar structure on right.

14.8 Pass cattle tank fed by electric pump.

16.6 Pass a road going right; riding surface improves.

21.1 Pass a major ranch complex on the right.

23.0 Cross the Continental Divide (C.D. crossing #21).

24.9 Merge left onto State Highway 603 toward Pie Town.

28.1 Route crosses U.S. Highway 60 onto unsigned Double Bar Road. Pie Town is just off route to the east. Services here include a café, free camping (with water) at Jackson Park, and the famous "Toaster House" cyclists-only lodging (ask for information and directions).

You'll see a lot of windmills and water tanks in southern New Mexico. Burros and bikers, not so much. (Candee Pearson)

307.8 MILES
Days 64 through 70 (seven days)
Eleven Continental Divide crossings

This section of the Great Divide route heads south from Pie Town through a corner of national forest lands before crossing the western edge of the barren Plains of San Agustín. From there it climbs back into the federal lands of the Gila National Forest.

For many miles the route toys with the Continental Divide, crossing it between Pie Town and Silver City no fewer than seven times. The mountains of the Gila National Forest are conspicuously different from any range you've encountered thus far on the route; they're packed with moderately long, immoderately steep climbs that give way to moderately long and equally steep downhills. Due to the demanding terrain, some previous riders have found days 66 and 67 to be too long, and have instead taken three days to ride from southeast of Collins Park to Silver City.

At Silver City, a town straight out of the nineteenth-century Wild West that has grown graciously and vibrantly to meet the twenty-first century, you'll finally say goodbye to mountain riding. The last 124 miles of the Great Divide route traverse that which you may have begun wondering if you would *ever* reach—real desert, that is, authentic Chihuahuan Desert, embraced by true desert mountains.

The final crossing of the Continental Divide, located between Separ and

The Pie-O-Neer Café in Pie Town, New Mexico, purveyor of pies and proprietary pie recipes (Etienne Theroux)

Hachita, is an anticlimactic blip in the topography that you may not even notice. But if you do, take some time to reflect on a few of the thirty-two (at least) times you've surmounted the Continental Divide on your Canada-to-Mexico adventure. And ruminate on this: The Great Divide Mountain Bike Route may end at Antelope Wells and the international border, but the Continental Divide keeps going south into Mexico, where an incredible bounty of country still awaits discovery by intrepid bicycle adventurers like you. Note: Because (1) the camping options are limited and not overly pleasant, (2) riders are generally in excellent shape by this point, and (3) State Highway 81 north of Antelope Wells has been known to be used at night by drug traffickers, a lot of cyclists cover the 124-mile distance between Silver City and Antelope Wells (much of which is paved) in two days rather than the three outlined below. The choice is yours.

Day 64
PIE TOWN TO VALLE TIO VINCES CAMPGROUND
29.5 miles

Although you will pass a possibly operational windmill at 24.0 miles today, be sure to fill all your water bottles before heading out. On leaving Pie Town you'll begin another long flirtation with the Continental Divide, this one 140 miles in duration. Today's route, all of it along dirt and gravel roads, crosses the divide three times (see map on page 227). The first 20 miles of the ride bring you ever closer to 9,854-foot Escondido Mountain, a distinctive volcano of Tertiary age that has been shaped, reshaped, and shaped again by erosion during the last several million years. In case you make camp early and have miles to spare in the legs of iron you've developed over the course of riding more than 2,400 miles, an intriguing side trip beginning near the recommended overnighting spot climbs east for a few miles to Mangas Lookout, elevation 9,500 feet.

Much of the area you've ridden through in New Mexico, as well as a good deal of the country still to come, is ecologically within either the upper Sonoran life zone or the transition life zone, or, quite commonly, somewhere within a mix of the two. Characteristic trees of the upper Sonoran, which prevails at elevations between 4,500 and 6,500 feet, are Gambel oak, Colorado piñon pine, and various species of juniper, including the extraordinary alligator juniper, which you'll immediately recognize if you encounter one, owing to its alligator-plate-like bark. These trees stand in contrast to desert plants like mesquite, yucca, and cholla cactus common in the lower Sonoran zone, which encompasses much of nonmountainous New Mexico at elevations under 4,500 feet.

Both piñons and junipers typically grow less than 30 feet in height and feature stunted, twisted trunks and broad crowns. At the lower elevations of their habitat, where moisture is at a premium, the trees grow well apart from one another; at the higher reaches, where moisture is more abundant, they grow in bunches, which prevents the understory from growing as thick as it does at lower elevations. The compact profile of both trees, along with the scaly leaves of the juniper, and the piñon's small number of needles per bunch, are adaptations aimed at reducing the surface area exposed to moisture-sucking winds. Despite the tough growing conditions they face, both species appear to be expanding their ranges in the West, as they're invading grasslands in many places. Some say this is due to overgrazing of grasses by stock, which has reduced the competition and made available additional moisture in the soil for the piñons and junipers.

Ponderosa pine, appearing at the higher elevations of the upper Sonoran zone, begins to really thrive in the transition zone, which stretches from approximately 6,500 to 9,000 feet above sea level. Spruce and Douglas fir, spurred on by greater quantities of precipitation and lower temperatures, prevail at the upper end of the transition zone.

DAY 64 ROUTE

0.0 From where you left the route near Pie Town, go south on unsigned Double Bar Road.

0.2 Continue straight after stop sign.

0.7 Cross cattle guard. The next several miles cross private lands.

3.0 Cross Continental Divide (C.D. crossing #22).

4.1 Continue straight where a road goes right into private place.

6.0 Road curves right.

6.5 Bear right uphill where a road of equal quality drops left.

7.3 Cross Continental Divide (C.D. crossing #23).

9.7 Ranch on left; continue straight.

10.3 Continue straight where another good road goes left.

16.7 Water available at cattle tank with spigot and pump (be sure to turn pump off).

17.5 Turn right away from Mangas Mountain at junction.

20.3 Turn left at T-intersection onto unsigned FR 214.

21.6 Old slab-and-mortar structure on right.

21.8 Turn up to right, crossing cattle guard (left goes onto private land).

23.5 Enter national forest lands. Camping permitted next 14 miles.

24.0 Windmill and huge old juniper tree.

24.6 Continue straight on FR 214 toward abandoned Mangas Work Center.

25.1 Continue straight toward Mangas Lookout; abandoned Mangas Work Center on left.

28.8 Good dispersed campsites on right.

29.1 Cross Continental Divide (C.D. crossing #24).

29.5 Valle Tio Vinces Campground (water available in stock tanks).

Day 65

VALLE TIO VINCES CAMPGROUND TO COLLINS PARK DISPERSED CAMPSITES

40.1 miles

On today's ride you'll drop from the Mangas Mountains to cross State Highway 12 between the one-horse settlements of Old Horse Springs and Aragon. Excepting where you turn onto and then immediately off the highway, the entire day will be spent on gently graded dirt and gravel roads. South of the highway you'll pedal briefly along the western fringe of the desiccated Plains of San Agustín, a mountain-ringed spread of flatness marking the bed of a Pleistocene lake that was 50 miles across. Technically a block of earth that subsided between two parallel faults, the valley once was subject to a major meteorite bombing, and many rocks from space have been recovered here.

Leaving the Plains of San Agustín behind at about 26 miles, you'll reenter mountain country via La Jolla Canyon, which leads to Collins Park. The flat character of this attractive, pine- and aspen-covered expanse of the Gila National Forest belies the fact that the Continental Divide runs right through. You'll pass at least a couple of windmills today, as well as a pair of small reservoirs.

Aragon, located a few miles west of where the route crosses State Highway 12, was the site of Fort Tularosa. In 1872 an unsuccessful attempt was made here at hammering out an armistice between the U.S. government and Cochise, chief of the Chiricahua Apache. The goal: put an end to Cochise's raids against Mexicans on both sides of the international border.

Old Horse Springs, situated east of the route, is the location of a natural spring that was an important water stop along the southern branch of the Beefsteak Trail, formally known as the Magdalena Livestock Driveway. (The trail forked at Datil, with the northern branch passing through the areas of Pie Town and Quemado.) With activity beginning in the mid-1880s, the driveway was used until the 1950s, making the Beefsteak the last regularly utilized major cattle-drive trail in the country. Along the trail cowboys

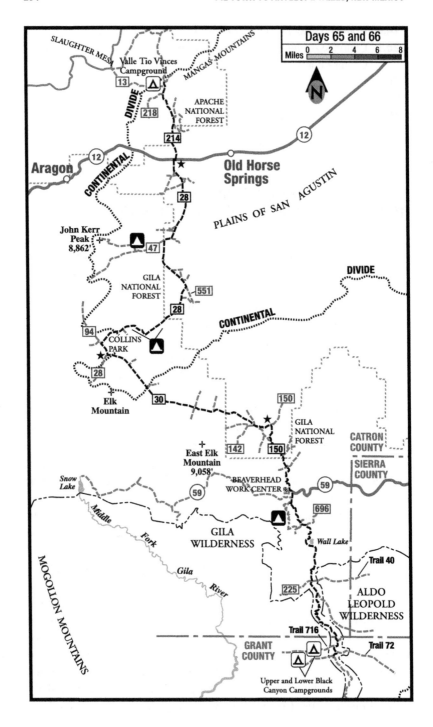

*A medley of earth-tone rock and brilliant blue sky—and a very hot rider—on the road
south of Valle Tio Vinces Campground (Etienne Theroux)*

herded semi-feral cattle and sheep from ranges in western New Mexico and
eastern Arizona to the railhead in Magdalena, New Mexico. Even after State
Highway 12 and U.S. Highway 60 were built through, many old-timers chose
to continue driving their cattle cross-country, rather than shipping them by
truck, despite the fact that it was often a tremendous ordeal to get the wild
cattle to cross the paved roads. The beasts would graze regularly throughout
the foot journey and arrive at the railhead in better shape than those trucked
in, thereby commanding a higher price per head.

If you're like most cyclists, by this time in your odyssey you're anxious
to make time to get to the end of this darn thing. But if you're one of those
rare individuals who has come to feel most at home on the Great Divide route,
you may be dreading finishing and returning to the "real world." If so, rest
assured that plenty of potential side trips await to foster dawdling. Take, for
instance, the loop up into the John Kerr Peak country of the Tularosa Mountains, accessed by following FR 47 west from 19.3 miles into today's ride.
Various options exist once you gain elevation, including that of taking FR
94 south to rejoin the main route in Collins Park (mile 38.5 below). Or, from

the vicinity of today's recommended end point, taking FR 28 and other roads to swing around the south sides of Elk Mountain and East Elk Mountain.

These only brush the surface of the options at hand—underscoring why the greatest challenge facing Great Divide route planners often was not finding a route, but settling on a single choice from the plethora of possibilities begging consideration.

DAY 65 ROUTE

0.0 Continue riding south on FR 214.

1.0 Fenced pond on left.

1.1 Continue straight where FR 13 goes right toward Slaughter Mesa.

1.7 Bear left, continuing on FR 214 toward Patterson Canyon where FR 218 goes right.

9.5 Turn right at T-intersection onto State Highway 12, then immediately left at the lonesome farmhouse onto gravel FR 28 toward Beaverhead Ranger Station.

15.3 House, windmill on right.

19.3 Continue straight on FR 28 where FR 47 goes right (informal campsite situated 2.6 miles west on FR 47).

20.3 Windmill on left.

25.1 Bear right following FR 28 toward Beaverhead Ranger Station where FR 551 goes straight.

28.6 Enter Gila National Forest.

29.4 Attractive campsite on left in an aspen- and pine-filled canyon.

34.3 Another nice campsite.

35.9 Small reservoir on left.

36.5 Cross Continental Divide (C.D. crossing #25).

38.5 Bear left on FR 28 into Collins Park where FR 94 goes right.

40.1 Bear left at Y onto FR 30 toward Beaverhead Ranger Station. Camp in this vicinity.

Day 66

COLLINS PARK DISPERSED CAMPSITES TO BLACK CANYON CAMPGROUNDS

55.0 miles

The landscapes encountered on today's ride offer further study in the sorts of contrasts New Mexico can dish up. Early in the day, in a pine-timbered setting in the canyon of O-Bar-O Creek, you'll ride through an area of grassy slopes reminiscent of certain portions of the Continental Divide country outside

Helena and Butte, Montana. Then, after cruising up yet another dry, rocky canyon, you'll enter the realm of the rugged Mogollon and Black mountains. The day ends in the protected confines of Black Canyon, where you'll find a constant stream and Forest Service campsites nestled amid stands of juniper, oak, and pine. (Earlier in the day, at mile 29.5 and 37.5, respectively, you'll pass the Beaverhead Work Center and Wall Lake, potential water sources.) Today's long mileage, combined with the challenging hills that characterize the second half of the distance, make for a tough row to hoe.

It's rollercoaster, up-and-down, grunt-and-grin riding along these gravel roads of the Gila National Forest, through places unlike those encountered anywhere else on the Great Divide route. The terrain is tight and heavily timbered, the roads steep and serpentine. (For an advance clue, pore over the Gila National Forest visitor map and note how closely webbed the drainage patterns are, compared to those of other national forests you've ridden in.) From the high ridgetops you can see dark ridges rolling away in every direction. Were it not for the bounty of plants characteristic of the high Southwest, those who've ridden back East might think they've unknowingly

The steep, rugged ridges of the Gila National Forest provide a physical challenge even to those who've ridden 2,500 miles to get here. (Etienne Theroux)

been whisked back to the Appalachians of West Virginia. Not surprisingly, this maze of mountains provided hideouts for outlaws and renegade Indians alike, including the legendary Apache chiefs Cochise, Geronimo, and Mangas Coloradas.

Approximately 5 miles past Wall Lake you'll enter a narrow non-wilderness corridor, often little more than a mile wide, that is surrounded by federally designated wilderness. To the west lies the Gila Wilderness of the Mogollon Mountains, set aside in 1924 as the first wilderness area in the United States. The impetus for the wilderness' creation was pioneer conservationist Aldo Leopold, who spent time as a forester in this region with the U.S. Forest Service. Befittingly, to the east, within the Black Range, sprawls the more recently dedicated Aldo Leopold Wilderness. Combined, these two wilderness areas offer enough trails to keep even the most energetic of hikers and horseback riders busy for years. Numerous trails beckon, both left and right, but please remember: Tread them only by foot, leaving your bicycle outside the wilderness.

DAY 66 ROUTE

0.0 Ride southeast on FR 30 toward Beaverhead Ranger Station.

0.4 Cross the Continental Divide (C.D. crossing #26).

5.5 Cross Continental Divide, elevation 7,670 feet (C.D. crossing #27).

6.9 Curve left where another road goes right.

18.7 Continue straight toward Beaverhead Ranger Station where FR 142 goes back/right and another road goes left toward State Highway 12.

20.5 Veer right onto FR 150 toward Beaverhead; left goes to "Magdelena 80 miles."

25.8 Gila National Forest sign.

29.1 Beaverhead Ranch on left.

29.5 Beaverhead Work Center (water). Curve right toward Wall Lake, as paved State Highway 59 goes left toward "Winston 42 miles." The road you're following is well graveled but narrow and potentially washboarded.

30.2 Continue straight where State Highway 59 heads right toward Snow Lake.

31.5 Pass road dropping right to potential campsites.

37.5 Wall Lake to left.

42.6 Continue straight where a road also goes right and Trail 40 goes left. (May have to ford Diamond Creek.)

50.6 Pass road forking left to landing strip.

53.0 Trail 716 on right. Tremendous view to where you're headed.

55.0 Upper and Lower Black Canyon Campgrounds.

Day 67

BLACK CANYON CAMPGROUNDS TO SILVER CITY

59.3 miles

Stock up on water before leaving Black Canyon to prepare for the steep hills between here and the Mimbres River, encountered at mile 21.6. Riding south from Black Canyon, you'll continue for 12 miles through the narrow passageway separating the Gila and Aldo Leopold wilderness areas. Beware of ruts and loose rocks on the steep descents and climbs. At mile 13.7 you'll surmount the Continental Divide for the twenty-eighth time since setting out from Banff, then proceed to ride directly atop the divide for 8 miles. Subsequently you'll turn northwest onto State Highway 35, a narrow, winding road that you follow for 12 miles to the junction with State Highway 15 at 34.1 miles—en route, passing through an area of campgrounds and other

An optional detour will take you to Gila Cliff Dwellings National Monument, which protects ruins first recorded by Adolf Bandelier in 1884. (Etienne Theroux)

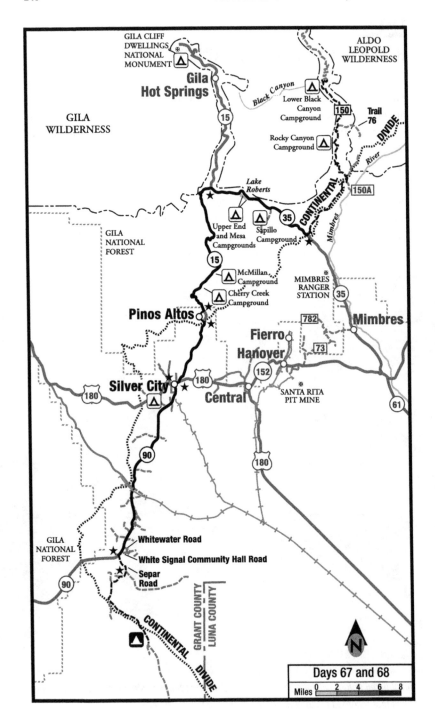

GILA CLIFF
DWELLINGS
NATIONAL
MONUMENT

ALDO
LEOPOLD
WILDERNESS

Gila
Hot Springs

Black Canyon

Lower Black
Canyon
Campground

150

Trail
76

GILA
WILDERNESS

15

Rocky Canyon
Campground

150A

Lake
Roberts

Upper End
and Mesa
Campgrounds

Sapillo
Campground

35

CONTINENTAL DIVIDE

Mimbres River

GILA
NATIONAL
FOREST

15

McMillan
Campground

MIMBRES
RANGER
STATION

35

Cherry Creek
Campground

Pinos Altos

782

Mimbres

Fierro

Hanover

73

152

Silver City

180

SANTA RITA
PIT MINE

180

Central

61

90

180

GILA
NATIONAL
FOREST

Whitewater Road

White Signal Community Hall Road

90

Separ
Road

GRANT COUNTY
LUNA COUNTY

CONTINENTAL DIVIDE

N

Days 67 and 68

Miles 0 2 4 6 8

tourist services in the vicinity of Lake Roberts. (Forest Service campgrounds are found at about 5, 7.5, and 8.5 miles west of where you turn onto State Highway 35.) You'll turn south onto State Highway 15, which leads to Silver City by way of the Old West town of Pinos Altos. Use special caution while riding State Highway 15, which is hilly, winding, and narrow. It can carry heavy traffic, and blind corners are common.

Pinos Altos could serve as a set for a Hollywood western. Founded ten years before Silver City, the town was the site of a September 1861 raid on residents by several hundred Apache Indians led by Cochise and Mangas Coloradas. Fifteen Indians and three miners were left dead in the wake of the attack. Because of continued harassment by the Indians, Pinos Altos was deserted by 1862 and the town wasn't resettled until 1866, after the forging of an uneasy truce with the Apache. Recognizable names with ties to early Pinos Altos include Roy Bean, who operated a store there before moving on to Texas to enforce the law west of the Pecos; and the Hearst family, which had mining, ranching, and mercantile interests in the area. The nearby Phoebe Hearst Mine was a namesake of William Randolph Hearst's mother.

And there's a lot more to see in this area. If, back at mile 34.1, you turned north off of the route onto State Highway 15, you would—in a serpentine, whoop-de-doo ride—find yourself at Gila Cliff Dwellings National Monument. It's a very worthwhile side trip, but by no means just an hour's diversion—the distance from where you leave the route to the national monument is a hilly 18 miles.

The prehistoric ruins encompassed by Gila Cliff Dwellings National Monument were first recorded by archaeologist Adolf Bandelier in 1884, and twenty-three years later President Theodore Roosevelt created the national monument. The monument holds the remains of dwellings built within natural cave overhangs around AD 1000, then abandoned around AD 1300. Hanging nearly 200 feet above the valley floor, the cliff dwellings can be visited by following a 1-mile foot trail. Their inhabitants were farmers who supplemented cultivated crops of corn, squash, and beans by gathering wild plants and hunting game. Ruins of other varieties of habitations—including pit houses and above-ground structures—are also located within the monument. Some, dated as old as AD 100 to AD 400, were built by members of the Mogollon culture, the first known human inhabitants of these mountains. Today's monument also boasts an outstanding museum, along with a pair of National Park Service campgrounds.

Like yesterday, big mileage and countless hills create a long and tough go of it; the good news is that almost 38 of the 59.3 miles are paved. Silver City has all services, including bike shops.

DAY 67 ROUTE

0.0 Begin steep climb out of Black Canyon.

2.6 Top out.

6.5 Trail 76 goes left. Start descent.

8.9 Rocky Canyon Campground.

13.7 Continental Divide (C.D. crossing #28). Road meanders along the C.D. for the next few miles.

14.3 Pass FR 150-A going left to Mimbres River.

19.5 Start dropping into main valley of Mimbres River.

21.6 Turn right onto narrow, paved State Highway 35.

21.8 Continental Divide (C.D. crossing #29). Cross cattle guard.

26.6 Road to Sapillo Campground.

29.2 Upper End Campground.

30.0 Mesa Campground.

31.1 Lake Roberts.

34.1 Turn left onto State Highway 15. Narrow, winding road with potential heavy traffic.

46.0 McMillan Campground.

47.0 Cherry Creek Campground.

51.3 Turn right onto Main Street/Business Loop.

52.0 Pinos Altos.

52.2 Turn right onto State Highway 15.

52.6 Continental Divide (C.D. crossing #30).

58.8 Silver City.

59.3 Junction with State Highway 90.

Day 68

SILVER CITY TO HIGH LONESOME CAMPSITE

30.0 miles

From here on out the terrain is relatively level, but there's a good chance that the temperatures will be hotter than those you've previously encountered. Before leaving Silver City, obtain adequate food to get you all the way to Mexico; also stock up on enough water to last to Separ (mile 21.2 tomorrow), in case the windmills, reservoirs, and stock tanks mentioned in the route descriptions are dry. Leaving Silver City and the mountains behind at last, you'll spin south for 18.4 miles on paved State Highway 90 before turning southeast to follow dirt roads into the heart of the Chihuahuan Desert. After climbing in some places through virtual forests of tall yucca—that ubiquitous

True desert at last. Not far to go, and over relatively moderate terrain. Just watch out for javelinas and tire-puncturing thorns. (Ben Yandeau)

and distinctively multisworded succulent of the desert Southwest—you'll meet the Continental Divide at 24 miles, then stay high along it for a few miles. As stated below, it's recommended that you make camp "somewhere in here" in the 30-mile range, which is more precisely somewhere in the middle of nowhere. (Note: You've entered thorn country, so be careful where you roll your bike off the roads to avoid flat tires.)

Alluring Silver City, a lively and prosperous town of approximately 10,000 residents, sits on the edge of the desert at the threshold of the mountains. Save for its fine Victorian homes and business buildings, Silver City appears rather modern, but it owns a compelling history filled with tales of Apache Indians, Spanish settlers, gold miners, gamblers, wranglers, and outlaws. It exploded into existence in 1870 after silver was struck nearby. Soon thereafter the county seat was moved from neighboring Pinos Altos to Silver City, which within a decade held eight taverns, two banks, three billiard parlors, four restaurants, two fur dealers, a half-dozen newspapers, and a host of other enterprises.

It is virtually impossible to visit Silver City without running across some reminder of the town's most infamous resident, Henry McCarty, a.k.a. William Bonney, a.k.a. Billy the Kid. McCarty moved with his mother and her new husband to Silver City in 1873, when Henry was thirteen or fourteen years of age. He was jailed for the first time in his new hometown after being arrested for robbing a Chinese laundry. So, naturally, he also made his first jailbreak here, escaping through a chimney. Billy the Kid–related sites you can visit include the Star Hotel (where he worked for a while), his family's home, and the Memorial Lane Cemetery at the west edge of town, which holds the remains of his mother, Catherine McCarty Antrim.

DAY 68 ROUTE

0.0   Ride southwest on State Highway 90.

1.0   College Avenue goes right to historic business district. As you leave town, road is four lanes with wide shoulder.

11.7 Road narrows to two lanes (still with fairly wide shoulder). Pass under railroad tracks.

17.5 Pass Whitewater Road on left.

18.0 Pass White Signal Community Hall Road on left.

18.4 Turn left onto sandy, smooth Separ Road, which begins winding in and out of a desert-canyon wash.

20.4 At fork, continue straight on unsigned Separ Road as main road goes left. Climb toward Continental Divide through yucca desert.

23.5 Corrals and windmill.

24.0 Swing left to trace the Continental Divide (C.D. crossing #31).

24.4 Stay high where another road drops right.

27.4 Reservoir to right.

27.9 Continue high along the Continental Divide where another road drops left.

29.3 Cross cattle guard.

30.0 Camp somewhere in here.

Day 69

HIGH LONESOME CAMPSITE TO BIG HATCHET PRIMITIVE CAMPSITE

59.2 miles plus 2–3 miles off route to camp

Today you'll continue pedaling through the desert outback, swinging southwestward at 8.6 miles to take aim at Interstate 10 and the settlement of Separ. From Separ, reached after 21 miles of dirt roads, you'll parallel the interstate for some 7 miles on a dirt/gravel frontage road before turning south onto paved State Highway 146, which you follow for nearly 20 miles to Hachita. A few miles before Hachita—although you might not even notice it—you'll cross the Continental Divide for the thirty-second and final time on this route. Remember to fill your water bottles at the trading post in Separ, south of which you'll roll past the occasional rural complex reminiscent of Australian bush camps.

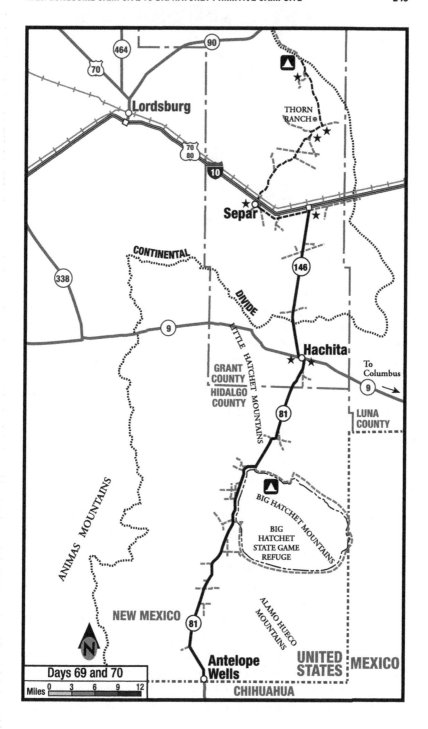

Thorn Ranch was probably named after the family that works—or worked—the land here. Or perhaps it's a namesake of local vegetation. (Doug Werme)

You're now well into one of the northernmost extensions of the Chihuahuan Desert. Roughly 1,200 miles long and 800 miles wide, the Chihuahuan reaches from southern New Mexico, southwestern Texas, and southeastern Arizona to just north of Mexico City. The largest and highest of the four deserts shared by the United States and Mexico (the other three are the Sonoran Desert, the Mojave Desert, and the Great Basin), the Chihuahuan Desert encompasses lots of empty country as well as several major communities, including El Paso, Texas; Las Cruces, New Mexico; and the Mexican cities of Chihuahua, Torreon, and Saltillo.

The majority of the Chihuahuan Desert is bordered by the Sierra Madre Oriental (east) and the Sierra Madre Occidental (west), Mexico's two great ranges. That is why the region is so dry: As warm, moist air pushes up and over the ranges from either direction, it quickly cools, resulting in rainfall over the mountains. By the time the air masses make it into the basins of the desert they have very little moisture remaining. Most of the rain that does fall in the Chihuahuan Desert comes during a single rainy season, extending from July into October. The other three deserts, largely due to their location closer to the West Coast, each have two rainy seasons, one in winter and one in summer.

One of the more unusual critters you may encounter out here is the javelina, or collared peccary, the only wild pig native to America. (The wild boars of the Tennessee hills and other places southern are escapees gone feral.) Considered the smallest of our big-game animals, an adult javelina weighs 40–60 pounds and is about 3 feet long and 2 feet high at the shoulder. Preferring rugged, scrub-filled hill and canyon country, and typically nocturnal in nature, groups of javelina will seldom be spotted any closer than 100 yards away. They'd rather not see you and you not see them; however, their eyesight is poor, especially during the daylight hours, so it is possible that you'll stumble upon a group at close range. If you do, and they're upwind of you, they still may not be aware of your presence, so yell and throw rocks or sticks to scare them off. If javelina are cornered, their natural reaction may be to attack. Recommended defense measures include standing tall and looking big by waving your arms overhead, and moving back slowly while speaking loudly. Another tip: If you smell something vaguely resembling the odor of a skunk, it might be nearby javelina. Make a lot of noise before entering tight places, particularly if you detect a musky smell in the air.

DAY 69 ROUTE

- **0.0** Continue riding southeast.
- **0.2** Stay high to the left toward Thorn Ranch rather than dropping right onto road of equal quality.
- **0.5** Go straight where another road descends to a water tank.
- **4.2** Continue on main road where another road drops to a water tank. Just past here, curve right going downhill where a two-track goes left.
- **7.1** Cross cattle guard.
- **7.5** Go straight toward Thorn Ranch where another road goes left.
- **8.6** Bear right at junction toward Thorn Ranch (left goes to "Deming 40 Miles").
- **9.2** Pass two-track going right to water tank.
- **10.1** Curve left away from Thorn Ranch.

The final Continental Divide crossing on the Great Divide route is scarcely a blip in the topography. (Doug Werme)

10.7 Stay on main road where another road forks left.

11.4 Cross wash. Pass ranch with windmill.

12.3 Cross cattle guard and continue toward "Separ 9 miles."

13.3 Pass under high wire.

13.6 Cross gas pipeline, then cross it again in 0.75 mile.

21.1 Cross railroad tracks.

21.2 Pass under interstate and turn left onto deteriorating frontage road in tiny Separ. Services include a snack shop and grocery with limited supplies. Possibly your last water source.

21.8 Road turns to dirt following I-10.

28.7 Curve around interstate exit and merge right onto paved State Highway 146. Remainder of route is paved.

42.5 Road widens and shoulder improves.

44.2 Indistinct crossing of Continental Divide (the final C.D. crossing, #32).

47.9 Turn left onto State Highway 9 toward Antelope Wells. Hachita; no services.

48.3 Turn right onto State Highway 81.

52.4 Enter Hidalgo County.

59.2 Road going left/east into Big Hatchet State Game Refuge. Primitive camping can be found within the refuge.

Day 70
BIG HATCHET PRIMITIVE CAMPSITE TO ANTELOPE WELLS

34.7 miles plus 2–3 miles returning to route from camp

On this, the final day of your grand adventure, you'll ride south on what just might be the loneliest paved road in America. Only at certain times of the week and/or weekend will there be any traffic, primarily when Mexicans or Mexican-Americans are traveling from one side of the border to the other to visit relatives. At other times—although it's not recommended—you'd probably be perfectly safe lying down in the middle of the road and taking a nap.

If you're a soon-to-be through-biker, you're nearing the terminus of a route you no doubt have occasionally thought might never end. Now that it is ending, you're probably having mixed feelings galore. Take it slowly today to savor the final moments. Pull over now and then to inspect a cholla cactus plant, or just to gaze around. If the day is hot—which it probably is—in the

Adventure Cycling's first organized group to complete the U.S. portion of the Great Divide route, circa 1999

barren distance you'll see heat rising in waves in front of arid mountain slopes, and desert mirages pooling on the flats. If you have a good map of Mexico, sit on the ground, spread out the map, and have a look. Ruminate on some of the poetic place names shown in close proximity to the Continental Divide in that foreign land, and imagine what they might be like.

That's all there is, but there's a lot more where it came from. Just try to fight that urge to keep going south when you reach Antelope Wells.

DAY 70 ROUTE

0.0 Return to route from Big Hatchet State Game Refuge.

4.5 Pass through Hatchet Gap, which separates the Big and Little Hatchet mountains.

4.6 Wildlife area loop comes back in on left.

12.8 Pass road on right, and several more going left and right over next 12 miles.

28.3 Pass windmill on left.

34.7 Antelope Wells; international border. Water and restrooms available. Southern terminus, Great Divide Mountain Bike Route. Congratulations!

It's been a few miles and a few days since you pedaled through Canadian terrain like this. Ready to turn around and do it in reverse? (Julie Huck)

INDEX

ABOUT THE AUTHOR

Photo by Nancy McCoy

Michael McCoy's bicycle-trail-research career spans more than thirty-five years. His first such gig was helping to plan Bikecentennial's TransAmerica Bicycle Trail during the winter of 1975–76. McCoy is the author of ten books, including *Montana: Off the Beaten Path* and *Insiders' Guide to Glacier National Park*, both published by Globe Pequot Press. He has written for the National Geographic Book Division and for many magazines, including *Men's Journal, Runner's World, Bicycling*, and *Powder*. Still serving as a writer and media specialist for Adventure Cycling Association, McCoy is also editor of *Teton Valley* and *Teton Home and Living* magazines. He and his wife, Nancy, live in Teton Valley, Idaho.

MOUNTAINEERS BOOKS SKIPSTONE BRAIDED RIVER

recreation • lifestyle • conservation

MOUNTAINEERS BOOKS, including its two imprints, Skipstone and Braided River, is a leading publisher of quality outdoor recreation, sustainability, and conservation titles. As a 501(c)(3) nonprofit, we are committed to supporting the environmental and educational goals of our organization by providing expert information on human-powered adventure, sustainable practices at home and on the trail, and preservation of wilderness.

MOUNTAINEERS
BOOKS

All of our publications are made possible through the generosity of donors, and through sales of more than 700 titles on outdoor recreation, sustainable lifestyle, and conservation. To donate, purchase books, or learn more, visit us online:

1001 SW Klickitat Way, Suite 201 • Seattle, WA 98134
800-553-4453 • mbooks@mountaineersbooks.org
www.mountaineersbooks.org

Leave No Trace strives to educate visitors about the nature of their recreational impacts and offers techniques to prevent and minimize such impacts. Leave No Trace is best understood as an educational and ethical program, not as a set of rules and regulations.
For more information, visit www.lnt.org or call 800-332-4100.

OTHER MOUNTAINEERS BOOKS YOU MIGHT ENJOY

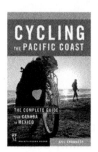

Cycling the Pacific Coast
Bill Thorness
Discover the most popular bike tour in the United States.

75 Classic Rides Washington
Mike McQuaide
Washington's best bike routes, ranging from paved biking paths to epic mountain-pass climbs. If you're seeking the best in Washington, you can bet your bottom bracket you'll find it here.

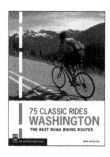

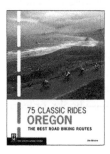

75 Classic Rides Oregon
Jim Moore
Classic cycle routes for one of the nation's top biking destinations. Find plenty of blacktop bliss in this full-color guide to the best bike trails in Oregon.

Biking Puget Sound, 2nd edition
Bill Thorness
Explore the 60 best bike tours in the Puget Sound area, from Olympia to the San Juans, with most tours located close to Seattle.

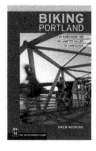

Biking Portland
Owen Wozniak
55 routes from downtown Portland along the river, into the greenways of the Tualatin basin, through the Clackamas countryside, and across the Columbia.

Adventure Cycling in Northern California
Adventure Cycling Association
44 classic on- and off-road biking routes in Northern California, featuring some of Northern California's most magnificent landscapes.

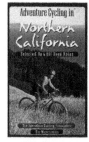

Mountaineers Books has more than 700 outdoor recreation titles in print.
For more details visit
www.mountaineersbooks.org.